WESTERN EUROPE: ECONOMIC AND SOCIAL STUDIES

series edited by Eleonore Kofman and Allan Williams

Western Europe: Economic and Social Studies is a series of introductory texts dealing with the major countries of Western Europe. It provides a concise overview of the economic and social geography of individual countries or areas, using contemporary social science theories to interpret the evolution of geographical patterns. Each book covers the political and economic context; post-war economic and social development; rural transformation; urbanization; regionalization; future development, and includes a detailed bibliography. Each is suitable for use on a range of courses, including geography, language, economics and social science.

The United Kingdom   Ray Hudson and Allan Williams
Scandinavia   Brian Fullerton and Richard Knowles
Ireland   Barry Brunt
Italy   Russell King

Christopher Flockton is Lecturer in Economics in the Department of Linguistic and International Studies at the University of Surrey, where he teaches courses on the French and West German economies. He has also taught at the University of Lyons III. He has long been interested in French economic and physical planning and regional policy, and has published a number of articles on these subjects.

Eleonore Kofman is Senior Lecturer in Geography and Planning at Middlesex Polytechnic. She has also been visiting lecturer at the University of Caen. Her publications have been in the areas of gender and geography and regionalism and nationalism, with particular reference to Corsica.

FRANCE

FRANCE

CHRISTOPHER FLOCKTON

Lecturer in Economics,
University of Surrey

ELEONORE KOFMAN

Senior Lecturer in Geography and Planning,
Middlesex Polytechnic

WESTERN EUROPE:
ECONOMIC AND SOCIAL STUDIES

P·C·P
Paul Chapman
Publishing Ltd

First published 1989
by Paul Chapman Publishing Ltd
144 Liverpool Road
London
N1 1LA

British Library Cataloguing in Publication Data
Flockton, Christopher
    France – (Western Europe: economic and social studies)
    1. France. Economic conditions, 1945–1988
    I. Title II. Kofman, Eleonore III. Series
    330.944'083

ISBN 1–85396–022–5

Typeset by Inforum Typesetting, Portsmouth
Printed by St Edmundsbury Press, Bury St Edmunds
Bound by W.H. Ware & Sons Ltd, Clevedon

To our respective parents, Dorothy and
Roy Flockton, and Rachel and Vladimir Kofman.

CONTENTS

PREFACE

As France approaches the 1990s, discussions have flourished both on the geographical and historical construction of national identity in the past, and on France in a future, more open Europe. The bicentenary of the French Revolution of 1789 has given rise to debates on whether the age-old social and political cleavages still apply, and on what role diversity and plurality have had in the construction of the nation state. In this book we have restricted our journey into the past to the more recent period of postwar reconstruction. However, during this period France was transformed from an inward-looking society and state to one whose frontiers have been broken down.

The transformation of postwar France has produced a voluminous literature by both French and foreign observers. What we would wish to add, as our contribution to this discussion, in addition to a much-needed socio-economic analysis is a spatial dimension that brings together the processes of change operating at different levels, in order to highlight the articulation of the local and the global, both national and international. In adopting this perspective, we will be questioning a narrowly Jacobin view of transformation, whereby it is solely the State which commands and local societies which react. Certainly the State did, at the height of the Gaullist epoch, seem to be overpowering and leave little room for civil society. Today, competition between localities and major cities is encouraged as part of the preparation for the Europe of the 1990s. Yet, competition is also supposed to be tempered by solidarity, enshrined in the multiplicity of local development initiatives.

It is obviously not possible to do justice to all aspects of postwar change. While we have given the spatial dimension its rightful due, we have not treated it in isolation from the wider, economic, social and political situation.

Both of us have spent long periods teaching and researching in different regions of France and we have brought this experience to the writing of the book. Eleonore Kofman wrote Chapters 1, 3 and 7; Chris Flockton, Chapters 2, 5 and 6. Chapter 4 was divided between us.

A number of people have given us help and advice in the preparation of the book. Keith Reader, in particular, read large chunks of the manuscript, and Pascal Buléon and Judith Still both read a chapter. All three have given us much appreciated suggestions. Steve Chilton, Drew Ellis and Malcolm Horne prepared the figures at a time when they were under considerable work pressure.

Eleonore Kofman would like to thank Isa Aldeghi, Michèle and Pascal Buléon, Jeanne Fagnani, Jacques Lévy and Monique and Michel Pinçon for material, discussions and hospitality. Without the studies undertaken by the Centre d'Etudes Régionales et d'Aménagement (CERA) at the University of Caen, the section on education could not have been written. She would like to thank all the postgraduates and staff associated with CERA for the help given during her six-month period of teaching in 1988. Her home institution, Middlesex Polytechnic, should also be thanked for granting her a sabbatical term and the Nuffield Foundation for a grant to study regional decentralization, in particular in Corsica.

Christopher Flockton

ONE

From National Reconstruction to European Integration

1.1 Introduction

According to Weber (1976), France acquired reality as a nation only after the 1870s, consisting until then of a set of relatively isolated and immobile communities typical of a rural society. Unification was achieved through integration into the urban world, new forms of communication and transport, and the work of institutions, such as the army and schools. Such a vision of the diffusion of urban mentalities and cultures into a static rural world is disputed by Tilly (1979). Rural France at the beginning of the nineteeth century no longer consisted of congeries of unconnected, immobile and agrarian localities. It was towards the end of the nineteenth century that rural deindustrialization and emigration created societies that corresponded to this agrarian vision. Furthermore, Tilly argues, it was capitalism and state-making, rather than urban diffusion, that finally unified France.

Debates over the nature of change and development have continued to provoke interest during the postwar period. The years after the Second World War stood in sharp contrast to the interwar years when the image of a rural *France profonde* still rang true. In popular mythology it was a society of artisans, small shopkeepers and peasantry, the latter comprising the largest group. Urban expansion proceeded slowly; it was only in 1936 that a majority of the French population (52 per cent) became urban dwellers.

On the other hand, economic and social change took place rapidly in the postwar period, especially after the mid-1950s when urbanization gathered momentum, consumption patterns altered and the economy began to be restructured in preparation for entry into the European Economic Community in 1958. Some socioeconomic groups expanded (the salaried middle classes); others declined, such as the artisans and small shopkeepers, who were squeezed out by the concentration of commercial outlets. Yet already from the mid-1950s, organized movements began to protest against and contest the nature of a transformation which left in its wake marginal socioeconomic groups and territories that failed to enjoy the fruits of modernization.

We should not, therefore, accept a simplified view of local societies, seen as blocking change and suffering the consequences of what had been decided by the all-powerful and centralized State and big business. The portrait of France has been for so long one of a Jacobin political system, denying the mediation of any territorial unit between the individual and the State. However, we are concerned with examining more closely the sources and impetus of socioeconomic and spatial transformation.

In the rest of this chapter we outline the major periods of economic, social, political and geographical change. The first section describes the years of the Fourth Republic from the end of the Second World War until 1958, which laid the basis for much of the later, more comprehensive, spatial and socioeconomic restructuring. The end of these years of political instability and difficult decolonization also witnessed the formation of the European Economic Community. The second section focuses on the key years of the Fifth Republic under Gaullist domination (1958–69), a time of major projects and programmes that altered the face of France. A transitional period under President Pompidou (1969–74) ushered in years of slower economic growth and urban development, and the liberalization of the economy and downgrading of planning, especially during the Presidency of Giscard d'Estaing (1974–81), which will be examined in the third section. From 1973 onwards, the economic crisis led to higher levels of unemployment, accompanied by attempts to liberalize the economy and make it more competitive. Yet certain social groups questioned the ideology of progress, while the expanding salaried middle classes increasingly made their presence felt politically, especially in local and regional initiatives.

The Socialist government, which came to power in 1981, also closed an era of 23 years of Centre–Right government. It faced greater demands for local development but in the context of an economy that was continuing to be drawn more fully into the international system. Many of the reforms promised in the Socialist programme were never delivered due to the imposition of an austerity programme and political and social opposition. As in many other advanced capitalist societies, subsidies were withdrawn from declining industries and social expenditure tightened. Modernization took over as the key slogan in the later Socialist governments. The return of the Right in March 1986 did not mean a total rejection of the policies of the past five years, despite the rhetoric of the increasing role of the individual and the private sector. The return of the Socialists in the 1988 elections, though not with the outright majority they had enjoyed after the 1981 legislative election, is likely only to modify, rather than substantially alter, existing economic policies. France has its sights fixed on the demands of a single European market as from 1993, which has virtually become political orthodoxy among all groups, with the exception of the extreme-right

National Front and, to some extent, the Communist Party.

1.2 From liberation to the collapse of the Fourth Republic

In 1944, after the liberation of France from German occupation, its level of industrial production had fallen below 1938 levels and many lines of communication were destroyed. While the economy was not exactly rebuilt along the lines proposed by the *Conseil National de la Résistance* (National Council of the Resistance) the temporary weakness of conservative forces and their collaboration during the war led to nationalization in certain key sectors, such as cars (Renault) and clearing banking, and the implementation of the core of a welfare state that would cover all salaried workers. It should be remembered, however, that at this time France still had a far lower proportion of salaried workers than, say, Great Britain, namely 60 per cent as against 80 per cent in the UK (Goubet and Roucolle, 1981, p. 139).

The State was heavily implicated in the First Five Year Plan which concentrated on rebuilding the infrastructure (1947–1953). However, already in the early stages of the Plan the composition of the government had altered; in May 1947 the Communists were pushed out of the government due, to a great extent, to Marshall Aid, leaving a government composed of radicals and conservatives (Rioux, 1983, p. 161). Furthermore, one of the two leading trade unions, the *Confédération générale du travail* (CGT), no longer participated in the Plan as from 1948. However, the Plan was indicative and optional; it was not intended to hinder private capital but to encourage a revived capitalism from its interwar Malthusianism.

The 1950s witnessed rates of sustained growth previously unknown in France. Productivity was extremely high in agriculture, 6.4 per cent per annum from 1949 to 1962, and 6 per cent for industry. The highest rates of growth were in the large-scale industries, for example 15 per cent p.a. in chemicals. However, mergers and concentration remained limited to 60 per year, although small firms of fewer than 10 employees were fast disappearing. In 1958 the 500 largest firms still contributed only 30 per cent of production, but by 1980 this figure had doubled. Economic growth in the 1950s was essentially internally fuelled and autarchic with no more than 6 per cent of the gross domestic product being concerned with exchange.

The change in living conditions brought about by this growth became visible by 1955 (Figure 1.1). National income, the purchasing power of the average hourly salary and consumption increased by 40 per cent between 1950 and 1958 (Rioux, 1983, pp. 168–70); France was now well into the 'trente glorieuses', a term coined by Jean Fourastié (1979) to describe the thirty years (1946–75) of relatively uninterrupted growth from

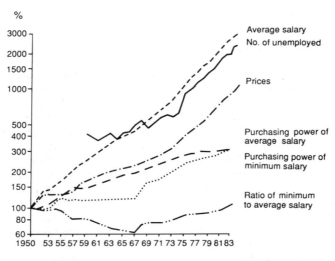

Source: INSEE- Revenue division

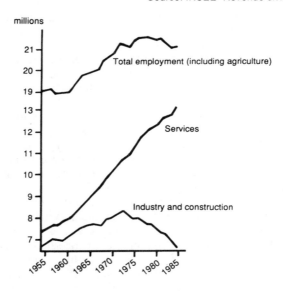

Source: INSEE Employment Division

Figure 1.1   a, Salaries, purchasing power and unemployment, 1950–83.
b, Employment of active population, 1954–85.

reconstruction to the economic crisis of the early 1970s.

However, the consequences of growth and increased well-being were unevenly experienced by different social classes and occupational groups. Two main groups suffered adverse consequences in terms of their overall standard of living and importance in the French economy. These were farmers and small shopkeepers and artisans. The silent revolution had begun to take place in the countryside. After the period of food shortages, farmers' income did not keep up with the French average. One in ten farmers left the land from 1949 to 1954, and then from 1954 the rate quickened with 30,000 farms disappearing annually, or 3 in every 10 farmers. These farmers would migrate to the small- and medium-sized towns and feed the increasing numbers of the working class.

The initial response of the corporatist leaders in the *Fédération nationale des syndicats d'exploitants agricoles* (FNSEA National Federation of Farmers' Unions) and in the chambers of agriculture resembled that of a pressure group, pushing for more political representatives from the agricultural world. However, the amplitude of changes confronting agriculture passed them by. Nor were the governments of that period able to conceive a coherent agricultural policy in response to the decline in prices for products, such as milk and meat. The challenge to the established leaders came from those who wanted to modernize in an orderly fashion, especially the members of the young farmers' group *Jeunesse agricole catholique* (JAC) which, in 1954, was transformed into the *Centre national des jeunes agriculteurs* (CNJA National Centre of Young Farmers). They wanted a more modern, technical and professional farming sector which would not be entirely dependent on public subsidies. In 1956 the CNJA joined the FNSEA under the leadership of Michel Debatisse, a member of the JAC, and proceeded to take it over and define a new strategy.

For the small shopkeepers, previously buoyed up by shortages and high rates of inflation, the 1950s marked the end of their golden age. They operated on high margins of profit and in 1950 covered 89 per cent of sales. It was the tightening of fiscal legislation that finally led to an organized movement of protest under the leadership of Pierre Poujade, owner of a stationers and bookshop in the Lot (Rioux, 1983, p. 80). The programme of this movement, termed '*poujadisme*', was popular and imprecise, calling on a French fraternity under the banner of independent workers. It was generally concentrated in south-western and central France in areas with lower levels of urbanization and high rates of rural exodus, namely the area south of the often cited line from St Malo to Geneva (Rioux, 1983, p. 96). At their parliamentary peak in the January 1956 elections, the Poujadists gained 11.6 per cent of the votes cast and 51 seats. However, despite this performance, the trend towards concentration in the commercial sector continued unabated with the Prisunic chain opening in 1958 and Carrefour in 1963 (Braudel and Labrousse, 1982, pp. 1533–4).

Agriculture and commerce were two of the archaic sectors that the modernizers aimed to push back. More than any other person, Pierre Mendès-France, Prime Minister from June 1954 to February 1955, incarnated a modernist tendency that found its adepts in the *Commissariat du Plan* (Planning Commission), among the liberal bourgeoisie and followers of social Catholicism. Mendès-France was the only political figure since 1950 to point out publicly that it was necessary to choose between economic growth and Indochina (Gauron, 1983, p. 46). As an ideology of economic development, modernism opposed the immobility of economic and social structures and values. Its objectives were to increase industrial production, speed up rural depopulation and urbanization, and provide the collective public services required by demographic expansion (Gauron, 1983, pp. 8–9). In the 1950s its ideas radiated out from the *Commissariat du Plan* to other state agencies, but it was in the 1960s, during the height of the Gaullist period, that its objectives were put into action among higher-level civil servants.

At the same time, under the governments of Mendès-France and Edgar Faure, action was undertaken to contain and remedy regional inequalities, forcefully publicized in 1947 by Jean-François Gravier in his book *Paris et le désert français (Paris and the French Desert)*. Gravier argued that centralism and the industrial revolution had reinforced regional disequilibrium, and that public bodies had to institute deconcentration, so as to bring about a national harmonization of economic space and the return of civic, social and political virtues. The 1954 census seemed to confirm the seriousness of regional inequalities, evident in variations of population density and per capita income. The highest population densities and growth rates were generally in the North and East as well as the Mediterranean fringe. Elsewhere, areas displayed signs of backwardness, rural depopulation and archaic structures. Indices of production, productivity and per capita income all showed that France was divided into two, based on a line from Le Havre to Grenoble. For example, for a national average of 100 in terms of per capita income, Paris ranked first with 148, the Centre and South with 73, while 25 departments had per capita incomes of less than 40 per cent of the national average. Yet, as Rioux (1983, p. 205) points out, we should not exaggerate the supposedly simple patterns, for the medium-sized towns tempered the dichotomy of archaism and modernity, while rural depopulation did not inevitably entail economic decline and lack of future prospects.

Already in 1951 mixed-economy agencies for rural, urban and even regional areas had been set up. As from 1956, when the reconstruction priorities had come to an end, regional considerations came more fully to the fore. Under officials from the *Commissariat du Plan*, France was divided into twenty-two programme regions in October 1956. It would be wrong, however, to highlight solely the initiatives of the State, for in certain areas regional study and liaison committees and committees for economic expansion had outlined regional programmes of their own and pressured the State to provide the adequate infrastructure. The best known of these was the *Comité d'étude et de liaison des intérets bretons* (CELIB Committee for the Study of Britanny and Liaison of Breton Interests), founded in 1949. These committees created their own national conference of regional economies in 1952 (Rioux, 1983, p. 209) and were influential in bringing a more regional dimension to planning. They were obviously able to exert more influence in the parliamentary system of the Fourth Republic which left more opportunity for initiatives from within civil society. Even so, the State took over and attempted to control regional initiatives through its regional action plans from 1957 onwards. Under the Fifth Republic these would transform the remaining peripheral zones, as in Corsica. Legislation in 1955 regulated the setting-up of new industrial establishments within an 80 km radius of Paris as well as giving public funds to firms moving to zones of under-employment. While this measure inaugurated a process of industrial decentralization, the main cause of the new spatial division of labour, which would develop in the 1960s, was the search for cheap, non-unionized labour shed by the restructuring of agriculture.

As the problems associated with decolonization came to dominate domestic policy, the demands imposed by an escalating involvement in Algeria scuttled domestic growth. At the end of the Second World War, the French Empire was the second largest in the world and extended from South-east Asia to sub-Saharan Africa and North Africa. Certain overseas territories (Guadeloupe, Guyana, Martinique in the West Indies, Réunion in the Indian Ocean) were designated as overseas departments (DOM) in 1946 so that French metropolitan legislation applied to them (Potel, 1985, p. 583).

The first defeat the French encountered was in Vietnam, where its refusal to negotiate with the Vietminh drew France into a guerilla war lasting seven years. The final defeat occurred in May 1954 when French soldiers were trapped in Dien Bien Phu. Due to US aid, the cost to the French economy was not too great. This was not to be the case with Algeria, where much more was at stake. The Algerian population included one million *pieds-noirs*, or white colonists, and formed part of metropolitan France. On the other hand, elsewhere in North Africa, as in Tunisia and Morocco, with their smaller settler populations, and in Black Africa, France managed to resolve the process of decolonization with less conflict. In Algeria, on the other hand, much of the most fertile land had been appropriated by the colonists, especially along the coastal belt. The *Front national de libération*

(FLN, National Liberation Front) was formed in October 1954 and on 1 November 1954 about 70 attacks broke out. By 1957 over 400,000 French troops were stationed in Algeria. It was estimated that from 1954 to 1960, the cost of the war comprised 28 per cent of the French national budget (Hanley *et al.*, 1984, p. 12).

1.3   The Fifth Republic: the Gaullist State

By 1958 the politicians of the Fourth Republic had lost control of the political situation, and called on de Gaulle to avert a civil war and resolve the Algerian situation. Thus from 1958, when de Gaulle first became President, to 1962 when the Algerian situation was finally laid to rest with the granting of independence, the political regime of France was changed to an executive one separated from the legislative, with power now passing to the former. Proportional representation was abolished, and replaced by a two-ballot system that yielded clear majorities. However, even more significant was the degree of State intervention in restructuring the French economy and territory, and the rise of the higher echelons of the administration, who could now finally carry through the modernist vision. The creation of special commissions, for example *Délégation à l'aménagement du territoire et à l'action régionale* (DATAR, Delegation for Territorial Planning and Regional Action), bypassed traditional local and regional élites. De Gaulle's use of the referendum at opportune moments, as in 1962 to electing the president by universal suffrage, exemplified the call on the direct expression of the national interest, unmediated by politicians representing particular interests. His foreign policy sought to restore France's position as an independent world power, for example by withdrawing from NATO's military command and giving France a nuclear deterrent force. His rejection of a supranational European sovereignty was both political and economic, for industrially the regime promoted concentration among domestic sectors, but did not encourage European co-operation in large-scale projects and mergers.

However, the Gaullist era, from France's entry into the Common Market until the turbulence of 1968, could not be crudely categorized as state monopoly capitalism as it was by the French Communist Party. This thesis rested on the argument that the State adopted policies at the behest of monopoly capital and formed an organic whole, linking economy, society and politics (Kesselman, 1980, pp. 181–2). While the State achieved a unity of purpose and action unknown in the Fourth Republic, its relationship with the different capitalist sectors and social groups was neither straightforward, nor without contradictions and protests. In particular, the unresolved tension between the drive to modernity and the persistence of archaic systems, as with education and industrial relations, would explode in 1968.

The pressure to rid France of economic Malthusianism and open up the various sectors of economic activity came from specific fractions of social classes and strata, and usually not from those with the most power and capital. As we have seen, the challenge in agriculture came from the medium-sized farmers, who rejected a policy based exclusively on prices, a policy favoured by the large landowners. The takeover of the FNSEA in the 1960s by Michel Debatisse, who became assistant general secretary in 1964, laid the basis of 'corporatist' decentralization, by which means the Gaullist regime was able to circumvent the traditional power bases of regional administrative structures of privilege and negotiate with professional bodies which shared its views (Keeler, 1985). However, in the embryonic stages of this relationship, violent confrontation occurred over the slow pace at which the new legislation was being applied (*Loi d'orientation agricole* 1960, see p. 155). Even in 1965, some in the FNSEA were still hostile towards de Gaulle, whom they saw as provoking a European crisis that brought to a halt negotiations over farm prices.

Despite the transformation of agriculture, the small producer, though contributing much less in quantity, still remained dominant numerically. The peasantry continued to enjoy a much lower standard of living. For some, the FNSEA was not seen to speak for their needs and so in 1959, twenty-three departments south of the Loire came together to form the *Mouvement pour la défense des exploitants familiaux* (MODEF, Movement for the Defence of Family Farmers). Its greatest support was mainly in left-wing areas south of the Loire, but also in certain areas of Brittany (Gervais *et al.*, 1976, pp. 492–6).

In the industrial sector, the emergence of a modernizing bourgeoisie to oppose the positions of entrenched familial capitalism took until the mid-1960s to develop. This industrial bourgeoisie had all the hallmarks of a closed caste, wary of allowing new capital to enter into family enterprises and deriving status from property and assets, for example de Wendel, Lip, Dassault, Michelin. Authority was not to be shared, the rights of workers to participate were denied. The young turks of industry in the *Centre des jeunes patrons* (Centre of Young Employers), on the other hand, argued for the opening of frontiers, competition and the recognition of workers' rights and their unions, unlike the traditional *Confédération national du patronat français* (CNPF, National Confederation of French Employers). In effect, economic liberalism and social authoritarianism went hand in hand during the mid-1960s when the pace of mergers and concentration began to quicken, but management refused to negotiate.

The State had increasingly to intervene in the 1960s. Key capital goods industries, such as steel, electronics and chemicals, could not attract sufficient investment capital from the market, precisely because they offered risky prospects due to their exposure to foreign competition (Hayward, 1986, p. 79). Dynastic family firms continued to maintain their control and were able to regulate carefully the introduction of outside capital. Their traditional views, expressed in the arch-liberal statement issued by the CNPF in January 1965, espoused a declaration of faith in self-reliance and freedom from state intervention. However, enormous difficulties of financing and losses, as in the steel industry, would make state intervention inevitable, and already by 1968 the CNPF had come to espouse intervention and assistance in the face of mounting international competition.

As from 1965, a whole series of measures was enacted to introduce easier availability of credit, a reformed banking system and to push through mergers in the public and private sectors. The Fifth Plan (1966–70) put forward clearly and forcefully the objective of restructuring so as to establish or reinforce, where they existed already, a small number of firms or groups of international size. In most industrial sectors, the numbers of these groups were to be very small, often reduced to even one or two. Firms were to be given the greatest manoeuvrability to shut down and reorganize production (Hayward, 1986, pp. 82–3). It is little wonder that one might consider a theory of state monopoly capitalism to have a certain plausibility.

The first round of mergers occurred at the time of France's entry into the Common Market, while the second, at a much more rapid pace, took place in the years 1966–72 with 213 mergers per year and a maximum of 263 in 1969. In the earlier phase, from 1958 to 1964, the main thrust was a redistribution of activities within the 500 largest groups but, after 1964–5, the pace of financial centralization and concentration quickened in industry and banking, in both the public and private sectors. Branch companies were also set up jointly and higher-level administrators exchanged to bring about a much greater interaction between firms. At the same time, family firms altered their status to limited liability companies, for example Peugeot in 1965 and de Wendel in 1967, although the original families still retained control and even management of the large companies (Gauron, 1983, p. 118).

New forms of capitalist organization and industrial restructuring in the 1960s were accompanied by new work practices and the formation of a more diversified working class. This was a period of rapid geographical mobility of labour, especially out of agricultural regions. It was in the 1960s that industrial decentralization in regions of reconversion (East, Rhône-Alpes), and those in the process of industrialization (Basse Normandie, Brittany and Aquitaine), took place. Of the 350,000 jobs decentralized from 1950 to 1964, almost half moved to within a 200 km radius of the Paris region. For

80 per cent of these firms, according to a survey conducted for the period 1960–70, the main attraction was the supply of cheaper labour (Gauron, 1983, p. 10). The Centre, the first region to receive employment resulting from decentralization, had a high proportion of less skilled manufacturing jobs and a relatively low level of engineers, technicians and foremen (Lipietz,1980, p. 39).

During the 1960s the total labour force finally expanded from its stable level of just over 19 million in the 1950s. In the 1950s, increased demand for labour was met, not so much by incorporating new sources of labour, but by extending the working week. Although the 40-hour week had been passed by the Popular Front in 1936, exceptions to these regulations were frequently made and overtime became common. Thus until 1968, France had one of the longest average working weeks in Western Europe (45.2 hours). The Fifth Plan (1966–70) spoke of the crucial importance of labour mobility for economic expansion, and certainly a much higher degree of mobility was evident in the late-1960s. Thus 13 per cent of the workforce changed their sector and 20 per cent their place of work in 1959–64, while 17.1 per cent and 33 per cent respectively did so in 1965–70 (Caron, 1983, p. 287).

At the same time, the goverment continued to apply pressure to keep wage increases, especially the minimum salary, low. This eventually led to a decline in disposable household income in late 1966 (see Figure 1.1) and had already provoked general strikes at Peugeot (Sochaux), PTT (post office), RATP (transport) and EDF (electricity). The combination of salary differentials between Paris and the provinces, and the effects of deskilling and loss of employment resulting from restructuring, also initiated a whole series of strikes in the provinces. These ranged from one at Dassault in Bordeaux in December 1966, to strikes in Mulhouse in the autumn, and in Fougères and the Caen region in January–February 1968. While experienced as local conflicts, they nevertheless went beyond these confines and were to lay the basis of the far more generalized strikes of May 1968. Other strikes had often won widespread local and regional support, for example the conflict over the Decazeville mines in 1961–2 or the foundry strike at Hennebont in Brittany. The struggles to preserve employment drew the attention of intellectuals to the lack of control over employment in the region and the role of the regional bourgeoisie.

Restructuring, of course, did not just entail the alteration of work practices and the use of a higher proportion of less skilled labour; it also involved the incorporation of new sources of labour, and hence a more heterogeneous working class, whose specific composition varied regionally (see Chapter 3). In the early 1960s, the increase in the active population was partly due to greater numbers of immigrant workers and the settlement of *pieds-noirs* from North Africa, especially Algeria. In 1954, 1.7 million foreigners were resident in France, the main groups still of Southern European origin. From 1954 to 1961, 72,000 foreign workers entered annually, this figure rising to 132,000 per annum for 1962–73. From 1962 onwards, Algerian immigration grew very rapidly, although Algerians did not constitute the largest single group until the 1970s (Table 1.1). Thus from 1962 to 1968 the percentage of immigrant labour rose from 7.7 per cent to 9.4 per cent on average. A much higher proportion of them were on the basic minimum wage (*salaire minimum interprofessionnel garanti*, SMIG) and were often underpaid. It has been calculated in a study published in 1973 that immigrant labour as a whole reduced the wages bill by 20–30 per cent (quoted by Goubet and Roucolle, 1981, p. 26). This is particularly relevant since immigrant workers were concentrated in sectors with lower levels of profit and often sheltered from international competition. Their main areas of concentration were in the highly urbanized regions of the Paris region, Rhône-Alpes and Provence-Côte d'Azur (Figure 1.2).

Elsewhere, the swelling ranks of the semi-skilled workers were filled by the formerly agricultural population, which towards the end of the 1960s acquired an increasingly female allure. At the beginning of this century, women constituted 36 per cent of the paid labour force in a society where agricultural, artisan and traditional industries were significant employers of female labour. By 1962, the proportion of women in the working population

Table 1.1   Composition of the foreign population, 1954–82

Nationalities	Percentage of the foreign population				
	1954	1962	1968	1975	1982
Europeans	81.1	73.4	72.3	61.1	48.7
Italians	28.7	29.0	21.8	13.4	9.1
Portuguese	1.1	2.3	11.3	22.0	20.8
Spanish	16.4	20.4	23.2	14.5	9.1
Africa	13.0	19.7	24.8	34.6	42.8
Algerians	12.0	16.2	18.1	20.6	21.6
Moroccans	0.6	1.5	3.2	7.6	11.7
Tunisians	0.3	1.2	2.3	4.1	5.2
Other	0.1	0.8	1.2	2.3	4.3
Asia	2.3	1.7	1.7	3.0	8.0
Others	3.6	5.2	1.2	1.3	1.4
Total number	1,176,298	2,169,665	2,621,088	3,442,415	3,680,100

Source: INSEE censuses.

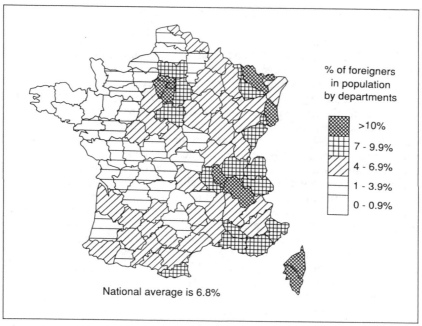

Figure 1.2   Distribution of foreign population, 1982.

had fallen to 27.6 per cent and their participation stood at 36.2 per cent.

1.3.1   A new spatial strategy

The 1960s were also the era of a spatial vision of a France of grandiose projects fit for a modern nation state. De Gaulle himself saw planning as a means of including social forces in the elaboration of economic and social policies. Planning would encompass all of society, set the objectives, establish a hierarchy of the most pressing and important needs and inculcate among administrators and politicians, and even among the public, a sense of what is global, ordered and continuous (Gauron, 1983, p. 73). These ambitious objectives, extending to the management of the whole of national space, can be clearly seen in the work of DATAR, which was set up in 1963 by Olivier Guichard and his successor Jérome Monod. Formally, this organization adopted the previous voluntarist policy of development, favouring the regions to the west of a line running from Le Havre to Marseilles and the zones of industrial reconversion. The hierarchical ordering of space was embodied in its earliest strategy of the *métropole d'équilibre* (counter-magnet city), which identified eight major regional urban centres (Strasbourg, Nancy–Metz, Lille–Roubaix–Tourcoing, Nantes–Saint Nazaire, Bordeaux, Toulouse, Lyons–Saint Etienne–Grenoble, Marseilles–Aix), to counterbalance the attraction of Paris and act as magnets for their respective regions. Five of these urban centres were further endowed with an *Organisation d'études et d'aménagement de l'aires métropolitaines* (OREAM, Strategic plan for the development and urbanization of metropolitan areas) and were given the task of drawing up a long-term plan until the year 2000. The empty spaces in between these metropolitan centres were to be filled in by regional action plans, some of which had already been instituted in the late 1950s (for example, Corsica, see p. 117).

Grandiose plans for the industrial development of Fos sur Mer, west of Marseilles, for the tourist development of the Languedoc coast and for the new towns of the Paris region were conceived during this period. For example, DATAR took charge of the Fos development from 1964 (Ferrier *et al.*, 1986, ch. 5) with the objective of recentring the Mediterranean on a decolonized France and challenging Northern Europe with a Europort of the South. The whole development of this area opened up possibilities for national and international capital, and so further marginalized the local bourgeoisie within its traditional activities. Not all these massive projections for the future were the work of DATAR. In the case of Paris, the *'District de la Région de Paris'* (District of the Paris region) was created in 1961 and headed by Paul Delouvrier, who had de Gaulle's support in his attempt to plan for the spectacular demographic growth that was envisaged for the Paris region. An enormous publicity campaign accompanied the publication of the *Schéma directeur d'aménagement et d'urbanisme de la Région,* (Control scheme for the development and planning of the Paris region) which some have suggested was an orchestrated attempt to win legitimacy in the face of opposition from elected local politicians (Amiot, 1986, p. 195). In all, five new towns in the Paris region and four in the rest of France (Lille-Est, le Vaudreuil near Rouen, l'Isle d'Abeau near Lyons, and Berre near Marseilles) were designated. Spatial reorganization was thus linked to the productive system.

At a regional level, *Commissions de développement économique régional* (commissions for regional economic development (CODERs) were set up parallel to the old regional expansion committees and sought to incorporate the modernizing economic and social forces. A regional mission was also established alongside each regional prefect so that, together with the external agents of DATAR, there was a sense of missionary zeal among those 'parachuted in'. Like the corporatist decentralization, these new institutions attempted to bypass the traditional notables and co-opt modernizing regional forces through a programme of functional regionalism (Hayward, 1986, pp. 54–5).

In general, then, the State took the initiative in economic modernization and spatial organization. We have already seen that the impetus to create larger economic units, initially within a national market, was at first often resisted by family-owned firms, as in the steel industry where a *Plan professionnel* (sectoral plan) was finally accepted in 1966. Yet, while high-level technocrats were able to im;:ose their economic and planning projects, the social conservatism and values of the French bourgeoisie remained more or less intact. As Gauron (1983, pp. 130–1) points out, de Gaulle may well have taken away some of the political power from the traditional represent-atives and given a much greater degree of autonomy to higher levels of the administration, now closley linked with the financial bourgeoisie, but conservatism and authoritarianism still prevailed in French society.

Furthermore, although social investment in collective consumption was supposed to be increased by 50 per cent under the Fourth Plan (1962–5), the reduction in public spending after 1963 had led to corners being cut. Priority was to be given to urban and rural infrastructure, education, health, sports and culture. The desire was to improve facilities as well as to provide more. However, in housing, for example, the huge increase and redistribution of population in the postwar years rendered these efforts inadequate after a period of a totally insufficient rate of construction up to the end of the 1950s. From 1949 to 1958 France built 160,000 dwellings on average per year compared to 280,000 in Great Britain (Goubet and Roucolle, 1981, p. 44).

Population increased from 40.13 million in 1946 to 42.89 million in 1954, largely due to natural increase (85 per cent in 1946–56). However, from 1958 to 1959, immigration increased and this was further augmented by the arrival of those who returned from Algeria, so that for the period 1960–6, immigration made up 47 per cent of the total increase in the population. In the years 1960–3, France experienced a most exceptional period of growth of 500,000–900,000 persons per year. Thus in the 1962 census, the official population stood at 46.42 million.

It was not just the overall population increase which would be important for the provision of collective consumption. By the 1960s, the impact of the postwar baby boom had begun to be felt in higher education after having strained the resources of primary and secondary school provision. The peak birth-rate was registered in the immediate postwar years, 21.1 per thousand population for 1946–9, but was still as high as 18.5 per thousand for the years 1954–7, a level higher than that of Italy (Beteille, 1986, p. 23) (Figure 1.3a). Hence from 1954 to 1962 the population under 20 years rose from 13.17 million to 15.38 million and then to 16.79 million in 1968.

a

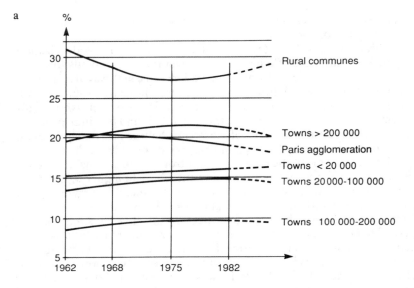

b

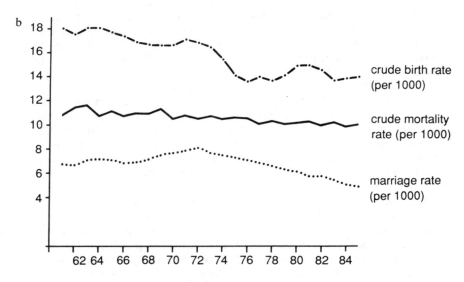

Figure 1.3 Demographic trends. a, Rates of birth, marriage and mortality, 1960–85. b, Rural and urban population by spatial distribution of primary residence, 1962–85.

The geographical location of this population also altered considerably during these years. From 1954 to 1968 urban communes grew by 1.8 per cent per annum compared to 1.1 per cent for the whole of France (Figure 1.3b). In between the censuses over 3 million people moved from one programme region to another. Yet in relation to housing and education, the overall population increase and its geographical redistribution do not alone allow us to understand the tensions in these sectors.

In education, for example, the explosion in the system stemmed, not just from the increase in the numbers of young people, but also from the greater rates of participation of each age group in the secondary schools, especially for women. The rate of participation for the age group 10–17 years rose from 22.2 per cent in 1950–1, to 35.2 per cent in 1958–9 and to 45.1 per cent in 1964–5 (Girard, 1981, p. 409). This rise was particularly due to girls entering the schools, for before the Second World War girls still formed a small minority in state secondary schools. By 1955 there were as many girls as boys within the education system. The school population in the second- ary sector was further boosted by legislation, fully implemented in 1967, making education compulsory until 16 years.

The huge expansion of the university sector did not occur until the 1960s. Until then, it increased at the rate of 3–4 per cent per annum, but then leapt up to an increase of 14 per cent per annum. Student numbers had risen from 136,700 in 1949 to 508,199 in 1967 (Hanley *et al.*, 1984, p. 36). While much has been said about democratization of the higher education system, the fact remained that this sector was still largely the domain of the bourgeoisie. For example, in 1967 57 per cent of the children of top management and liberal professions, but only 3.4 per cent of those from the working class attended university. The educational system in general reproduced *en masse*, and within a highly centralized system, what it had done in the past. It is no wonder, then, that students were at the centre of the May '68 events. The complaints of '68 were that all decisions emanated from faceless bureaucrats in Paris, with rigidly standardized syllabuses and virtually no autonomy and participation (Hanley *et al.*, 1984, p. 261).

1.3.2 *Archaism and modernity in collision*

The explosive combination of economic restructuring, decomposition of rural societies and social immobility of French institutions came together in the events of May 1968. While the violence of 1968 took everyone by surprise, some authors have traced its roots back to 1965, the year when industrial employment ceased to provide the necessary increase in jobs and when the effects of restructuring and increased capital intensity (ratio of capital to labour) combined to produce higher levels of unemployment.

From 300,000 people in search of a job in 1965, unemployment rose to 400,000 in 1968. The government's attempt to minimize salary increases was one of the factors, together with differentials between Paris and the provincial branch plants, that led to a whole series of local conflicts from 1965 onwards.

The political opposition had also begun to co-ordinate its efforts and to gain strength. Mitterrand presented himself as the candidate of a united Left in the 1965 presidential elections and managed to force de Gaulle to a second round, which the latter won with 55 per cent of the vote. Despite disunity on the Left, the Gaullists needed support from everyone else in the 1967 elections in order to form a government based on an extremely thin majority, namely 244 seats in an assembly of 485. Opposition to internal economic and social policies had grown to such an extent that de Gaulle's government, under Michel Debré as Prime Minister, ruled by ordinance in economic matters from April to October 1967. Students paved the way for the standstill that paralyzed the whole of France in mid-May 1968. Trouble had started at Nanterre, a new campus that had exceeded its capacity to accommodate students. More generally, however, students were concerned about the implementation of the Fouchet reforms for higher education and the threat of selection instead of the automatic right of entry from the *baccalauréat* (except in the *grandes écoles*, the select higher education establishments). In addition to this, there were massive demonstrations against American offensives in Vietnam. Confrontations between police and students in early May gained public sympathy for the students against police over-reaction. From 13 May, action switched to the workers, and from 15 May, factory after factory, beginning with Sud-Aviation in Saint Nazaire, went on strike. By 23 May millions of workers were on strike, some not returning to work until almost mid-June.

What, then, were the effects of May 1968 and the challenge to the immobility of French society? In the short run, a government was elected with an overwhelming Gaullist majority – 358 seats out of 485 in the National Assembly and politically to the right of the previous government. Before the strikes had ended, the Grenelle agreements had been made with the unions and these were eventually to form the basis of agreements in a whole series of industries. These gave a 35 per cent increase on the minimum wage for a theoretical 40-hour week, reduction in hours worked, a general wage increase of 10 per cent and greater recognition of shopfloor union rights. It also showed that the CNPF, the employers' organization, was able to negotiate, if forced to, and thus pushed them into a more united position. In education, a *Loi d'orientation* (November 1968) sought to change the higher education system. Although it set up more scope for the universities to decide their own teaching programmes and assessment, and enabled new interdisciplinary subjects to be included, administration remained as centralized as ever.

De Gaulle attempted to assert his authority through a referendum on regional institutions. In his March 1969 speech delivered in Lyons, he had argued that the centuries-old centralization efforts were no longer required. In reality, what he was trying to do was to break the power of the local and regional notables through the abolition of the Senate, which would no longer be able to legislate and would not be fully elected. In exchange De Gaulle offered a measure of regional decentralization, though even this did not go so far as regional elections, and left intact the existing urban and departmental organization. The combined votes of the Left and conservatives thus led to de Gaulle's defeat in the referendum (46.8 per cent in favour) and his immediate resignation (Nivollet, 1982, pp. 20).

What did de Gaulle's departure represent? The events of 1968 overturned the way the State viewed civil society and revealed its inability to control and transform various economic and social structures. The reminder of the persistence of archaic and authoritarian structures in France led to a questioning of what the modernizers were attempting to achieve through planning. Hence '68 also brought the technocrats and planners back to earth, though not entirely scuppering their Faustian vision of gigantic monuments. Fos, agreed in December 1968 by the Prime Minister, and the 'new towns' went ahead in the early 1970s. Above all, the power of the planners, substituting for elected officials, was much diminished. This was one of the lessons of the victory over de Gaulle by conservatives and local notables, and his replacement by the socially conservative Pompidou as the next President. The autonomy and means at the disposal of planners and technocrats at the full height of the Gaullist regime, together with the power of the executive at the expense of elected bodies, left little room for channelling protest. The events of May 1968 had expressed a multiplicity, albeit often contradictory, of critiques of society, ranging from the Marxist critique of capitalism, the anarchist critique of state power and the more specifically '68 critique of consumer society.

Various ideas on alternative societies had germinated pre-'68 but were to be more fully developed and radicalized in the post-'68 era. In 1965, the CFDT launched the notion of *autogestion* (self-management), a suggestive but ill-defined idea of a self-managing society. It was to be taken up by many of the countercultural movements, such as the regionalists and the *Parti socialiste unifié* (PSU) (United Socialist Party), and later by the rest of the Left. For the CFDT, self-management did not simply involve new relations in the workplace, but extended to other domains of society. Unlike the Communist Party (PCF), their objective was not the seizure of the State, for it is civil society, and thus social transformation, which should take priority over the State.

The social rethinking, crystallized by the events of 1968, politicized a number of groups, turning environmentalists into political ecologists, and regionalists into nationalists, and also linking the two more closely, as in the case of Larzac in the southern Aveyron. The *comités de défense de l'environnement* (committees for environmental protection) of the 1960s did not question the nature of society, but confined themselves largely to the consequences of industrial society on the environment. However, '68 questioned the objectives of industrial society and advocated a revolution of everyday life. So in 1970, several new groups were founded, such as the *Amis de la Terre* (Friends of the Earth). The first antinuclear demonstration was organized in Fessenheim (Alsace) in April 1971, and massive demonstrations against the extension of a military camp on the Larzac plateau, where 103 sheep farmers were threatend with expulsion, became a national affair, uniting many protest groups, including regionalists (Chafer, 1982, pp. 202–5). By this time, environmental concerns had even reached the government, leading to the establishment of the first Ministry for the Protection of Nature and the Environment, dubbed by Poujade, its first Minister, '*le ministère de l'impossible*' ('ministry of the impossible') (Chafer, 1982, p. 205).

Regionalist movements, especially the Breton one, emerged in the 1960s. Their early analysis was based on internal colonialism, an idea derived from a comparison of the treatment and situation of French peripheries with those of the French colonies, especially in North Africa (Reece, 1979). This thesis was also taken up by Occitanian movements. After 1968, the splits hardened between those who wanted to participate in development and those who took a stronger position against the State's development policies. Social and culural conflicts were integrated into the regional struggle, such as agricultural and environmental issues in Corsica, and the viticultural crisis and Larzac in Languedoc. As with environmental issues, the regionalist theme and demands gradually made their way into the Left's programme, for example the adoption of the slogan '*vivre et travailler au pays*' ('live and work in the local area') by unions, especially the CFDT, and the Socialist Party as from 1974.

The third major social movement of the 1970s was the feminist movement. Questions of reproduction and sexuality had been aired by politicians and the press in the 1960s. Indeed, Mitterrand was the first politician to open up the debate on more liberal contraception in his 1965 presidential campaign. Legislation revoking the highly restrictive 1920 Act on contraception was passed in 1967, but without specifying how information or access to contraceptive measures would be provided. However, in 1970, the Women's Liberation Movement (MLF) took onto the streets the invisibility and rights of women. Much more radical demands were voiced on contraception, and increasingly abortion, by organizations such as the French Family Planning Movement (MFPF), set up in 1956, and later, in 1973, with the formation of the Movement for Freedom in Abortion and Contraception (MLAC). Thus in 1974 the Chirac government passed further legislation on contraception and a restricted bill on abortion in 1975. From 1973 to 1974, the MLF tackled issues of battered wives, rape, homosexuality and economic independence, but it was slow in considering one of the major changes to occur after 1968, namely that of women's entry into the workforce and, particularly, their position in the worst remunerated jobs in manufacturing.

1.3.3. The end of Gaullism and the 'industrial imperative'

1968 and the end of a Gaullist regime did not just signify a flowering of social movements, but also altered the economic orientation, especially industrial policy, under the Pompidou presidency. The Sixth Plan, initiated in the aftermath of the May events, gave many of the most influential positions on its commissions to representatives of finance capital, and especially Roger Martin, President of the Industrial Commission. The protectionism and distribution of resources of previous plans were rejected; industrial development should be given priority and international competition taken seriously, instead of being vaguely espoused (Quinet and Touzéry, 1986, pp. 54–5). The State's role was to ensure the smooth regulation of the market, while those sectors which, for historic reasons, exist outside of it, should also be forced to operate competitively (quoted in Gauron, 1983, p. 178). National independence would have to give way to the industrial imperative. France certainly lagged behind in its international openings, especially in its exports. In the technologically advanced industries in 1972, only between one-quarter and one-third of production was exported, so that France still tended to export semi-finished products and import finished ones (Parodi, 1981, p. 113). It was during this period that the State encouraged public companies to set up subsidiaries with French and foreign capital, for example Elf–Erap, les Charbonnages de France, EDF (Parodi, 1981, p. 127), as had been suggested in the Montjoie-Ortoli Report (1968).

Growth was rapid from 1968 to 1972 so that the 1972 report of the Organization for Economic Co-operation and Development (OECD) noted a promising situation for France. However, Pompidou was mindful of the social tensions that he might not be able to control if growth proceeded too rapidly. This was not without foundation for in 1969 there had been large-scale strikes, and since then, the more worrying militant action occurred from a quarter which had provided the Gaullists with considerable electoral support. These were the small shopkeepers and artisans under the leadership of Gérard Nicoud. Gaullist reforms of the commercial sector in the 1960s had facilitated the expansion of larger stores, which operated on lower profit margins and therefore helped to keep down the rate of inflation. Hence from 1966 to 1971, the number of small shops fell by 20,000, while supermarkets and hypermarkets (more than 2500 m^2 and dealing in general merchandise) increased by 1987 and 143 respectively (Keeler, 1985, pp. 268–9). Government attempts to give this group of organized small shopkeepers some advisory role proved inadequate to stem their growth from 23,000 members in 1970 to over 200,000 in 1972. Most significant was the decline in support for the Gaullists among this group in the 1973 legislative elections. Pompidou, indeed, replaced Prime Minister Chaban-Delmas with the more conservative Pierre Messmer, in the hope of bolstering his appeal to the *France des profondeurs* (deepest rural France) and those who felt threatened by rapid economic growth.

The response of the government to the militancy of the artisans and shopkeepers was the *Loi Royer* in 1973. This law aimed to facilitate three forms of equilibria in this sector: modern/traditional, centre/periphery in urban areas and the human, between artisans and shopkeepers and other social categories. The cornerstone of the reform centred on expanded powers conferred on the commissions that had been set up in 1969 to control commercial development. In this way, and through the elected chambers of commerce and industry, the goverment hoped to co-opt this sector, as had been successfully achieved through corporatist decentralization in agriculture (Keeler, 1985, p. 271).

Another example of Pompidou's cautious approach, mindful of his need to ensure political support and try to win over centrist local notables, yet not antagonize Gaullists, was the regional reform passed in 1972. The legislation created public regional bodies that were indirectly elected, primarily administrative bodies to carry out some of the State's regional development functions. They had few resources, little legitimacy and, most importantly, preserved the departments, and therefore did not challenge the power bases of the local notables. Pompidou's fear for national unity mirrored that of most Gaullists, who were not particularly enthusiastic about this reform. Concern for the quality of life, now adopted by planning agencies and ministries, and the need to foster a sense of local community, were themes stressed in the development of a policy for medium-sized towns. Following the six towns chosen for pilot studies, the programme was opened up in 1973 to allow any town that so wished to apply for a contract. This form of centre–local relations represented a change from the earlier Gaullist policy, where only a few were selected within the urban hierarchy, to a policy that focused on individual urban centres, enabling them to improve their environmental and sociocultural conditions, but showed no interest in their economic functions. Though not placed in the foreground, economic considerations were certainly not absent from this policy. The lower costs of infrastructural provision and labour were recognized, especially the fact that many of these medium-sized towns reached deep into rural areas with substantial reserves of cheap labour for industry.

The Socialist Party (PS), too, finally united under Mitterrand's leadership at the conference held in Epinay-sur-Seine in 1971, also turned its attention to urban and environmental issues and espoused many of the qualitative and alternative demands resulting from the May '68 events. In July 1972 the PCF and the PS signed a Common Programme, which outlined a manifesto they would implement if they won an election. In economic policy, they promised wage increases, improved benefits and more extensive nationalization, a strategy pushed most strongly by the PCF (Kesselman, 1980). In the following March 1973 elections, the PCF with 21.3 per cent of the votes gained 73 seats, whilst the PS with a lower percentage of the vote did well with 101 seats (see Table 1.3).

Although the Gaullists won the elections (36.4 per cent of the votes and 238 seats), there had been considerable criticism of what was called the 'UDR state', and various scandals involving property development, which were reshaping many of the large cities (Hanley *et al.*, 1984, p. 44). Unemployment and prices were rising even before the impact of the increase in energy prices and the worsening situation of the world economy. We examine these trends more fully in the next section dealing with the Giscard presidency and the implementation of liberal economic policy. Pompidou died before the end of his term in April 1974, and before the effects of these economic trends had worked themselves out.

1.4 Giscard and advanced liberal society

In the second round of the presidential elections in May 1974, Giscard d'Estaing narrowly beat Mitterrand with 50.6 per cent of the votes. However, in Parliament, Giscard had to contend with a Gaullist majority and therefore appointed Jacques Chirac as his Prime Minister. Giscard had campaigned under the slogan of 'change without risk' and the promise of reforms.

In many aspects of economic policy there was little radical change, although the quadrupling of oil prices led to an acceleration of the nuclear energy programme, the curtailment of public spending and a greater emphasis on the private sector, for example in housing and urban development. Thus a programme for the rapid construction of nuclear power stations, which would make France 70 per cent dependent on internally generated energy, had already been announced in February 1974. National independence replaced dependence on international oil supplies in an attempt to counteract the heavy reliance on imported energy (75 per cent). However, we should not rashly jump to the conclusion that this programme was determined primarily by oil price rises for *Electricité de France* (EDF) had had proposals in hand for an 'all-electricity' energy policy using electro-nuclear power. All the obstacles to this policy were removed with de Gaulle's departure and a new openness towards American products.

The nuclear programe in its present form dates from 1975, when the effects of France's dependence on imported oil added a further impetus to this policy. France also had, after all, 3 per cent of the world's uranium resources. The squabbles in the 1960s over the choice of nuclear-reactor technology (gas-cooled or the American Westinghouse pressure water reactor (PWR) were finally settled in 1975, when the latter was adopted. Alongside the network of PWR reactors was built a nuclear fuel-cycle facility, comprising a uranium enrichment plant at Le Tricastin, completed in 1979. A uranium reprocessing plant for spent fuel at La Hague was also built in 1969 and its capacity doubled in 1980.

On the other hand, the CFDT put forward an alternative plan in 1975 which, while accepting the necessity of nuclear energy, none the less suggested ways in which energy could be economized and accused the EDF of pursuing a commercial policy, simply aimed at boosting household consumption of electricity (Parodi, 1981, pp. 107–8). Even before the announcement of the acceleration of the nuclear programme, the first antinuclear demonstration had taken place in Alsace in April 1971.

A beneficial consequence of spiralling energy costs was a rethinking of transport policy. Since 1962, investment in public transport, especially the railways (SNCF), had stagnated, leaving France with the lowest investment in relation to traffic carried of the six EEC countries (Parodi, 1981, p. 144). The age of the individualized form of transport had taken over, but the infrastructure provided for the new needs was inadequate. In the period 1962–77 the number of cars increased from 7 million to 19 million. By 1971, France had constructed 1600 km of motorway, the first one linking the North with the Mediterranean. Air traffic on the longer routes also competed with railways, so that from the 16,000 passengers carried on internal flights in 1960, the figure multiplied to 2 million in 1968 and continued to expand in the 1970s.

While the rail network was pruned in the 1960s, the intraurban services were gradually improved, especially in the Paris region, where the *Réseau Express Régional* (RER) was extended to the western and later the eastern inner suburbs. It was clear that, with depopulation from the centre of Paris and vastly increased commuting distances, the public in the 1960s were becoming increasingly dissatisfied with transport provision, as evidenced by the consumer protests over price rises and the quality of transport in Paris. The inadequacies of urban transport were not surprising given the rapid and often unplanned growth of the urban population in the 1960s (see Chapter 5).

Although urban growth slowed down overall in the years between the 1968 and 1975 censuses, it had done so particularly in the larger cities with a population of over 200,000 (see Figure 1.3b). As the urban population comprised 72.9 per cent of the total population in 1975 (63.4 per cent in 1962, 71 per cent in 1968), the medium-sized towns became the most attractive and Paris the least. Obviously, although Paris only registered an increase of 11 per cent compared to, say, Grenoble with 48 per cent or Montpellier with 46 per cent, there existed within the Paris region a massive demand for improved infrastructure and housing. The shift in population involved not only an extension of urban zones but also a social redistribution within urban areas, particularly the expansion of large peripheral estates (see Chapter 5), and the gentrification of old centres. In Old Lyons as well, the first city to have declared a *secteur sauvegardé* (conservation area) in 1964, only one-fifth of the original population remained after the renovation of this sector (Scargill, 1983, p. 128). Similarly, in the urban renewal schemes begun in the 1950s and 1960s, the immigrants and unskilled working class were for the most part dislodged and settled in the vast peripheral estates (Castells, 1978). Urbanization and new socioeconomic structures were producing a new social landscape.

1.4.1 The new social landscape

Since the Second World War, two major groups had been steadily declining as a proportion of the active population and in their economic influence. The agricultural population experienced an even more rapid decrease in the early 1970s (5.7 per cent per annum for 1968–75), leaving farmers and farm workers in 1975 representing no more than 7.6 per cent and 1.7 per cent, respectively, of the total population (Table 1.2). The number of small shopkeepers had also declined from 943,000 in 1945 to 771,000 in 1975.

However, the major debates about the composition and political importance of social classes in the 1970s concerned the working class and the new salaried middle classes. In the late 1960s, Serge Mallet (1969) in *La nouvelle classe ouvrière* (*The New Working Class*) had argued that new technological processes and the evolution of the capitalist system had engendered a new working class (male), much younger, better qualified and in the high-technology sector. This new working class, with more control over the work process, could be contrasted with the traditional (male) working class,

Table 1.2   Socioeconomic composition of the active population, 1954–75

	Percentage of the active population			
	1954[1]	1962	1968	1975
Farmers	20.7	15.8	12.1	7.6
Farm workers	6.0	4.3	2.9	1.7
Industrialists, shopkeepers, artisans	12.0	10.6	9.6	7.8
Liberal professions, intellectual professions, higher management	2.9	4.0	4.8	6.7
Middle management, intermediate professions, technicians	6.8	7.8	9.9	12.7
White-collar employees	10.8	12.4	14.8	17.7
Workers	33.8	36.7	37.7	37.7
Personal services	5.3	5.4	5.7	5.7
Other	2.7	2.9	2.6	2.4
Total no. of active population	19,184,764	19,251,195	20,397,976	21,774,860

Source: INSEE censuses.

[1] The definitions of the 1954 census are not the same as subsequent ones, nor were its data as reliable.

usually older and concentrated in declining industries. What became clearer in the 1970s was the even more pronounced territorial and social fragmentation of the working class. On the one hand, the proportion of foremen and skilled workers increased as a percentage of the working class to 43 per cent in 1975, yet, on the other hand, the unskilled and semi-skilled categories were increasingly filled by women and immigrants (45 per cent of these two categories in 1975).

By 1975 immigrants formed 18 per cent of the workforce; 90 per cent of the active immigrant population (1,642,800) in 1976 were employed as semi-skilled or unskilled workers. This represented the peak employment of immigrants since, after racist attacks in France, Algeria stopped migration in September, and this was followed in July 1975 by the curtailment of new immigrants seeking employment in France. At work, immigrants were concentrated in particular sectors, while in housing they were often allocated the less desirable HLMs and hostels, *habitations à loyer modéré*

(HLMs, social housing) from which the skilled working class had moved out (Hargreaves, 1987).

Another dimension of fragmentation, with significant consequences for trade union and political activity, was the growing proportion of the working class whose origins lay in the agricultural sector. Two-thirds of those who left the land became industrial workers. Agricultural workers, in particular, occupied the unskilled positions. The consequence of the postwar formation of the working class was to reduce the proportion of workers from working-class backgrounds. As Thélot noted (1982, pp. 213–14), this section of the working class had tended to vote to a greater extent for the Left, especially the Communist Party, while those from an agricultural background have a much weaker working-class identification (Terrail, 1984, p. 18), seeing their current position as transitory. It is also among the recent recruits to industry that unionization is lower. Yet even among the traditional working class, the spatial cohesion and solidarity, resulting from the association of work and residence, have often disappeared with the break-up of old patterns of working-class urban segregation, the displacement of their inhabitants to peripheral housing and economic restructuring in industries such as steel and coal mining. Mallet and others also pointed to the integration of the working class arising from higher average living standards (see Figure 1.1a) and the consumer society diffused through the mass media.

The other group that has generated much discussion is the salaried middle class. It was among middle and upper management and professional groups that the increase was most spectacular between the 1968 and 1975 censuses. For example, tertiary and secondary school teachers recorded an 8.5 per cent increase, higher-level administration and management 5.3 per cent, and social and medical services 8.1 per cent. Interest in this heterogenous grouping stemmed precisely from the difficulty of placing its various fractions in relation to the two traditional classes of the bourgeoisie and the proletariat, and its growing political importance in the 1970s, which expressed itself in involvement in local politics, social movements and associations of all sorts, whose membership was overwhelmingly middle class. As with the working class, but to an even greater degree, feminization of the lower and middle echelons of the salaried middle class occurred. By 1975, 63.5 per cent of infant and primary teachers, 79 per cent of social and medical personnel and 47 per cent of secondary and tertiary sector teachers were women.

1.4.2   *New patterns of consumption*

The service sector and the salaried middle classes continued to expand, albeit at a slower rate, even after the impact of the first increase in oil prices. Since the 1960s, the public sector has added a large number of new jobs in education, post and telecommunications and finance, although the private sector remained the largest employer of the salaried workforce (67 per cent in 1975). Certain sectors, such as health, maintained their spectacular growth rate in terms of expenditure per household unit and employment (Figure 1.4). While health insurance had been implemented after the Second World War, as part of the social security programme of the National Council of the Resistance, its extension to various sections of the population had proceeded slowly; by 1960, 24 per cent of the population did not enjoy social security benefits. However, bringing the agricultural population and the self-employed into the social security net substantially reduced the

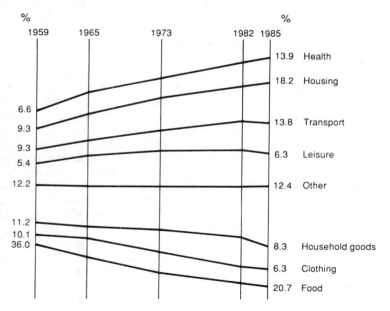

Figure 1.4 Household expenditure, 1959–85.

population not covered to about 1 per cent, although these categories still tended to use medical services to a far lesser extent than the salaried middle class and skilled workers (see p. 89).

In relation to the provision of housing, the level of construction remained high in the immediate period after the increase in oil prices (546,000 dwellings completed in 1972, 515,000 in 1975), and government policy encouraged the trend towards the private provision of housing (see Tables 5.1 and 5.2). After 1972, conditions of social housing allocation had become less favourable at a time when accession to home ownership increased by 216,000 per year. However, from 1973 to 1978, the rate of accession slumped from 115,000 dwellings in 1975 to 69,000 in 1978. The complicated system of subsidies led to the commissioning of a report on housing finance in 1975. The Barre Report recommended a reform of housing finance away from aid to those building dwellings towards aid to the individual. It was argued that the French spent too little on housing and that this reform would give the individal greater choice in housing and help to break down the high levels of social segregation in many cities, by making the individual less dependent on the HLM organization (Arnaud, 1988). Housing was one of the priority programmes of the Seventh Plan and typified its discourse of quality rather than quantity.

The Seventh Plan (1976–80) had taken a long time in preparation due to the sudden change of presidency in 1974. It marked a clear disengagement of the State from earlier forms of planning and collective consumption, reasoning in terms of the impossibility of quantitative objectives in a world beset by the uncertainties of external economic constraints. Yet it went much further in limiting state action to improving the quality, as in housing, or reducing excessive inequalities and spreading responsibilities (Quinet and Touzéry, 1968, p. 57). The programmes supported by the Plan were to be limited and selective, recommending desirable policies and measures rather than defining objectives in quantitative terms (p. 58). However, even these more restricted objectives of state intervention had to be modified in the light of the Barre Plan, the key justification of which was the necessity to fight inflation.

1.4.3   Political alignment

Chirac 'resigned' in 1976 due to his economic policy and political and ideological differences with Giscard, leaving an inflation rate running at 9.5 per cent p.a. in the last year of his office. Barre, the new Prime Minister, introduced a counter-inflationary plan in September 1976, reflecting a liberal economic approach that stressed a balanced budget and moderate wage increases. However, the effects of his policy were to lower purchasing power with only a marginal slowing-down in retail prices from 9.8 per cent in 1976 to 8.6 per cent in 1978.

Really fundamental changes and a supposedly more decisive withdrawal of state intervention in the economy did not come about until after the Right's surprising victory in the 1978 legislative elections (Table 1.3). The 1977 municipal elections brought considerable gains for the Left, leaving them in control of two-thirds of the municipalities with over 30,000 population, even in regions identified with the Right. The Left had managed to win not only those seats where it had already received a substantial vote in the 1973 legislative elections, but also those in cities where it previously had only a weak presence. The Left also made gains in rural communes, for the arrival of new, often middle-class inhabitants produced a more politicized election. One of the most notable outcomes of these elections was the inroad made by the Socialist Party in the traditionally conservative and Catholic West, where detachment from the Church proved favourable to the PS. Devout Catholics remained immune to the Left's message with only 2 per cent voting for the Communist Party and 14 per cent for other left-wing parties, as we know from the surveys conducted after the 1978 elections (Michelat and Simon, 1985, p. 36).

It was widely thought that the Left was poised for victory after its series of successful elections since 1974 and Giscard's unpopularity. Yet victory was snatched from it in the 1978 legislative elections even though it polled more

Table 1.3   Elections in the 1970s: percentage of votes cast

Political party	Legislative (first round)	
	1973	1978
Far left	3.28	3.27
PC	21.41	20.61
PS + MRG	19.2	24.98
Diverse Left	1.5	2.88
Ecologists	—	2.18
RPR	23.93	22.43
UDF	10.69	20.42
Diverse Right	3.30	3.22
Extreme Right	2.83	
Registered electors	29,901,822	34,394,845
Votes cast	23,751,213	28,098,113
Abstentions (%)	18.76	16.68

votes in the first round than the Right. Furthermore, the Left entered the elections divided, negotiations over the renewal of the Common Programme having broken down in September 1977, leaving the electoral pact unspecified at the beginning of the 1978 elections. With the deepening of the economic crisis, the different views of the PS and PCF on economic policy, especially the extent and purpose of the nationalized sector, diverged more openly. The Communist party wanted an enlarged public sector which would weaken the power of monopoly capitalism and bring about changes in the means of production and exchange (Kesselman, 1980); the Socialists were primarily interested in selective nationalizations without large-scale changes of property. In political terms, the muting of social conflicts and restraint on working-class demands had seemed not to pay off for it was the Socialists, and not the Communists, who made the spectacular gains in the local elections. Thus the Communist Party entered the 1978 elections as the weaker partner on the Left. It was for all these reasons that the pact was suddenly broken, resulting in dismay and disillusionment on the Left.

Though tensions existed on the Right between the Gaullists, with Chirac leading the *Rassemblement pour la République* (RPR), and the Giscardians, associated with the President and the newly formed *Union pour la Démocratie Française* (UDF), they managed to disguise their divisions. Compared with the earlier local elections, the 1978 results show a greater support for the Right from the middle management and white-collar sectors. This was not just due to Giscard's call for social consensus or the tempering of ideological divides, outlined in his book *Démocratie Française* (*Democracy in France*). Giscard had ably steered his way through these contradictory values by combining 'property and liberty' in which he undertook to '*rendre les Français propriétaires de la France*' (to make the French owners of France) (Capdevielle *et al.*, p. 12).

The Right emerged with a comfortable majority so that Barre then set about gradually abolishing price controls and reorienting state intervention. Competition was the key word and sectoral policies were dropped. The State would limit itself to macroeconomic policy and only exceptionally intervene in specific sectors. The objective of intervention was to supplement market forces, not to replace them. Furthermore, it was only with the continuation of Barre's austerity programme that, for the first time, internal demand was dampened. The problem was that the competitive sectors (electronuclear, armaments, telecommunications) had little effect on the rest of industry, and so the proportion of imported industrial products continued to increase from 20 per cent in 1971 to 30 per cent in 1978 and 35.7 per cent in 1981 (Potel, 1985, p. 341).

In reality, the State did not withdraw from a major role in restructuring.

Agencies such as CIASI (Interministerial Committee for the Development of Industrial Structures) handled 660 corporate rescues involving a total of 300,000 jobs during the Giscard presidency (Hall, 1985, p. 92). For the steel industry, the government finally proposed a 'steel plan' in September 1978 which led to the shedding of more than 21,000 jobs by 1980, hitting the steel-producing areas of Lorraine hardest (see p. 114). After violent protests in Longwy and Paris in 1979, the steel unions agreed to the plan in exchange for substantial redundancy payments and retraining schemes. Effectively the steel industry was a nationalized sector, for over two-thirds of the equity was now in the hands of the State and financial institutions under its control. Similarly, funds were also provided for restructuring the textile industry in the Vosges (Green, 1980, pp. 165–6). However, the cost of the austerity packages and restructuring programmes was increased unemployment, 5.2 per cent in 1978, reaching 7.6 per cent in May 1981. While household expenditure increased by 3.5 per cent p.a. for the period 1975–80, it was the unemployed who bore the brunt of the austerity measures (see Figure 1.1), for Barre hesitated in imposing them on the middle classes before the 1981 elections (Hall, 1985).

1.5   The Socialist years, 1981–6

Political power was finally gained by the Left in the 1981 presidential and legislative elections. Mitterrand proved to be lucky third time, and in his second contest against Giscard d'Estaing won 52 per cent of the vote in the second round on 10 May 1981. A number of departments outside the traditional left-wing zones had voted for Mitterrand–Burgundy and the Franche–Comté, the Centre, the edge of the Massif Central and in the West, Calvados and Charente-Maritime. The new elections in June 1981 gave the PS its best-ever result (37.5 per cent of voters), confirming its dominance of the Left and the continual decline of the PC, which polled only 16.2 per cent in the first round. On the Right, the RPR under Chirac's leadership managed to remain the largest party (with 20.7 per cent in the first ballot) as against the UDF's vote of 19.2 per cent. As yet, the extreme Right was insignificant, polling only one-third of 1 per cent of votes. The result gave the Left an overwhelming majority and, for the first time in the 23 years of the Fifth Republic, the chance of governing (Table 1.4).

The government set about implementing a radical change in the nature of society, based primarily on the 110 propositions of Mitterrand's electoral programme, hammered out with the Communist Party in the years in opposition. Economic and social aims were to be linked and represent a break with past policies such that a new style of citizenship would emerge. Respect for human rights would accompany a new society; not exclusively

Table 1.4   Elections in the 1980s

| | Legislative elections | | | | Presidential elections | |
| | 1981[1] | | 1986[2] | | 1988[1,3] | |
	% of votes cast	No. of seats	% of votes cast	No. of seats	% of votes cast	No. of seats
Far left	1.33		1.56		0.36	
PC	16.12	44	9.69	35	11.32	27
PS + MRG	37.77	285	31.61	214	35.87	276
Diverse Left	0.57	5	0.25		1.65[4]	
Ecologists	1.09	88	1.24		0.35	
RPR	20.91	62	42.03	147	19.18	128
UDF	19.16	7		132	18.49	130
Diverse Right	2.66		2.71	14	2.85	13
Extreme Right	0.36		0.16		0.13	
FN			9.87	35	9.65	1
Total no. of seats	491		577		575	

[1] Results of first ballot.
[2] Proportional vote using single ballot.
[3] Excludes French Polynesia.

devoted to production for the profit of a small group, so leading to a rupture with the previously capitalist system.

In economic terms the new model of economic growth called upon a statist strategy based on the revitalization of a decentralized and more participatory style of planning, and the expansion of a dynamic public sector through the nationalization of key sectors of industrial and finance capital. In cultural terms, the rights of minorities and the reality of a plural France were recognized. Decentralization, including a new regional tier of representation, was to be a major piece of legislation (see Chapter 4). Yet, while several environmental projects were cancelled, for example Larzac in May 1981 (Ardagh, 1988, p. 326), the nuclear programme was only slowed down. Five, including Plogoff, of the fourteen proposed new constructions were halted, but France continued to expand its nuclear capacity so that it was 60 per cent dependent on nuclear energy and had 44 PWRs in operation in 1985 (Bunyard, 1988, p. 4). In fact, capacity doubled between 1981 and

1985 despite the reduction in demand for electricity, leaving France with a significant generating surplus, part of which was exported.

After the honeymoon period in 1981, the Left set about reflating internal demand, especially increasing the purchasing power of the worst-paid workers, and attempting to reconquer internal markets through a modernized state sector. Its nationalization programme came unstuck through the unpalatable fact of France's international dependence. The Left had not fully appreciated either the extent of France's involvement in the international order or the increasing penetration of its internal market. By 1983 imports and exports represented 23 per cent of gross domestic product while the increase in internal demand (1.7 per cent in 1981 and 3 per cent in 1982) was increasingly filled by imports, thus worsening the balance of payments deficit. This was the period of a second international recession, following the second oil price rise in 1979, and France was in a particularly bad position due to its dependence on imported energy needs, paid in dollars. The situation was not helped by the inexorable rise of the dollar in the period 1981–4.

An initial austerity programme was announced in spring 1982, to be continued much more resolutely in March 1983 when a series of measures was put into practice to reduce internal demand, curtail public expenditure and reduce the balance of payments deficit – all classic instruments of balancing the books. Equally fundamental was the change in rhetoric from the discourse of change with the past to a discourse of modernization, competitiveness, the blessing of the mixed economy and the rediscovery of the talents of the entrepreneur.

The introduction to the Ninth Plan (1984–8) gives a flavour of this new thinking: 'The old world dies, a new one is born'. The Plan's main objectives are to maintain France's frontiers open as a fundamental element of its international strategy and, second, to modernize the country through industrial investment, research and education. Similarly, nationalized industries were also to abide by rules of profitability and competitiveness, just like any other company. It should be remembered that there had been relatively little investment by the private sector in many of the newly nationalized, industrial sectors and that state funds supplied a total of FF 20 bn to the nationalized sector between 1982 and 1984. At the same time, losses amounted to FF 10 bn in 1981 and FF 17 bn in 1983, so that with the switch to an emphasis on technological change and modernization, rather than employment and investment, the share of the budget for nationalized industries was reduced as from late 1983 (Stoffaes, 1985, pp. 162–3). In particular, plans for the coal and steel industries were revised, putting further pressure on already badly hit regions to continue shedding labour. Thus in the decade 1975–85, 60,000 jobs were lost in Lorraine (see p. 114);

this loss was only slightly compensated by employment gains in the service sector, and often these occurred in the metropolitan zones, such as Nancy and Metz, rather than in the industrial zones.

These austerity measures resulted in an average loss of 2.4 per cent in purchasing power for the salaried population between 1982 and 1985. The impact of the austerity programme and the abrupt turnabout in industrial and social policies, for example the reduction in unemployment benefits by 10 per cent from 1982–4, led to disillusionment and disenchantment with the Socialist government, both from its staunch supporters and those who had voted for the Left in 1981, especially among the salaried middle class.

Translated into more concrete social and political terms, this meant a loss of electoral support as early as the cantonal elections in 1982. In the 1983 municipal elections (see Table 1.4), Socialists and Communists lost a number of important cities, some of which they had governed for a long period, for example Nîmes, lost by the Communists. Other cities that were lost remained symbolic of the new, dynamic France, for example Grenoble (Ardagh, 1988, pp. 152–6), where Hubert Dubedout was defeated by Alain Carignon, a rising star on the Right. However, in western France, many of the gains of the 1977 elections were retained, for example Rennes led by Edmond Hervé.

1.5.1 Changes in the political landscape

The major features of the political landscape during this period were the meteoric rise of the National Front (FN) (Figure 1.5; see also Table 1.4) and the progressive eclipse of the Communist Party. While these two trends have often occurred in the same localities and regions, it would be facile to jump to the conclusion that support has directly shifted from the Communist Party to the Front National as certain interpretations tended to suggest.

Despite the presence of large numbers of foreigners in France (see Table 1.1), political parties focusing on racism had little success in the 1970s. Under Giscard, a series of regulations had restricted immigration from outside the Common Market, although from 1975 to 1982 the number of immigrants continued to grow. One-third of immigrants came in order to work, one-third for family reasons and one-sixth for political reasons. None the less, the foreign active population did decrease to 1.55 million, or 6.6 per cent of the active population. As in the past, a high proportion of this population is without qualification (over 40 per cent of men and 32 per cent of women), and so highly susceptible to unemployment. In 1987, for example, the rate of unemployment among the active workforce was 9 per cent for the French population, but 16.6 per cent for foreigners, with higher levels still for Algerians and Tunisians (Brunet, 1987).

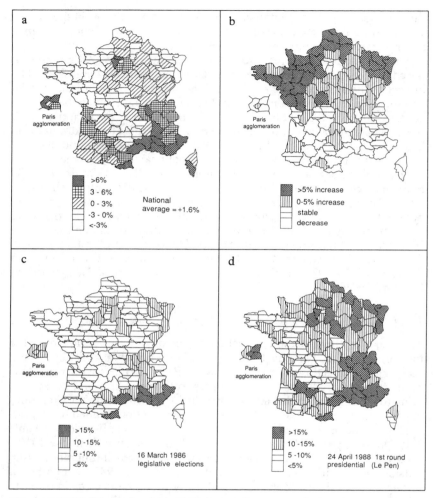

Figure 1.5   Political change, 1981–8. a, Progress of the Right, 1981–8. b, Evolution of support for Mitterrand, 1981–8: second round of presidential elections. c, National Front, 1986 legislative elections. d, National Front, 1988 presidential elections.

In the first few months of the Socialist government, a number of measures were passed giving immigrants greater rights (they could form associations and had rights against arbitrary expulsions) as well as the maintenance of

Table 1.5   Socioeconomic composition of the active population, 1982

	% of active population including unemployed		Women (%) of employed	
	Total population	Women	population	Foreigners (%)
Farmers	6.2	6.6	37	0.4
Industrialists, shopkeepers, artisans	7.7	6.9	33	3.1
Liberal professions, etc.	7.8	5.6	25	3.7
Middle management, intermediate professions	16.6	19.5	40	2.2
White-collar employees (including personnel services)	27.2	47.0	72	4.7
Workers	32.4	14.4	19	13.6
Skilled			8	11.5
Unskilled			34	16.5
	100.0	100.0		
Total	21,379,200	1,557,400	40.7	6.7

Source: INSEE censuses.
Note: The census categories were altered with the 1982 census to account for social and economic changes.

legislation against new work immigration (Hargreaves, 1987). But the rise of the extreme Right and pressure from the Right pushed the government from a policy based on legalisation of those without papers to the hunting down of illegal immigrants, over which a sort of consensus prevailed.

From the 1981 presidential elections, when Jean-Marie Le Pen could not gather the 500 signatures necessary to stand as a candidate and when the extreme Right parties only picked up one-third of 1 per cent in the legislative elections, the National Front came to acquire recognition and notoriety in 1983 (Schain, 1987). The rerun of the Dreux municipal elections in September 1983 gave the FN 17 per cent of the votes cast in the first round and led to its incorporation in the Right's victorious list. Openly racist programmes also seemed to be paying off in the Paris region, for example Aulnay sous Bois where Peugeot employed a majority of immigrant workers in its plant. Until after the FN's success in the European elections in 1984, when it scored 11 per cent of votes cast, the RPR and UDF on the Right were prepared to conclude alliances with it.

The rapid rise of the FN has given Le Pen numerous opportunities in the media to air his views on the role of immigrants in French society. Since February 1984, for example, Le Pen has appeared several times on the political programme *L'Heure de Verité (Hour of Truth)*, where he was judged favourably by those polled after the programme. The slick slogan equating two million unemployed with two million foreign workers exaggerates their numbers conveniently, but underplays their indispensable role in the economy and the high levels of unemployment they experience. Finally, another vote-catching theme is that of the climate of insecurity.

Race and law and order by no means exhaust the basis of support for the FN. Certainly, since 1984, when it was supported most strongly by artisans, shopkeepers and the liberal professions, its base has widened to include the young and the old. While xenophobia fuels a large group of FN supporters (38 per cent in an exit poll at the European elections in 1984), economic issues also loom large (Schain, 1987, p. 247). The FN plays on xenophobia, insecurity, decline of national identity and protest against exclusion and the political system. Le Pen's politics are effectively derived from the traditional political Right, on to which he has grafted elements of national populism (Schain, 1987, p. 246). Thus at every election the FN has consolidated and broadened its social and geographical base (see Figure 1.5).

Centres of FN strength are often found near, but not coterminous with, immigrant presence, in what has been called the 'halo effect'. Studies in the Paris region, especially in the former 'red belt' in the department of Seine-Saint Denis, have argued that the success of the FN is due to a complex process of disintegration of a local hegemonic system. In this process the weakening of the previously dominant party produces a generalized modification of political responses well beyond its own electorate (Rey and Roy, 1986, p. 38). Such an analysis enables us to understand how the FN has done well in both left- and right-wing areas. In left-wing areas it is the collapse of the Communist Party which has left a social and political void.

While already evident in the early 1970s, the slump in PC support manifested itself from the time of the 1978 legislative elections, when it polled 20.6 per cent of votes cast in 1978, but only 16.1 per cent in the 1981 legislative elections. That was only the beginning of its dramatic downward spiral, for in 1983 it lost a number of old urban strongholds. Only in the heart of its rural stronghold in the Limousin did the PC manage to attract one-fifth of the vote in the 1986 regional elections. The causes of the spectacular decline cannot just be sought in the sociospatial transformation of the electorate, namely a decrease in the importance of the traditional working class, particularly hard hit by the economic crisis, or the small peasantry in certain regions. It was not merely the rise of the salaried middle class, attracted more by the PS, that played a part in the PC's failure to win over a younger electorate. The weakness of its analysis and strategic thinking, the failure of its policies and its internal fights over how to adjust to current realities of French society and construct a democratic socialism all contributed to the Party's decline.

Other changes in the political landscape and a muted social mobilization were symptomatic of the trade union movement. A lower rate of unioniza-tion and participation in the union and social security elections, as well as a record low level of days lost in strikes, reveal the changes taking place in the world of work and the effects of durable and high levels of unemployment in the 1980s. From 1976 to 1983, the various unions lost a good percentage of their members, the *Confédération Générale du Travail* (CGT) declining by 30 per cent, the CFDT by 17.8 per cent. At the same time, the days lost in strikes entered a low phase, not encountered since the mid-1960s. In general, there was a tendency to hold back from strike action so as not to cause too many difficulties for a left-wing goverment. The greatest con-centration of strike action occurred in areas most heavily hit by restructur-ing (Lorraine, Nord-Pas de Calais, Haute Normandie and the Paris region), although the regional distribution demonstrated a higher degree of 'na-tionalization' than had previously been the case (Buléon, 1986, pp. 218–20).

If a degree of social and political disengagement and muted reactions characterized the response of unions and workers to the government's austerity programme and strident emphasis on technology and moderniza-tion, much more open confrontation prevailed in other sectors. This was especially the case in education, concerning the battle over the rights of the public versus the private educational system. The battle lines between Church and State and the role of religious bodies in education go back to the nineteenth century in France. Two pieces of legislation, the *Loi Debré* in 1959 and especially the *Loi Guermeur* in 1977, had given certain rights to the, overwhelmingly Catholic (93 per cent) private sector (Potel, 1985, p. 425). The 1977 legislation, passed in anticipation of a left-wing victory in the 1978 elections, forced local authorities to finance private schools which did not need to take into account the overall provision of educational facilities in the relevant area. This was, of course, highly favourable to the private sector which, since 1977, has been expanding and now educates 17.5 per cent of the school population from nursery to secondary school (see Chapter 3).

The conflict first broke out in Nantes in 1982 between the Socialist municipality under Alain Chenard and the Catholic educational system. When Alain Savary, the then Minister of Education, attempted to promulgate legislation integrating more fully the public and private sectors, the issue provoked some of the largest demonstrations seen in France with an estimated 1.3 million protesters assembling in Paris on 25 June 1984. The upshot of this conflict was the resignation of Alain Savary and his replacement by Jean-Pierre Chevènement, who put aside many of his predecessors's reforms and reverted to the traditional Republican values of education and emphasis on the basic skills of reading, writing and arithmetic. However, this issue also contributed to the downfall of the Mauroy government and his replacement by Laurent Fabius, who was far less closely associated with socialist aspirations and projects. The formation of this government and its pursuit of austerity led to the withdrawal of the Communists from the government in July 1984.

In terms that could be judged successful by a right-wing government, the Socialist government had by 1985 brought the balance of payments and inflation under control through its austerity programme, particularly the reduction of public spending. Nevertheless the Socialists continued to be attacked by their detractors and supporters. Purchasing power began to pick up in 1985 but favoured the better-paid salaried groups. Pressure on benefits also eased, but the system of unemployment benefits, based on an insurance principle and negotiated between the State, employers and the unions, was not designed for the long-term and recurrent unemployed. The principle of a minimum guaranteed income had been applied to groups such as the elderly, the disabled and young children, but neglected the unemployed (Collins, 1988, pp. 82–3), who had to fall back on local assistance and charities. In 1985, for example, 39 per cent of the unemployed, among whom the young and women were over-represented, were not entitled to any benefit. Unemployment no longer constituted a transitional state, for in 1986 47.8 per cent of those unemployed had been so for over 2 years (Brunet, 1987).

The growth of those excluded from work brought to light the existence of the so-called 'new poor' who were, as from July 1984, propelled into the political arena. Even before the economic crisis, it had been estimated that about only one-fifth of the French population benefited from the crumbs of prosperity (Clerc and Chaouat, 1987, p. 19). Almost half a million of the unemployed live in total poverty, receiving no income whatsoever (p. 88). Local authorities, especially those in the North-east, have implemented a number of minimum revenue schemes, but these are obviously limited (Charbonnel and Lion, 1988).

The limited reduction of inequalities and the persistence of poverty, despite the high level of social security contributions and income tax, provided ammunition for upholders of neo-liberal economic thinking who denounced the heavy and all-pervasive hand of the State. However, in reality the latter years of the Socialist regime had been accompanied by a rapid liberalization and deregulation of the economy, especially in financial markets and work conditions, not to mention the supremacy of the market as the regulator of the economy. Gone were the days when the Left thought it could make a break with capitalism and its belief in the value of national planning. The State may have disengaged itself to some extent from economic regulation and decentralized some of its powers, but it remained very visible in defence matters and the protection of its territorial integrity.

In relation to the latter, the hopes of independence expressed by the Melanesian minority (kanaks) in the overseas territory of New Caledonia did not materialize with the Left's victory, and thus exploded in a cycle of violence in 1984–5. A compromise seemed to have been achieved through a regional division agreed by the pro-independence *Front de libération nationale kanake socialiste* (FLNKS) and the anti-independence *Rassemblement pour la Calédonie dans la République* (RPCR). In the September 1985 vote the FLNKS gained control of three of the four regions. France's reputation in the South Pacific was troubled by the scuttling by French agents in New Zealand in July 1985 of the *Rainbow Warrior*, the ship of the ecological movement Greenpeace (Larkin, 1988, p. 376). Thus the Socialist government came to the end of its five-year period buffeted by various incidents and criticized by opponents and supporters alike.

1.6 The joys of 'cohabitation', 1986–8 and beyond

The March 1986 legislative elections witnessed the defeat of the Left, although the Socialists emerged as the largest single party (almost 32 per cent of the votes cast) (see Table 1.4). A right-wing majority in Parliament in conjunction with a left-wing President now produced a completely new situation in the life of the Fifth Republic.

Jacques Chirac was appointed Prime Minister of a government consisting of two parties, the RPR and the UDF, both proclaiming the virtues of a less interventionist, but more efficiently run state. Its programme highlighted the need to denationalize the banks, privatize nationalized companies (not limited to those privatized by the Socialists), deregulate prices, including rents, facilitate changes in the workforce and reduce public expenditure, so as to lighten the burden of fiscal and social taxes and motivate those who work and take risks. Yet, reduced in its powers of economic intervention, the State was certainly not destined to disappear for its powers were reinforced in relation to the police, the control of illegal immigration and delinquency (Julien, 1988, p. 25).

The first round of privatizations met with some approval from small investors (St Gobain and Paribas). Others, on the contrary, provoked more dissension, such as the privatization of TF1, one of the three state-owned television stations (Berger, 1987). The course of privatization did not in the end run smooth, for the stock exchange crash of October 1987, and again in January 1988, brought the value of shares on the Paris exchange tumbling by 40 per cent, and forced the Minister for the Economy and Finance, Edouard Balladur, to call a halt to the process. Popular capitalism would not be the pot of gold in the short run.

Already in its first year, the government had confronted massive opposition from students and pupils who were demonstrating against the university reform outlined by the Secretary of State for the university sector, Alain Devaquet. The show of force was not at all a replay of 1968; the students were protesting against greater selectivity of university entry and concern for employment opportunities. Moral issues, more than the desire to overturn society, motivated the students of the 1980s. Other grassroots discontent, which initially bypassed official union channels, seriously disrupted public transport in Paris and the rail network in December 1986 and January 1987.

Economically, the results were very mixed, with unemployment continuing to rise quite sharply in the first half of 1987, reaching a peak of 2.65 million and the balance of payments heading for a large deficit (FF 31,400 million francs in 1987) (*Le Monde*, 1988a, pp. vi–vii). The budget deficit itself had been reduced, partly due to an end to payments for the nationalization programme, while income and company taxes were lowered. However, the social security deficit of FF 19,000 million reappeared in 1987. The suggestion, made not long before the presidential elections in 1988, that the social security system would have to be radically rethought, was not at all well received. The withdrawal of full coverage for medicines for the long-term ill seemed to presage the future.

Mitterrand's opening remark of his presidential campaign in March 1988 about the 'RPR State' rang true. The distribution of favours to friends was quite clear in the media, as was the nomination of directors and officials in a whole range of institutions. In contrast, Mitterrand stressed Republican values, the refusal of exclusion and solidarity, and projected himself as a person above the mêlée of clannish interests, and the one who could unite the French and lead them into Europe in 1992, the year when a more unified Common Market becomes a reality. The idea that the age-old divisions were no longer relevant for French society had, of course, been initially propounded by Giscard d'Estaing in the mid-1970s (see p. 23), but his attempt to create a centre in French politics had not succeeded. By the late 1980s, the Left–Right division could no longer be demarcated so clearly; both sides of the divide had embraced doses of economic liberalism and the necessity to prepare France for the European market of the 1990s, the latter becoming a political myth to justify a whole range of economic and social changes. Rather, the Right found itself divided into three wings (*Le Monde*, 1988b, pp. 41–3): the conservative, led by Chirac; the liberal, headed by Barre; and a populist right, appealing to non-salaried groups as well as workers, championed by Le Pen. Just as the Communist Party had been the albatross of the Socialist Party, wheeled out conveniently at each election, so the National Front would this time bedevil the Right.

The major shock in the presidential elections was the performance of the National Front, which scored 14.38 per cent nationally but equally significantly extended its support throughout France (see Figure 1.5). However, the period between elections reminded the French of their colonial past for New Caledonia once again erupted in violence between the FLNKS and the police and army. Independence is largely supported by the Kanak population (43 per cent in 1984), who are concentrated in rural areas and in the north, east and the islands (Loyauté and Ouvea), while the European population (37 per cent) (Potel, 1985, p. 584) overwhelmingly favours remaining an integral part of France. The differing attitudes of these two groups towards independence have been resolved, if only temporarily, with Mitterrand's victory (8 May 1988) and his appointment of Michel Rocard as Prime Minister. An agreement was reached in August 1988 that a referendum would be held in 1998 to decide the future of New Caledonia. Thus the vital and geopolitical interests of France, represented by its presence in the South Pacific and control over vast maritime resources, have been preserved. In metropolitan France, issues of a guaranteed minimum income, education and professional training and the construction of a more integrated Europe are high on the social and political agenda.

The celebration in 1989 of the bicentenary of the beginning of the French Revolution brings to the fore questions of national identity, the persistence of geographical and political divisions and France's contribution to the modern world. Is the universally applicable 'Rights of Man', declared by the Revolution, the focus of this commemoration, or is it a more limited national examination of French society's continuing divisions? It is clear that the nation-state is being profoundly influenced by France's key role in European unification and its international interdependence. Ever since the adoption of the single European Act in December 1985, the idea of France in a Europe without frontiers has become part of daily conversation. Yet, a Europe entirely dominated by the logic of the single market is likely to exacerbate tensions within the nation-state. And the decade ahead, in which every year will recall further events in the revolutionary calendar, will be a time replete with geography and history. 1993, the first year of an economically exposed France, is also the bicentenary of probably the most contentious events of the Revolution when Republicans and Royalists were pitted against each other most violently in 1793, the year known as the Grand Terror.

TWO

The French Economy: From the *'Trente Glorieuses'* to Near-Stagnation in the 1980s

2.1 Overview

As the fourth largest economy within the Organization for Economic Co-operation and Development (OECD), the contemporary French economy outstrips that of the UK at current exchange rates, but much less so in purchasing power parity terms. Its manufacturing labour productivity in 1981 was almost double that of the UK. This rise to prominence is testimony to the near-miracle rates of growth achieved during the 30 years of rapid growth and to France's good output performance in the turbulent 1970s – it is only in the 1980s that semi-stagnation and a poorer output potential have set in. Admittedly, the growth optimism of those earlier years has evaporated. It has been replaced by anxiety concerning a pur-ported deindustrialization, or at least a significant weakening in industrial capability; the French wonder now if they are slipping back from their lead position in the second rank of industrial nations. The strength of foreign competition and heavy dependence on imported energy and raw materials have engendered a sense of frustration among the French. They feel that they can no longer isolate themselves and reachieve those rapid rates of growth experienced in the early postwar period when industry benefited to a considerable extent from protection. But this is to disregard the fact that it was the very opening of the economy to world trade, the strength of foreign demand for French exports, which did much to promote rapid industrializ-ation after 1958 and particularly from 1968 to 1973. Once opened to world trade, however, France in the 1970s really discovered the 'external con-straint': the years of unprecedented growth were at an end.

Outside influences are only a part of the story, though it is clear that 1973 brought a halt to growth, and then after the 1979 oil shock all the indicators turned to negative. The real interest lies in the fact that the international challenges to the French economy since 1973 illuminate these difficulties of adjustment, and the problems posed for economic policy by the near-stagnation of the 1980s and the growing trade deficit on industrial goods. GDP growth, inflation and unemployment rates for key postwar periods are

Table 2.1 Macroeconomic trends

	1952–9	1959–69	1969–73	1973–9	1980–7
GDP (% annual increase)	4.2	5.7	5.6	3.0	1.5
Inflation consumer prices (% annual increase)	3.3	3.9	6.2	10.7	8.9
Unemployment rate (% of labour force)	2.0	1.8	2.6	4.5	8.6
Manufactures (% growth):					
Imports/consumption	n/a	12.5	17	22.5	32
Exports/production (approx.)	n/a	13.5	18	24	35

Source: INSEE.

illuminating (Table 2.1). The growth path is high, relatively stable to 1973 but accelerating in the 1960s. The difficulties since are apparent, and are revealed also in the unemployment and inflation indicators. Unemployment rose steadily in the late 1960s and then jumped after the two oil crises. Inflation has clearly been a continuing feature, being quite high in an OECD comparison, and the effects of the oil shocks have magnified the problem. In recent years, the battle against inflation has been at the expense of growth and employment. Finally, the progressive opening to world trade is apparent in the rising export and import quotients.

The French economy has been modernized and transformed beyond recognition since 1945 as growth and structural change have brought a fundamental shift from a partly agricultural to an industrial and service economy (see Chapter 1). The 1982 census revealed an active labour force of 23.5 million or 43.2 per cent of the total population (see Table 1.5). For the first half of the century, this varied little, remaining at around 20 million, and then grew somewhat, especially from 1962 to 1982, when it increased by 22.4 per cent. The baby-boom generation had reached working age, 'pieds-noirs' and immigrants swelled the workforce, as did the rising female activity rate (Guillauchon, 1986). Occupational changes reflected the relative growth and decline of branches of activity (Table 2.2). The clearest shifts, for 1959–86, are those from a partly agricultural to a service economy, with the relative weight of industry (broadly defined) remaining constant. The fall in the agricultural workforce by 2.83 million, the 4.8 million growth in the tertiary workforce, and the shifts within manufacturing in favour of capital goods at the expense of consumer goods industries are all clearly revealed. Similar changes occur in the structure of value-added (Table 2.3).

Table 2.2   Structure of employment by branch of activity, 1959–86

	1959		1975		1986		% change	
	No. (000s)	%	No. (000s)	%	No. (000s)	%	1959–75	1975–86
Agriculture, forestry, fishing	4,344	22.1	2,109	10.0	1,513.0	7.1	−51.5	−28.3
Industry	6,927	35.2	8,074	38.6	6,501.5	30.6	16.6	−19.5
Food industry	588	3.0	603	2.9	622.6	2.9	2.6	3.1
Energy	398	2.0	302	1.4	286.6	1.4	−24.1	−5.1
Intermediate goods	1,420	7.2	1,729	8.2	1,253.1	5.9	21.8	−27.5
Capital goods	1,300	6.6	1,941	9.3	1,579.6	7.4	49.3	−18.6
Consumer goods	1,714	8.7	1,593	7.6	1,261.9	5.9	−7.1	−20.8
Construction	1,507	7.7	1,906	9.1	1,497.7	7.1	26.5	−21.4
Tertiary	8,411	42.7	10,762	51.4	13,220.6	62.3	28.0	22.8
Market services	5,161	26.2	7,347	35.1	9,022.9	42.5	42.4	22.8
Non-market services	3,250	16.5	3,415	16.3	4,197.7	19.8	5.1	22.8
Total	19,682	100.0	20,945	100.0	21,235.1	100.0	6.4	1.4

Source: INSEE, census and *Annuaire statistique*.

Table 2.3   Value-added by branch of activity, 1959–84

	Structure of value-added in 1959 in current prices (%)	Structure of value-added in 1984 in current prices (%)	1959–84 Average annual growth in value-added by volume (%)	1959–84 Average annual growth in value-added by price (%)
Agriculture	10.6	4.1	2.0	5.5
Food industry	4.8	4.8	4.8	6.7
Energy	5.9	4.8	5.0	5.6
Intermediate goods	8.9	7.7	4.6	6.3
Capital goods	8.0	8.7	6.3	5.5
Consumer goods	6.8	4.2	4.0	5.4
Construction	6.9	5.9	2.3	8.6
Wholesale, retail	13.4	9.4	3.9	6.1
Transport, tele-communications	6.2	5.3	5.0	5.9
Other market services	17.3	30.8	4.9	9.0
Non-market services	11.2	14.3	2.4	10.3
Total	100	100	4.1	7.3

Source: INSEE, *Tableaux de l'économie française.*

Here the changes are magnified because of shifts in relative prices in favour of services, especially to the detriment of agriculture. The volume growth, 1959–84, omits this relative inflation effect and reveals the change in physical output.

Of course, the years of rapid growth and the years of industrial crisis have had an effect. The employment effects of the crisis in industry are apparent in the changes since 1975 (Table 2.2). Moreover, throughout the 1980s industrial job losses have been occurring at a rate of 2 per cent per year, with a peak loss of 150,000 jobs in 1984. The transformation in foreign trade structure, in terms of commodities and geographical area, is illustrated by the decline in the share of the Franc Area (the old French Empire) among French export markets from 38 per cent in the early 1950s to 5 per cent recently. The European Community (EC) has gained prime importance among France's clients, now taking 60 per cent of her exports (Table 2.4). In terms of the commodity composition of exports, farm products have

Table 2.4   Trade patterns by area, 1986

CIF/FOB (FF bn)

	Imports	Exports	Balance	Coverage of imports by exports
OECD	708.827	635.311	−73.516	89.6
EC	531.299	477.119	−54.180	89.8
Other	177.528	158.192	−19.336	89.1
Non-OECD	178.675	190.106	−11.431	106.4
Centrally-planned economies	34.929	23.984	−10.945	68.7
OPEC (Middle East)	22.843	18.059	−4.784	79.1
Other	120.903	148.063	27.160	122.5
Total	887.502	825.417	−62.085	93.0

Source: INSEE, *Annuaire statistique.*

retained their share (about 15 per cent), while capital goods, including vehicles, have doubled in share to over 35 per cent of total exports.

If we return then to the years of unprecedented growth up to 1974, we can begin to identify some of its causes. The strength of investment and foreign demand was clearly crucial. The early heavy investments during the First and Second Plans bore fruit in a rapid rise in industrial output in the mid-1950s and so established an industrial base by 1958 from which France could benefit from the establishment of the Customs Union. The higher GDP growth rate of 5.7 per cent per year from 1959 to 1968 was under-pinned by a rise in investment of 8 per cent per year, while foreign demand led to a burgeoning of the export sector. Even by 1963, France's industrial weight and international presence bore little resemblance to the pre-1958 position. Especially strong gains in international markets explain much of the acceleration of GDP growth to 5.9 per cent p.a. from 1965 to 1973.

We can take the analysis further by looking at the relative contributions of factors of production (Carré *et al.*, 1976). Carré *et al.* could only explain one-half of growth by these 'supply' factors and labour force growth played little part before the early 1960s. The main factors accounting for growth were investment and improved skills and mobility of the workforce. But the unexplained residual of one-half of the growth actually achieved points to the true complexity of development, which must include government policy. This latter is expressly emphasized in the notion of 'Keynesianism–Fordism' by which Boyer (1987) describes the virtuous circle of growth and the social consensus in favour of growth of those years. He stresses that real wages, productivity and profits all grew in tandem during the 30 years of growth, and that underlying this were relatively constant wages and profit shares in national income. Hereby investment was sustained, leading to future productivity improvements, and workers' rising incomes ensured a market for the output. Governments maintained a high pressure of aggregate demand and made social transfers to consumers. (Boyer proceeds to make the point that it was the very disturbance of this wage/profit relation after May '68 and, he claims, the slowing of productivity gains from the assembly line system, which account for the crisis in growth after 1974.)

In practice, how Keynesian was the policy, and what was the contribution of state intervention? From a situation of low consumption in the immediate postwar years, French governments until 1974 pursued objectives of high demand growth and tolerated relatively high inflation in the pursuit of employment. The associated recurrent balance of payments problems were resolved by devaluation and temporary stabilization (i.e. anti-inflation) programmes. In the postwar reconstruction period payments crises and devaluations recurred; subsequently, the Rueff Plan of 1958 (establishing de Gaulle's 'new franc') and the 1969 stabilization plan (after the May 1968 concessions) proved highly successful, combining 'offensive' devaluations with budgetary and monetary tightening. The Giscard Plan of 1963 also succeeded in restraining inflationary pressures. Typical of such demand management was an unwillingness to break the growth momentum by abrupt stop–go measures. In fact, France could only maintain a medium-term pressure of demand in line with the plan projections – the legal rigidities surrounding the budgetary procedure made 'fine tuning' impossible – and the ideology of the balanced budget still held sway, though it was rarely observed.

Within this broadly Keynesian approach, what was the role of state intervention? In 1945, the nationalizations gave the government a dominant role in the productive economy; through its control of the banking and credit system it channelled one-half of productive investments, making full use of the planning system and the nationalized industries which had a pre-eminent position in the basic infrastructures of energy and transport. The full range of industrial policy instruments at the government's disposal, external protection, public purchasing, favourable investment and export credits and state initiatives in the high-technology sphere were all actively used. Yet from 1958 a retreat from this reconstruction-period type of interventionism began: the need to force firms to compete in Europe led to an emphasis, in rhetoric at least, on market discipline, and the Rueff Plan of

1958 was imbued with liberal economic thinking. It saw in the high deficit spending (which heavy state budgetary support for investment entailed) a prime source of French inflation. This reasoning, buttressed by liberal economic convictions, lay behind Finance Minister Giscard's acceleration of the State's withdrawal from productive investment after 1963. 'Debudgetization' involved the transfer of expenditure from the government budget to parastatal organizations such as the *Caisse des dépôts et consignations* (CDC) and to the banking system after the fundamental 1966–7 bank reforms. Market criteria should, it was said, increasingly govern investment decisions in place of the strategies of the politicians and technocrats. In practice, of course, the role of the State continued to grow over a wide area, but the State ceased to dominate industrial investment and no longer sought to integrate industrial plans in a single state strategy. There remains the question of the contribution of planning and industrial policy.

The French economy was in a state of very unbalanced growth well before the oil crisis struck. Investment rates of 25 per cent per year reflected the boom in manufacturing after the 1969 devaluation, but in spite of unprecedented rates of growth, unemployment edged up and inflation reached 8 per cent. France had come to acquire the rigidities known as the 'social monopoly' (Flouzat, 1984) in which, after May 1968, wages became increasingly indexed on prices and the more oligopolistic character of manufacturing enabled corporations to push through price rises. Prices for labour and goods (which had always been administered to varying degrees) only poorly reflected market forces. When the oil crisis struck in 1973–4, these rigidities were exposed and became the source of 'stagflationary' conditions – both unemployment and inflation soared and the old Keynesian instruments for pulling out of recession lost much of their effect. The history since then is one of painful adjustment (of course as elsewhere) to the new world economic conditions, and of a delayed renunciation of the old French model of growth. This model of high growth, with relatively high inflation and periodic devaluation, was dangerous or even self-defeating in the world conditions after 1973. France's chronic dependence on high-cost energy imports, and the need to cover these with competitive exports, ruled out the high inflation and 'offensive' devaluations of earlier policy as they risked a wage–price spiral and widening deficits. The very dependence on world markets meant that France was constrained by the prevailing international recession. The slow acknowledgement of this, and the adjustments required, in particular surrounding the social-justice consensus concerning maintenance of living standards, were all the stuff of the fierce ideological debates and policy switches occurring during the 1970s and early 1980s. As we shall see, these were polarized in particular around the Barre Plan of 1976–81 and the Keynesian stimulus of the Socialists in 1981–2.

The recent history of slow growth has arisen as France absorbs the costs of the mistimed, and possibly misconceived Socialist budgetary stimulus and tries to produce the conditions for non-inflationary growth, of which deregulation and the renunciation of the debt economy are policy options, leading to a further retreat of the state from economic interventionism. The distinctively French characteristics of economic management fade as France acknowledges international constraints and harmonizes policy with its European Monetary System (EMS) partners.

2.2   Industry, services, the balance of payments and unemployment

As French primary mineral production now makes only a small contribution to domestic requirements, we will focus on the secondary and tertiary sectors.

2.2.1   The manufacturing sector

Given that we have stressed so far both the rapidity of French industrial development and the scale of the recent slowdown leading to fears of 'deindustrialization', then any assessment of the French manufacturing sector requires a nuanced view. On the credit side, French manufacturing productivity exceeded the British as early as 1960 and the West German in 1980, yet manufacturing as a proportion of national output is not high, and has fallen. And there are export weaknesses in French industry. The transformation of France into an exporter of high-technology goods (engineering, electronics and consumer durables), similar to Japan or West Germany, certainly remains unfinished. France has shown a failure (with notable exceptions) to win through in those markets where exports are relatively price insensitive and where demand continues to grow. By contrast, France continues to export middling value-added, price-sensitive goods and her recent lack of competitiveness is evidenced in the trade deficit on industrial goods since 1987.

The industrialization effort and the export successes were carried by the capital goods industries (general engineering, aerospace, armaments, nuclear power plant), and vehicles and intermediate goods (steel, glass, rubber, chemicals). While the car industry, glittering symbol of the growth years, expanded on the strength of consumer demand, the remaining branches of industry tended to benefit from the heavy capital investment programmes at home and abroad. And so certain French firms, enjoying scale economies and expanding markets, grew into large groups, sometimes oligopolistic and multinational in character. If Renault, CGE (electricals), Rhône-Poulenc (chemicals) and Alsthom (rolling stock) took their modern

form in the early years of this century, much of French capitalism under-
went radical regrouping and restructuring in the 1960s, when Saint Gobain-
–Pont à Mousson and BSN, for example, emerged. The sustained public
and private investment programmes led to more than a quadrupling of
productive investment, from 1945 to 1985, permitting French manufacturing productivity per person to rise faster than in any other OECD country
except Japan, up to 1983. The opening of the economy from 1958 and the
'offensive' devaluations of 1958 and 1969 gave a tremendous boost to the
export of manufactures, while the cheap investment credit policy (including
the banking reform of 1966–7) and tax reliefs for mergers all sustained the
momentum of industrialization.

The contemporary picture now includes a number of branches in structural decline, whose difficulties were exacerbated greatly by the oil crisis
and competition from newly industrializing countries (NICs). Since 1973,
investment has fallen annually by 4.5 per cent in intermediate goods
industries and by 3.7 per cent in consumer goods industries. Job losses here
have ranged from 20 to 40 per cent of the workforce from 1973 to 1983, and
more than 1 million industrial jobs have been lost. Growth industries since
1973 have been principally those which the State has favoured in its answer
to the oil crisis – nuclear power construction, telephones and the aerospace,
armaments and large civil engineering projects which were to lead the
export offensive in OPEC and less developed countries (LDCs). The
present fortunes of French firms reflect this period: the collapse of Boussac
Frères in textiles; the liquidation in 1985 of Creusot-Loire (special steels,
nuclear engineering, shipbuilding); the catastrophic losses of Usinor and
Sacilor in steel-making; the cuts at Renault, Peugeot and in the chemicals
giants Rhône-Poulenc and Roussel-Uclaf, which had all expanded in the
1970s and faced financial haemorrhage in the 1980s. The star performers in
a technical sense are to be found in the aerospace, armaments and nuclear
engineering fields, where Aérospatiale, Dassault, Matra, Thomson-CSF,
Framatome and CGE–Alsthom dominate. With the exception of one newly
privatized company, all are nationalized and depend heavily on state
procurement programmes and on officially supported export contracts.
Such markets are heavily protected, revealing a dependency and fragility
which will be under threat in the single European market after 1992.
Finally, Thomson Grand Public (consumer electronics) and Bull (com-
puters) are examples of French groups which have failed to achieve a
substantial presence in high-technology markets.

Mention has been made of the wave of mergers in the 1960s, which led to
a more pronounced concentration in industry. Business concentration
remains less pronounced than in the UK, but displays the typical pattern of
oligopolistic structures in many capital goods branches, in some intermedi-

ate goods (steel, heavy chemicals, rubber, glass) and in energy. (The consumer goods industries remain fragmented.) Here the oligopolistic character is apparent from the fact that, typically, the four largest firms in each branch had, in 1980, shares in employment and investment of more than 50 and 60 per cent respectively. Since firms often belong to groups, then the 500 leading firms at the head of France's largest groups have doubled their share in total industrial assets to 61 per cent in the period 1958–77 (Guillauchon, 1986). If we exclude foreign-owned and nationalized industries, then much of the capital remains in family hands (Eck, 1988). Of course, the scale of the nationalized sector in France distorts these results: the extended nationalized industrial sector after 1981–2 accounted for 23 per cent of those employed, 30 per cent of sales, 30 per cent of exports and 40 per cent of industrial investments.

Finally, there is the question of the degree of internationalization of the French economy and of the strength of its multinationals, particularly in the context of the Single European Market at the end of 1992. France's international presence is often underestimated – France's international banking network is the world's third largest, as is that of its insurance companies. Certain groups have a pronounced multinational character such as Renault, Saint Gobain, Péchiney, CIT-Alcatel, although overall France's foreign industrial investment amounts to only 0.3–0.5 per cent of GDP, equivalent to that of Germany, but far behind the US, UK and the Netherlands. The main periods of international growth have been from 1973 to 1983, and strongly since 1986. A study by Delapierre (in Michalet, 1984) conducted in 1978 of 4000 French non-financial companies with foreign holdings, showed that 17 per cent of firms were in the metals and engineering sectors, 13 per cent were in chemicals and pharmaceuticals, and roughly 6 per cent each in the construction, electrical and food industries. Delapierre found that French investments were concentrated mainly in the EC and francophone Africa: this reflected traditional sales imperatives, though in its African investments the security of food and materials supplies was also a consideration.

The recent wave of mergers and acquisitions reflects newer preoccupations, as global competition becomes sharper. Presence on the US market is essential and French firms must consolidate their position in their home market, which is the EC, if they are not to fall behind and suffer takeover. Firms in mature industries seek a substantial market share internationally, while firms in new product markets seek competitive advantage by new innovations, but need large markets to spread devleopment costs. Both the US and EC markets play a role in these international strategies. In the early 1980s, French public sector groups such as Elf-Acquitaine, Renault and Péchiney made heavy US investments, while more recently, Thomson,

Rhône-Poulenc, Bull and Saint-Gobain, all nationalized, increased their US presence. In Europe, the food industry has made strategic investments, Saint-Gobain has rationalized Europe-wide, and Thomson has made major consumer electronics and semiconductor acquisitions (making it Europe's second electrical giant). CGE-Alcatel is, of course, on a par with Siemens in telecommunications equipment, after taking over ITT-Europe. Overall, though, there remains the feeling that French groups are lagging behind in the 1992 acquisitions race for reason of lack of funds (L'Usine Nouvelle, 21 April 88). Of course, speaking more generally, there has always been a strong current of opinion, particularly on the Left, which has feared the effects on employment and the trade balance of a 'delocalization' of production, especially that to low-wage countries.

The long-term strength of foreign investment in France has been the source of antagonisms and government restraints on inward investment, though this was welcomed by Giscard, and by Mitterrand after the U-turn. Under Chirac, foreign takeovers of French groups in anticipation of 1992 reached a furious pace, especially in the food industry. Foreign shareholdings of 20 per cent and more in French manufacturing firms in January 1985 amounted to 20 per cent of the sector's employees, 25 per cent of sales, 24 per cent of investment and 28 per cent of exports (SESSI, 1987). Largely of US, EC and Swiss origin, foreign-owned companies, against stereotype, are of medium-to-large size, tend not to be engaged in oligopolistically-organized markets, and have a better export rate than French firms.

In any comment on the purported 'deindustrialization' of the economy in recent years, attention must focus on the interrelationship between profitability, investment and unfavourable specialization (Capul and Meurs, 1988; Guillauchon, 1986). Much has been made of a crisis of productivity whereby ever-greater productivity gains, it is asserted, can no longer be reaped under the assembly-line system (Boyer, 1987). However, productivity per hour worked has not fallen since the late 1960s, while the profit rate has. The sharp decline in private investment between the two oil crises was disguised by the large State nuclear energy and telephone programmes. The modernization of private industry therefore slowed, with a consequent failure to incorporate the latest electronic- and computer-controlled processes – there was also a very slow switch in output to the new products demanded. R&D expenditure is low (2.25 per cent of GDP compared with 2.7 per cent in the USA) and only 57 per cent of this is conducted by firms. Clearly, the poor recent supply response of French industry, its problems of price and structural competitiveness, find their origins here.

2.2.2 The service industries

The heterogenous group of activities (retailing, wholesaling, transport, telecommunications, finance and insurance), that comprise the tertiary sector, now represents over 60 per cent of value-added and employment, and is thus greater than total industrial employment. We should not forget that on the world market, French service groups have a substantial presence, helping to sustain France as the world's second services exporter, and making an essential contribution to the balance of payments. Likewise, the French tourist industry, which is Europe's second largest, is a mainstay of 'invisibles' income, but unlike other countries relies on a very significant internal tourist demand. Only 15.4 per cent of French went abroad out of a total of 29.3 million French who took summer holidays and 13.6 million winter holidays. In the Paris region alone, more tourist nights were recorded (127 million in 1984) than for the whole of Spain.

The main expansion in service employment has taken place since 1960: at 2 per cent per annum it has compensated for the employment losses in agriculture and industry (Guillauchon, 1986) (see Tables 2.2, 2.3). In essence, these reveal that in terms of value-added, the contribution of retailing/wholesaling, transport and telecommunications has been falling, while 'other' market services and non-market services (public administrations, public hospitals) have seen a rapid growth (often because of high price inflation). In terms of labour force growth, the non-market services have caught up since 1975 with the market services. Areas such as the medical, teaching, business consultancy and financial services have grown strongly, while 'traditional' services have fallen back in employment terms. Fifty-four per cent of services employees are women.

This change to a service economy reflects the growth in the role of government (health, social security, education, police and military), the provision of ever more refined services and the very complex interactions between an industrial sector in constant change and adjustment, and the service sector itself. It is often said that the demand for services seems to grow independently of growth in income (e.g. factors of old age, social assistance) but since 1979, the French tertiary sector has seen its growth reduced by half, compared with the period from 1975 to 1979, as the industrial crisis has struck and real incomes have stagnated (Capul and Meurs, 1988).

The great changes in the service sector are apparent in the rise to prominence of some of the key names in French business. The rise of supermarkets and hypermarkets (Carrefour, Auchan) from the mid-1950s stimulated small shopkeeper reaction (see pp. 5). Club Méditerranée and Nouvelles Frontières in package tourism and Cap Gémini-Sogéti (Europe's largest software house) have been in the vanguard of these underlying structural shifts, while the world's largest construction firm, Bouygues, contributes substantially to the balance of payments in offering civil engineering consultancy to LDCs. Lastly, we should not forget that French banks and insurance companies are in the first rank internationally.

2.2.3 The trade balance

France is the world's fourth largest exporter of goods and second largest exporter of services and agricultural products. Unlike Britain, she has managed to sustain her share of world trade relatively successfully, though the recent deficit in manufactures has accompanied a falling world market share in these goods. As we have seen, the share of imports and exports in GDP has risen strongly to well over 26 per cent, in particular after the 1973 oil shock, since when the proportion of GDP exported has doubled. Typically, a large surplus on services has moderated or covered a deficit on visibles (Table 2.5). The historic evolution reveals the impact of the two oil crises, the success of the Barre government in re-establishing the balance by 1978, and the effects of the Socialists' 1981–2 stimulus, which were only absorbed in 1986.

2.2.4 Unemployment

Unemployment in France has risen strongly in the past two decades and especially since 1973 (Table 2.6). At its simplest, we can see how a steady rise in the economically active population has been accompanied by a stagnation and decline in total employment. At the end of 1987, unemployment stood at 10.7 per cent, compared with 4.1 per cent in 1975 and 2.7 per cent in 1972. In a historical perspective, two broad periods can be detected: the postwar period to 1973, when unemployment was low and stable, but rising slowly after 1965; and from 1973 to the present, when rapid rises have been experienced (Guillauchon, 1986). In the first period, after 1965, unemployment increased when a rapid increase in the labour force ceased to be matched by employment growth: and indeed the restructuring of industry increased frictional unemployment. Moving to the period of accelerating unemployment after 1973, the numbers of registered unemployed rose sixfold to mid-1985. The years of greatest rise were those following the two oil shocks and 1984, when domestic demand was tightly constrained and industrial cutbacks began in earnest. In contrast, the effects of the two Keynesian budgetary stimuli of 1975 and 1981–2 can be detected. The very mismatch between the increase in the labour force and the stagnation in total employment reveals the scale of the problem. From mid-1973 to mid-1984, the workforce grew by an annual 170,000 (though

Table 2.5 Balance of payments, 1973–86

Balance of payments (FF bn)

	1973	1974	1975	1976	1978	1980	1981	1982	1986
Trade balance	1.9	-23.2	4.6	-24.2	0.3	-56.6	-54.0	-103.8	-15.3
Visibles and invisibles balance	14.3	-7.9	22.7	-4.6	46.4	0	-2.7	-49.0	56.2
Current balance	6.6	-18.8	11.5	-16.4	31.6	-7.6	-25.8	-79.3	25.8
Long-term capital balance	-11.0	-2.3	-4.8	-8.4	-14.9	-6.0	-21.0	24.7	-70.4
Short-term capital balance	8.0	2.2	4.9	5.0	5.7	11.8	-12.4	13.9	3.9
Change in the external monetary position (public and private sectors)	-1.2	0.2	-21.8	19.1	-26.8	2.1	71.3	46.1	39.3

Source: INSEE, *Annuaires statistiques*.

early retirement programmes since 1982 have begun to limit this effect, albeit without creating vacancies for the young); the number of jobs meanwhile has stagnated during this period of crisis and slow growth (Guillauchon, 1986).

Since 1973, the average length of period of unemployment has risen by more than one-third to 331 days. However, the long-term unemployed are not the largest group among those without work; 40 per cent of the total, a proportion double that in 1976, comprises workers, generally young people, whose employment contract (temporary or fixed-term) has come to an end. This reflects employers' recourse to 'flexible' arrangements in their recruitment policy. Part-time labour has grown since 1982, encouraged by Socialist legislation which gave better protection to such workers (INSEE, 1987, p. 114). The risk of unemployment is concentrated as ever among certain sociodemographic groups. Young people of under 25 years have an unemployment rate (25 per cent in 1987) four times that of adults (see

Table 2.6   Unemployment by age, sex and nationality

	Unemployment rate (%)	
	1981	1987
Males		
15–24 years old	13.1	20.7
25–49 years old	3.6	7.0
50 years and older	4.2	6.7
Total number	692,000	1,172,000
Females		
15–24 years old	23.8	28.5
25–49 years old	7.4	11.5
50 years and older	5.7	8.0
Total number	960,000	1,395,000
Total number (%)	1,652,000 (7.1%)	2,567,000 (10.7%)

Unemployment by nationality, 1982 (% of active population)		
	Male	Female
French	6.2	11.4
Foreigners	12.1	20.1
Italian	7.2	16.1
Spanish	8.0	13.0
Algerian	18.6	44.8
Tunisian	16.3	35.5

Source: INSEE, Employment surveys.

Table 2.6). Women in every age-group are also much more liable to be unemployed than are men; they therefore represent more than one-half of the unemployed (Capul and Meurs, 1988). Young women suffer very high rates of unemployment and women generally experience longer periods of unemployment. On the other hand, the young in total have much shorter periods of unemployment, only one-half those of the unemployed aged over 50 years. Immigrant workers also experience more unemployment (Cahiers Français, 1985, p. 58), though the National Front makes them the scapegoats for unemployment among the French-born.

As is well known, unemployment also varies according to employment status. It rises in inverse relation to the level of qualification, and so affects manual workers three to four times more seriously than management grades and technicians. In 1984, 40 per cent of the unemployed were manual workers and 30 per cent clerical and administrative workers (whose employment security had clearly worsened substantially since the late 1970s).

2.3   The contribution of national planning and industrial policy to the years of growth

It was often asserted in Britain that the French system of national planning and industrial interventionism had accounted for much of France's postwar dynamism. Within the protected economy, the State controlled credit creation, and as in the reconstruction period conducted one-half of all productive investment, particularly through the Plan and through nationalized industries. It was claimed that the economy's growth rate had been raised by the channelling of investment into strategic industries and infrastructures, as well as by the creation of a consensus in favour of expansion. This image may describe the immediate postwar period, but as we have already seen, the retreat from an all-pervading state interventionism began relatively early, in 1958 and 1963. Thus the FDES (Economic and Social Development Fund), which had provided more than 60 per cent of long-term industrial financing in 1950, provided only 30 per cent in 1972. Only the First Plan was of an imperative, command nature; later Plans were indicative, which meant that they were designed to inform and guide private investment and consumption decisions.

Planning as created by the early Commissioners for the Plan, Monnet and Massé, sought to associate the modernizing social groups in a common project of economic and social modernization. The Plan would act as a 'reducer of uncertainty' and a form of 'collective market research' (Bauchet, 1986). Quinet and Touzéry (1986) see three main types of justification for planning. First, it would improve on the imperfections of the market economy, and so stimulate growth, by increasing information and reducing uncertainty among producers concernin᷉ 'emand and cost conditions. It would also help to achieve a balance of s..pply and demand. Second, the Plan would mobilize a project for society as a whole; and lastly, it would ensure much greater coherence in government investment programmes.

The informational, educative aspect of the planning procedures was apparent from the outset. Modernization commissions, organized on a tripartite basis, and serviced by the *Commissariat Général du Plan* (CGP General Commissariat for the Plan), brought together large numbers of decision-makers from the productive economy, and made them forecast demand and supply conditions for the coming five years for their branch. They did this within an overall macroeconomic forecast for the economy prepared by the CGP, which included assumptions concerning government spending and monetary policies. Finally, these elements were merged to produce a coherent forecast of the economy as a whole and by branch. One should add, however, that the unions withdrew from the planning machinery in the mid-1960s when the government tried to introduce discussions on incomes policies.

After the First Plan, subsequent Plans became indicative, progressively more technically sophisticated, and they broadened their coverage to include more sectors of the economy and government social provision. The Fifth Plan (1966–70) incorporated econometric modelling for the economy in aggregate, and subsequently ceased to give detailed forecasts by industrial branch. Finally, from the Eighth Plan onwards (1976–80), detailed forecasts were omitted and only a range of possible 'futures' was given, without choosing a central projection for the coming five years. The Plans did then gain sophistication in modelling the economy in aggregate, at the expense of detailed information valuable to industrialists. One might add that this also represented a divorce between a 'market forecast' plan and industrial policy, which required detailed, case-by-case information.

The loss of influence of planning was fully apparent in the 1970s when the Sixth, Seventh and Eighth Plans were rendered meaningless by the oil crises; the problems of forecasting the path of a heavily trade-dependent economy in a turbulent world were manifest. There was also considerable ideological opposition to planning in the 1970s, but other factors played a role. More often than not, the Plans had to be 'adapted' to take account of government stabilization ('austerity') programmes, and the Fifth Plan was thrown off course by the events of May '68. It is generally accepted that planning became increasingly difficult as the productive economy became more complex and as France opened up to the world economy. One might recognize in the Fifth Plan a turning point, for here was 'exhaustive' planning – targets for all branches and for government spending broken down by region. The Plan sought to speed France's insertion into the world trading system and to create large groups, often multinational, which would doubtless be able to produce forecasts of greater relevance to their own sector. Of prime significance is the fact that the Finance Ministry profoundly mistrusted the CGP and its ambitions, and so under Finance Minister Giscard from 1962 to 1974 it ceaselessly sought to curtail the CGP's influence. It is often forgotten that spending targets in the Plans were not binding on the Finance Ministry and so were expressions of general intent only, which were rarely, if ever, fulfilled.

Estrin and Holmes (1983) undertook various tests of the degree to which targets were realized. Common to all Plans was a difficulty in forecasting investment and trade. The Fourth Plan was probably the most successful, and then from the mid-1960s onwards Plans were increasingly wayward for a variety of reasons: firms could have constructed more meaningful plans for themselves from freely available data, especially in the case of the disastrous Seventh Plan (1976–80).

'Industrial policy' was not a term widely used in the 1950s and 1960s by government, who considered discretion to be important here; it belongs more to the vocabulary of the Left. In practice during this period there were three different foci. First, policies concerning industry in general (commonly designated 'environmental') sought to improve the operating conditions for industry as a whole. Measures included protectionism, public purchasing, export credits and the widespread availability of low-interest investment credits from the nationalized banking system and from sectoral credit institutions. Second, the large nationalized corporations had clear strategic objectives and were responsible for ambitious investment programes, incorporating the latest technologies. Renault apart, these were primarily in the energy and transport sectors. If they made a firm contribution to growth, they were nevertheless subjected to daily interventionism and price restraint. Finally, the Gaullist large-scale programmes sought to establish a French lead by state organizations in high-technology areas where French private industry was absent – SNECMA (aero-engines), SNIAS (aeronautics), CEA and COGEMA (nuclear power) all have a Gaullist parentage. Under the Fifth and Sixth Plans, as we have seen, the 'industrial imperative' became paramount: 'environmental' industrial policy, in particular the formation of internationally competitive groups, gained prominence under the Fifth Plan, while in the Sixth, sectoral plans in steel, aeronautics and computing took a large share of expenditure (Dacier *et al.*, 1985). There can be little doubt that such programmes, especially in aerospace, space research and nuclear energy, have pushed France to the forefront of world technological leadership in these fields. The computer plan, in contrast, showed grave strategic errors, as did, of course, a succession of over-optimistic steel plans.

In assessing the impact of planning and industrial policy on French growth, a healthy scepticism is probably required. It is clear that the very stability of French growth indicates that the Plans did achieve something, but their concrete influence is often difficult to discover. The years to the late 1950s, covered by the first three Plans, were the time when planners are thought to have widely affected expectations in favour of modernization, expansion and international trade. From 1963, the disengagement of the state budget from the financing of the econony, and the associated reform of banking as a source of capital for industry, marked an important retreat from central direction. The links between plan strategies and industrial policy appear very tenuous and, other than in the case of 'national champions', there was precious little evidence of a concerted industrial strategy in the 1960s (Estrin and Holmes, 1983). Most firms record that the impact of the Plans on their production decisions was 'slight' or 'zero'; in this case, what were the real forces for growth in the years of rapid expansion? It is obvious that state intervention and the use of the nationalized industries did contribute greatly to the investment boom in the reconstruction period and the first half of the 1950s. But with the new markets of Europe, exports increasingly contributed to the growth momentum. And we should not forget that the virtuous circle of growth, the so-called 'Keynesianism–Fordism', rested on a number of conditions – macroeconomic policy, wage and profit shares and productivity growth, which were all favourable until the late 1960s.

2.4 Economic adjustment and the oil crises: reversals in macroeconomic and industrial policies

By 1973 the French economy had become relatively open to world economic influences; still less so than Germany or the UK, but it was far more heavily dependent on energy imports. The challenge posed by the oil crises and the economic turbulence of the 1970s and early 1980s was not always clearly perceived, and policy adjustments were made only after some delay. The appropriate response was vigorously debated and we see in the marked switches of policy by successive governments different analyses of the problem and radically different policy prescriptions. The Barre Plan, a counter-inflation programme, purported to take an economically liberal approach to France's problems in the world economy, while the Socialist strategy of 1981–2 rejected this analysis and adopted a statist, protectionist stance. Macroeconomic policy was far from being the only economic area of ideological confrontation; industrial policy too showed marked shifts. Before focusing on these two areas, let us assess the nature of the challenge.

The French economy was subject to four external shocks in the 1970s and

1980s: the oil price rises of 1973 and 1979, the raw material price boom of 1976–7, and the rise in the dollar at the end of the decade, which magnified the import price rise. The two oil crises each represented a tax on France, by the Organization of Petroleum Exporting Countries (OPEC), of 2 per cent approximately of GDP. This produced problems of overall demand, of the balance of payments and of rampant inflation. The 'tax' on industrialized countries reduced their purchasing power as OPEC did not recycle the oil income by buying Western exports (which would have maintained global demand unchanged and equilibrated the balance of payments). In reality, demand in the West became depressed, and recession ensued, not solely for the reason of inadequate recyling, but also as governments acted to restrain the inflation caused by producers passing on the oil price increase. In a French context, exceptionally damaging was the prevalence of the indexation of wages on prices, leading to a wage–price spiral set off by the oil price rise. The result of this maintenance of real wages was a marked fall in profits, to which we have alluded, for wages had risen without any corresponding increase in output.

In the period 1974–6, France experienced stop–go policies in reaction to the oil shock. With the election of President Giscard d'Estaing in 1974, an austerity package was introduced, when the West was already moving into recession. Industrial output fell by 15 per cent from mid-1974 to mid-1975 and unemployment reached 1 million. Prime Minister Chirac therefore reversed policy by giving a huge budgetary stimulus to demand of 2.1 per cent of GDP in September 1975. The recovery was rapid, short-lived and unbalanced. Inflation reached 10 per cent, with wage rises of 16 per cent and the trade deficit reached the level immediately prevailing after the oil crisis! Here then was evidence of stagflation and of a balance of payments constraint. This burst of growth made no dent in unemployment, but led to rapid inflation (i.e. stagflation), and the rise in demand sucked in imports. This was a clear demonstration that there are difficulties with Keynesian solutions in an open economy, where wage-earners can absorb much of the demand injection in the form of higher wages. Here then was a lesson for the Socialists in 1981–2 when they too engaged in a large Keynesian stimulus.

After the resignation of Chirac, the new Prime Minister Raymond Barre introduced his counter-inflation programme – the 'Barre Plan' – in September 1976. Of a more monetarist persuasion, Barre lectured the French on the need to renounce the traditional French model of growth – of high growth, relatively high inflation and devaluation – in the adverse international climate. The oil dependence imposed a heavy balance of payments constraint, and if the external deficit was to be redressed, the competitiveness of French exports was imperative. The old practice of inflationary budgetary deficits and devaluation (which fuelled a wage–price spiral and exacerbated import costs) harmed France's competitiveness. This was then a 'plan of rejection' – a rejection of budgetary deficits, a rejection of external deficits and of devaluation as an instrument.

We have already referred to the Barre Plan in Chapter 1, the key points being that Barre implemented at first a classic austerity programme and price freeze, followed after the 1978 legislative elections by a more economically liberal programme. Price controls on manufactures were lifted progressively, a Competition Commission was instituted to fight restraints on competition, monetary targeting on the West German model was introduced. In addition, the parity of the franc was fixed, in particular against the Deutschmark, in the newly launched European Monetary System (EMS), for which Barre and the West German Chancellor, Helmut Schmidt, claimed parentage. As we have seen, the Barre Plan was largely unsuccessful, though it was badly hit by the second oil crisis. In particular, inflation rarely dropped below 10 per cent, and the intention of raising the share of profits as a route to new investment was a failure. Profitability fell rapidly during the 1970s as real wages rose and the firms had to shoulder much of the social security burden of rising unemployment. The consequences of the fall in private investment (an average of 1.5 per cent per year from 1973 to 1981), masked by heavy public investment in nuclear energy and the telephone system, were serious for competitiveness and jobs. The unemployment rate trebled, from 1973 to 1981, to stand at 7.8 per cent.

This orthodox, market-liberal approach by Giscard and Barre was fundamentally rejected by the Left, which came to power in 1981. Deflation hit the living standards and employment prospects of the weaker social groups; the stress on facing international competition coupled with an overvalued franc had left the French domestic economy wide open to penetration by multinational corporations and by low wage economies. The policy of the Left combined 'redistributive Keynesianism' (Hall, 1985) with protectionism under the slogan of 'reconquest of the home market'; it was by this means that the Left intended to confront the employment and balance of payments problems over the medium term. Underlying the Keynesian orientation of the policy was the belief that even if the boost to home demand did lead to balance of payments difficulties, these would be temporary and could be met by borrowing. French and OECD forecasters predicted that OECD GDP would rise by 2 per cent in 1982 and world trade would rise by 4.6 per cent. The Left, therefore, sought only to anticipate this upturn by one year. This 'redistributive Keynesianism' involved a budgetary boost equivalent to 2 per cent of GDP in 1981–2, to the benefit primarily of the minimum wage-earners (the minimum wage, the SMIC, rose by 38 per cent, 1981–3), and family allowances, pensions and housing allowances were substantially improved. A further facet of the redistribution was the imposition of a wealth tax which would in small part meet these costs. Public expenditure also met the cost of the 200,000 newly created public sector jobs, while the introduction of a 39-hour week and a fifth week of holiday were intended, mistakenly, to lead to a rise in the demand for labour.

What went wrong and why were the Socialists forced into a policy U-turn? It is clear that the external constraint, which brought the Chirac government's stimulus to an end in 1976, was felt forcefully in 1981–2, within a matter of months. The stimulus was short-lived, petering out in mid-1982, and a balance of payments problem appeared in October 1981 when the franc was devalued. 1982 had been termed the 'year of all the deficits', when the balance of payments deficit reached FF 104 bn, the government deficit equalled 3 per cent of GDP, the social security deficits snowballed and inflation accelerated to 13 per cent. It appears that one-half of the deterioration was the result of the world recession and the vertiginous rise in the dollar. The forecasts had gone awry (Muet and Fonteneau, 1984). Of equal importance was the manifest failure of French industry to meet the increase in demand. This very poor supply response must be explained by the previous years of low profitability and low investment, together with the fact that it was industry which bore the brunt of the costs of the stimulus. The costs of the SMIC increases, the reduced working time and higher social security payments equalled FF 34 bn in 1981–2, or a rise in costs of 25 per cent. The U-turn in policy came in stages (see Chapter 1), with a four-month wages and prices freeze in June 1982 and the decisive shift to austerity in the shape of the March 1983 Delors Plan, which sought the deindexation of wages in order to break the wage–price spiral.

If we turn to industrial policy, the ideological oppositions were as intense. Giscard and Barre were both market liberals and found little role for national planning. It is during the 1970s that the demise of planning became assured. And as for industrial policy, the rhetoric pronounced the disengagement of the State from interventionism, but in practice the Barre government became engaged in shoring up French capitalism to an extent never before countenanced. Both Giscard and Barre placed no faith in the ability of planning to improve on the imperfections of the market. They distrusted the Keynesian orientation of the forecasting models and contested the 'hexagonal', i.e. French, context of the Plan, given the openness of the French economy and its susceptibility to international forces. Clearly these models were ill-suited, for the Sixth, Seventh and Eighth Plans (the latter was never voted in Parliament) were rendered useless by the oil crises. The neo-liberal attack on planning was mounted first by Giscard in 1974 when he set up a presidential Central Planning Council to rival the CGP, and in the same year all industrial influence was removed from the CGP when the Ministry of Industry was created. Critics argue that the Seventh Plan was scuppered deliberately: the post of Commissioner for the Plan was held vacant for 18 months, and the government adopted the 'rose' strategy for the Seventh Plan, which was wildly optimistic in the post-oil shock years. The Barre Plan came to substitute for the Seventh Plan.

In industrial policy, the neo-liberals obviously stressed their opposition to interventionism and to the grand projects of the Gaullist years. The Barre government in particular, stressed the need for 'positive adjustment'; in order to redress the external balance, France must pursue her comparative advantage in world markets, shifting to high-technology branches and abandoning industries facing Third World competition. Known as 're-deployment', the strategy sought niches of competitiveness in a hostile trade environment. Under the pressure of events, and for political reasons, this austere policy was hardly implemented. The grand Gaullist pro-grammes were continued to sustain a French lead, but far greater emphasis was given to the vastly expanded nuclear programme and to the moderniza-tion of the telephone system. As for the promotion of high-technology industries, aid to these from the Committee for the Development of Strategic Industries (CODIS), established in 1979, bore no relation to that given to sectors in decline (Dacier *et al.*, 1985). The CIASI fund, estab-lished in 1975 to assist sectors in difficulty, merely retarded the inexorable decline of the machine tool, leather and shoe and watchmaking industries, while the aid to sustain shipbuilding and to salvage the steel industry in 1978 absorbed a sizeable part of the public budget, without offering any longer-term solution. As for the much-vaunted assistance for small- and medium-sized firms, the 1979 Hannoun Report found that in 1976, six industrial groups employing no more than 25 per cent of the industrial labour force gained more than 50 per cent of the industrial assistance.

In direct ideological opposition to this policy, the Left proceeded to reverse it. Redeployment, they argued, benefited a few large multinational groups at the expense of the army of workers employed in industries threatened by foreign competition. Closures and redundancies had simply exposed the French markets to import penetration and had torn up the tissue of interrelationships between supplier and customer firms which, they argued, were an essential part of French industry's supply capability. The Left's counter-proposals focused on the network of linkages, compris-ing the stages of vertical integration from raw material to final product and incorporating the diagonal integration links with process plant manufac-turers (Morvan, 1985). The network could also be a means of rejuvenating sectors in decline by the transmission of technical progress for, to adopt a commonly used slogan, 'there were no sectors in decline, only those suffering technological obsolescence'. It can easily be grasped that by the mastery of these linkages a protectionist policy, excluding foreign suppliers, could be implemented.

The nationalization programme was to provide the spearhead: nationalized enterprises would speed up investment and R&D programmes and by their purchasing and investment power would stimulate whole networks. Bound to a strategy by planning contracts, they would be a key instrument in a renewed planning system. In 1982, eleven of France's largest manufacturing firms, many of them multinational companies, became state-controlled, together with the remainder of the banking system not already in state hands. Six large conglomerates were nationalized fully, the two quasi-nationalized steel companies changed status, and the State took majority interests in Matra, Dassault and CII–Honeywell–Bull. In Roussel–Uclaf, it could take only a 40 per cent interest. The expanded state holdings in the energy and manufacturing sectors accounted for 23 per cent of employees, 30 per cent of sales, 30 per cent of exports and 40 per cent of industrial investments, giving the State the leading role in industry. But the economic climate and U-turn quickly dictated a shift in policy towards retrenchment and restructuring, euphemistically called 'modernization' (see Chapter 1). A succession of four Ministers of Industry ensured that there was no strong policy continuity and the notion of networks found expression, if at all, only in the field of electronics. In practice, the Socialists adopted a policy of national champions in accordance with time-honoured tradition. And in view of the losses of FF 77.1 bn between 1981 and 1985, in addition to the FF 86 bn total cost of acquisition, we have to agree with Cohen (1986) that the nationalizations rescued French capitalism and, after a restructuring at public cost, the nationalized industries then became suitable for privatization!

2.5   Problems of slow growth, uncompetitiveness and unemployment in the 1980s

Economic stagnation, deindustrialization and mounting unemployment have been the focus of French anxieties in recent years, and reflect in part the need for France to get back into step with her EMS partners after the failed Keynesian stimulus of 1981–2. A consensus has been revealed among the successive governments of different political complexion on the need to get to grips with the external constraint in the direction charted by the 1983 Delors Plan. The achievement of international competitiveness is pursued through a tight rein on home demand, and by anti-inflation policies (wage restraint, monetary discipline exerted by a fixed franc: Deutschmark parity in the European Monetary System) as well as by deregulation. This has had a certain success – low inflation of 2.5 per cent, a notable reduction in the external deficit – but at the expense of very slow growth of 1.1 per cent (1981–5), soaring unemployment (jumping by 875,000 between May 1981 and February 1986, to stand at 10.7 per cent) and a decline in living standards in 1983 and 1984. This is clearly a policy for the longer term, where growth will then be carried by investment and exports. Many people question, however, whether France is not fixed on a slow growth trajectory, which is insufficient to reduce unemployment.

The continuing balance of payments difficulties, especially the deficit on industrial goods, are a constant reminder that the success of the policy is not assured. For a range of manufactures, the import share of the French market now exceeds 50 per cent. In part, the balance of payments deficit reflects the demand differential – the fact that French demand cumulatively had risen faster than in its partner countries (OECD, 1987). However, the deficit in manufactures has its origins in poorer price and structural competitiveness. A strong franc (overvalued by about 16 per cent in 1981) is unhelpful when exports are price sensitive. More interesting, though, is the question of structural competitiveness, reflected in the heavy deficit with OECD countries and in the strong domestic import penetration (Lafay, 1987). Analysts speak of France having few 'poles of competitiveness' – related branches of manufacturing in which France specializes and dominates world markets. The explanation focuses again on the years of low profitability and underinvestment which have led to a present weakening of French industry.

The inexorable rise in unemployment, and the poor short-term prospects of any substantial improvement, have focused debate on its causes, for only an accurate diagnosis can guide employment policy. Malinvaud (1983) makes two broad distinctions in the origins of unemployment – Keynesian and classical. Keynesian unemployment arises, for example, in a recession when demand is low, and so policies of budgetary stimulus such as the Socialists' of 1981–2 or Chirac's stimulus of 1975 seek to remedy the demand deficiency. The close limits on the efficacy of these policies have focused attention on 'classical' unemployment, which arises when firms will not invest in further capacity nor take on new workers because it is unprofitable; here attention focuses on 'wages being too high' or other costs such as social security contributions and interest rates. Does the minimum wage – the SMIC – push up wage costs? Has wage indexation damaged profits and investment? Have the hefty rises in social security contributions since the mid-1970s led to high indirect wage costs? Do French administrative controls over redundancies make employers unwilling to hire labour?

The inexorable rise in wage costs might seem to support the 'classical' case – unit wage costs stood 12 per cent higher in 1983 than in 1973. Let us review briefly the findings. The hypothesis of real wages being too high (a 'real wage gap' in relation to productivity) finds no strong econometric support (Hénin, 1986), and the effects of the SMIC in raising youth unemployment can be easily exaggerated (Martin, 1983). In contrast, Keynesian causes, when recession is a worldwide phenomenon, have plainly been at work. There seems little doubt that 'classical' unemployment was predominant from 1969 to 1974; since then and until recently, the sharp falls in profitability have led to serious underinvestment, and therefore to a shortage of jobs. But overall, the narrow scope for treating this diagnosis by demand-led expansion was revealed by the 1981–2 'boost' to the economy, and years of underinvestment have left France with a completely insufficient capacity to employ all those without work.

Given these constraints on policy-makers, it is hardly surprising that they have searched for growth in efficiency improvements, by deregulation, rather than by risky macroeconomic measures. The 'liberal wind' started blowing towards the Socialists even before the market-liberal ideologies under Chirac gained power. The objectives of this 'supply-side' approach are to improve the supply of labour and capital, to enable prices to fulfil their function (abolition of price, exchange and dividend controls) and to stimulate enterprise through competition and incentives. Here then was a reversal in the Socialists' statist policies, and a further retreat from traditional interventionism. Reforms in financial markets were begun under the Socialists and culminated in the stock-market reform under Chirac (see Chapter 1). The expressed aims of the privatization policy from 1986 to 1988 were to raise technical efficiency in the companies themselves, and expose them to market discipline, while contributing to a flood of dealing on the stock exchange. In relation to employment reforms, apart from a widening of the early retirement and youth employment schemes, which followed in the direct line of policy since 1977, Chirac sought to raise flexibility in the labour market by two principal innovations: (1) the abolition of administrative approval of redundancy proposals, which had imposed delays and uncertainty; and (2) the relaxation of restrictions governing fixed-term contract working and part-time working.

This new policy orientation of competitiveness, a strong franc and the search for growth through exports, investment and greater liberalization, seems likely to be pursued in the longer term. Many French people wonder when the benefits of low inflation will feed through into expansion and jobs. In particular, their dependence on the West German market and on the franc–Deutschmark parity, when West Germany seems destined to slow growth, raises further doubt about future French growth possibilities. An upturn in growth and investment became apparent from early summer 1988 and promises a more sustained growth performance. The international constraints remain, however, and an improvement in employment will take time.

THREE

New Social Practices, Continuing Sociospatial Inequalities

Twenty years after the turbulent events of 1968, many commentators have concluded that French society has matured and discarded the old battle-grounds and lines of conflicts, especially those centred on class, religion and institutions. The age-old divisions have supposedly given way in a modern society to a greater emphasis on individualism and its related values. Traditional institutions founded on a more collective sense of belonging, such as the Church, have entered into a period of crisis in which they can no longer impose their values and priorities. An overwhelming number of those who declare themselves Catholics say it is their conscience which dictates their actions (SOFRES poll quoted in *L'Etat de la France*, Verdié, 1987, p. 294). The young are said to be no longer desirous of overturning society, but content to adapt to and find a place in it (*Le Monde*, 1988, p. 132) in a decade when unemployment has taken a particularly heavy toll in the younger age-group (see Table 2.6).

Yet the evolution of French society is contradictory, complex and geographically variable. For example, the regular practice of religion is confined nationally to a small minority; in 1981 only 13 per cent of Catholics went regularly to mass compared to 37 per cent in 1952. The decline in the West has been even more catastrophic, as a recent study of Basse Normandie highlighted with attendance falling from 51 per cent to 11.5 per cent in the Manche in the past 30 years. The young employees and workers and those living in urban peripheries display extremely low levels of observance. It is above average among farmers, the middle classes, in urban centres and small towns (CERA and INSEE, 1987). Yet, despite this collapse of religious observance and the demise of the parish culture (Hervieu-Léger, 1987), the four solemn occasions marking stages in the life cycle – baptism, communion, marriage and burial – are still religiously celebrated. In the religious areas of the rural West, civil marriages and burials remain the object of scandal. Even in localities where religious practice has virtually disappeared, these traditions are still followed (Lambert and Willaime, 1986, pp. 191–2).

The decline and changing role of institutions exemplify tensions between the individual and multiple collective groupings and institutions, between state and society, between equality, solidarity and identity. The cohabitation and realization of different tendencies have not proved easy, as, for example, in the desire for the right to a distinct identity, which was originally the basis of a post-68 critique by feminists and regionalists who argued that equality had to incorporate identity (Viveret, 1985). More recently, the extreme Right has adopted this idea as a justification for the exclusion of those who are different. A simple notion of equality has itself been rejected, and partially replaced by the idea of solidarity which would encompass and respect diverse groups and prevent the exclusion of poorer and marginal groups.

A good example of respect for plurality is to be found in the movement SOS-Racisme, with its punchy, easy-going motto of 'Hands off my pal', founded by a group of Parisian students in 1984 after Le Pen's success in the European elections and an increase in racist incidents (*Le Monde*, 1988a, pp. 106–7). The duration and severity of the economic crisis, especially the continuing high levels of unemployment, have engendered an exploitation of themes of law and order, security, exclusion of immigrants and national identity. A return to the solidity of traditional values, in particular those of the family, is also extolled as a bulwark against the rising tide of delinquency, which has been highest in the past decade in large cities of over half a million people (INSEE, 1987, pp. 60–6).

3.1 The diversity of family models

The existence of a single family model, consisting of two parents and children, is a far cry from current reality. It is ironic that the State itself should have contributed through its wide-ranging and generous family allowances to the plurality of family forms and personal relationships. Family allowances, instituted in 1946 but with antecedents in the 1930s, sought to encourage the reproduction of the French population (Prost, 1987). This included an allowance for families on single salaries and reached 50 per cent of a monthly basic salary for three children. In general, the real value of family allowances declined in the 1960s, and it was only in 1972 that the legislation was rethought so as to be more selective in terms of family incomes and order of child (Collins, 1988). Two initiatives were implemented to take account of the changing family structure – an allowance for child care and one for the single parent. In the 1978 reforms, the third child was the focus of attempts to favour a higher birth rate, which had been dropping steadily since the 1960s (see Figure 1.3). The Socialist government reaffirmed the neutrality of subsidies in relation to family situations.

Furthermore, Chirac's government in 1986 extended child-care allowances to those couples where both, or one if a single parent, were working and who employed a person in the house for child-care purposes.

Today family situations are highly diverse. A large number of young adults are single (24.8 per cent of women in the age-group 25–29 years and 12.7 per cent of those aged 30–34 years), while over 40 per cent of the over-60s are single or widowed. The increase of cohabitation, divorce and single parents is quite striking since the mid-1970s. What this means is that a substantial proportion of the population will at some time in their lives go through one of these experiences.

The rate of marriage has declined steadily from a peak in 1972, a fall that is attributed partly to the widespread use of modern means of contraception and a consequent reduction in the number of unions resulting from an unplanned child. While the rate of marriage decreased from 76.9 per thousand in 1973 to 54.9 per thousand in 1983, the number of divorces has risen sharply from 46,047 in 1973 to 110,000 in 1985 (265,000 marriages celebrated that year). There has also been an increase in the number of unmarried couples, from 2.9 per cent of all couples in 1962 to 6.3 per cent in 1982. The trend is far more pronounced among younger age cohorts for whom cohabitation has become quite common. In 1985, almost one-third of women and over 40 per cent of men in the age-group 20–24 cohabited, varying from a low level among farming couples, but comprising almost one-half of women from the liberal, scientific and managerial professions and over 60 per cent of men. Similarly, there are important geographical variations from rural communes (just under 30 per cent of women aged 20–24 years living in couples cohabit) to the Paris region (over 40 per cent) (Figure 3.1b). These rates subsequently decrease by almost half for each successive age-group (7.8 per cent of women and 9.5 per cent of men in couples aged 35–39 years) (INSEE, 1987, p. 506).

Although for a majority cohabitation still represents a temporary stage, a growing number of couples are choosing to bring up children outside of marriage. From 63,000 births outside of marriage in 1975, the number has shot up to 135,000 in 1984, or almost one in five births. Similarly, single-parent families have also increased and in 1982 constituted 6.3 per cent of families, or an increase of 14.3 per cent in relation to 1975. The vast majority (85 per cent) are headed by women. As with cohabitation, the greatest concentration and highest percentages are found in the Paris region and Provence-Alpes-Côte d'Azur, the latter with a high percentage of divorced single parents (Figure 3.1a). Thus in the Paris region, and especially central Paris, these new family situations have become acceptable, if not virtually dominant.

To find our traditional, large family, we would have to look to the families

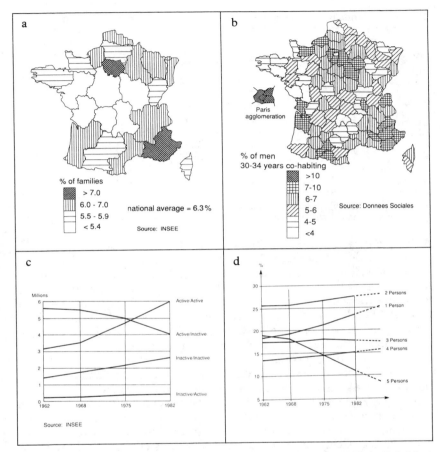

Figure 3.1 Diversity of family forms. a, Single-parent families, 1982. b, Cohabitation (men, aged 30–34 years). c, Working and non-working couples, 1962–82. d, Household size, 1962–82.

of recent immigrants for it is among these that the proportion of large families reaches its peak. For example, 5.9 per cent of foreign families have five or more children (17 per cent among Algerian families) as opposed to only 0.6 per cent of French families and 0.9 per cent of naturalized French families (INSEE, 1987, p. 29). Furthermore, the extended family is very much a vestige of the past, significant only in certain rural areas as in the South-west. Indeed, the fastest growing category among household types is

Table 3.1   Women's participation in the workforce by family size, 1986

No. of children	Age of women*				Proportion of women working part-time
	25–29	30–34	35–39	40–44	
0	89.0	84.6	81.6	74.9	17.4
1	80.6	85.1	81.4	72.3	20.1
2	62.4	70.3	73.1	64.1	30.2
3	30.2	42.7	50.5	49.8	
4	20.9	27.3	37.0	39.0	38.7
5 or more	11.9	10.8	13.2	14.3	
Average	72.5	68.1	68.5	67.3	

Source: INSEE (1986) *Enquête sur l'Emploi.*
* Women living in couples with children under 18 years.

the single-person household (Figure 3.1d). Emphasis has been placed on trying to encourage more couples to have three children. Women's employment is often interrupted by the arrival of a third child, especially if children follow on closely. A sharp drop occurs in the participation rate in the workforce for women with three children, since over 60 per cent of women between 25 and 44 years living in a couple and with two children continue to work, while only about one-third are able to do so with three children (Table 3.1). The degree to which this pattern applies varies according to social class and type of commune.

The family and its associated values of solidarity and primary socialization have once again come to the fore in the political discourses of the Right. The classic Right vaunts the family as the best insurance for the 1990s, able to counteract various social problems, such as delinquency, and to provide the resources necessary to look after an aging population (Barzach, 1988). The extreme Right, on the other hand, closes its eyes to the diversity of family forms and irreversible trends, such as women's employment. Its programme ironically extols the virtues of the large family and the return of women to the home. It is unlikely that women's participation in the labour force will be voluntarily reversed, although the recent trend has been to push women into part-time and temporary jobs (13.6 per cent in part-time employment in 1975, 23.1 per cent in 1986; Table 3.1).

However, it was the existence of two salaries and the rapid increase in working-class salaries, especially in the years after 1968, that contributed to the increased purchasing power of households in the 1970s (see Figure 1.1a). From 1966 to 1979, the average standard of living of households rose by 55 per cent, even more so for the less favoured groups – farmers,

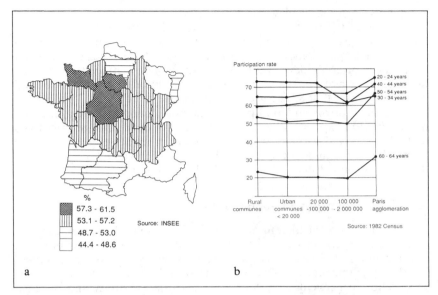

Figure 3.2 Women's participation in the workforce. a, Proportion of women working in the age-group 15–64 years. b, Female participation in the workforce by age and size of settlement.

agricultural workers, manual workers and the retired – and thereby reduced the extreme disparity of salaries between the better paid and the worst paid (INSEE, 1987, p. 366).

During this period basic household goods (refrigerators, televisions), which today are possessed by over 90 per cent of households, became widely available. The diffusion of the consumer revolution levelled out certain class distinctions and ended the exclusion of groups such as the peasantry and the working class. Yet various INSEE surveys (1987, pp. 397–9) have shown that income strongly determines consumption for the vast majority of household goods, and that two basic cleavages continue to structure forms and styles of consumption and demarcate a hierarchy of class distinctions. The first separates out households in terms of the proportion of their budget devoted to basic expenditure in contrast to those for which cultural expenditure is an important element. The second cleavage is related to the social and cultural environment, so that with equivalent incomes, forms and types of consumption will vary. For example, in relation to cultural expenditure, the working class and peasantry favour expenditure on entertainment, while intellectual groups put their taste and social judgement on display (Bourdieu, 1985).

Geographically, patterns of consumption and social practices differentiate rural and urban populations. Rural populations tend to be less disposed towards the acquisition of appliances, to eat more basic foods and to go on fewer and shorter holidays. Yet these variations stem as much from the size of settlements as from the geographical distribution of social classes and groups. The fact that 82.9 per cent of Parisians, but only 50.7 per cent of those in small towns and 40.3 per cent in rural communes went away on holiday in 1985 expresses the general tendency of those in large cities to go on holiday, as well as the presence in large urban centres of a much higher proportion of the middle classes and those who spend a high proportion of their income on culture and leisure (INSEE, 1987, pp. 383–4).

3.2   The geography of social classes

Few studies have taken into account the geographical distribution and grouping of social classes, and the way in which the social environment, thus created, influences forms of consumption and structures inequalities. Yet the geography of social classes underscores the concentration of classes and groups in particular types of areas and the proximity and distance between various groups (Table 3.2).

Nicole Tabard (1987) has drawn up a typology of three sociospatial configurations based on the 1975 census[1]:

(1) The *agricultural*, defined by the proportion of agricultural households (at least 19 per cent), comprises 20 per cent of the total population. Here, the retired, artisans, shopkeepers and unskilled workers are all strongly represented, live in proximity and thus share a rural space. Within this category, several subgroups stand out. Those localities with a high proportion of workers, many of whom are unskilled and of agricultural origin, are characteristic of the West (1960s industrial decentralization), Rhône-Alpes and Franche-Comté. On the other hand, those with the highest percentage of workers (41 per cent of heads of households), but which have maintained a higher proportion of skilled workers (42 per cent of workers), dominate the zones of earlier industrialization in the North and North-east.

(2) The *intermediate* category, covering 5000 communes and 16 per cent of the population, is characterized by a salaried workforce in the service sector. Within this type of locality, there are further sub-sociospatial groupings, of which the most demographically dynamic comprise skilled workers, supervisors and technicians in urban peripheries.

(3) The *non-agricultural* comprises 60 per cent of the population and all of the large cities. Despite a relatively balanced range of groups represented in

this configuration, two groups at the extreme of the social hierarchy vary considerably in their spatial distribution. On the one hand, semi-skilled workers range from as little as 4 per cent in the chic suburbs of western Paris to up to 23 per cent in the most working-class areas. On the other hand, higher management, scientific and intellectual professions display a similar polarization, attaining 22 per cent of the total population in certain residential areas near cities, such as Paris, Lyons, Metz and Aix-en-Provence. Within the urban system, higher social classes tend to gravitate towards the centre, leaving private sector employees and intermediate professions and management, skilled workers and technicians dominant in outer urban areas.

The significance of this sociospatial configuration is that it is closely related to the demographic and economic vitality of communes, highlighting the link between level of qualification and spatial location. As Frémont (1988) has pointed out, it is the middle classes who are shaping the contemporary geography of France. They use up much space through their adoption of new practices of work, residence and leisure. On the other hand, unskilled workers, self-employed producers and the elderly live in localities which are experiencing depopulation and are reliant on agricultural and traditional industries. The disadvantages faced by the social groups occupying these declining or slow-growth localities are numerous, ranging from poor educational provision (see pp. 85) to a lack of professional training and cultural facilities. In contrast, qualified workers, technicians, etc. tend to live in more dynamic communes, which are relatively well endowed with various services. Hence the spatial dimension reinforces the reproduction of social classes and groups, especially through access to educational opportunities.

Although French society has, since the postwar period, shed some of its most extreme forms of social rigidity and seen its middle classes expand, the two extremes of the social hierarchy remain remarkably self-reproducing. The dominant classes continue to ensure a promising future for their children; at the top of the hierarchy, the liberal professions see to it that 70 per cent of their children do not leave the dominant classes. At the other end of the spectrum, the picture is slightly more complex. The peasantry is self-recruiting, but its disintegration has pushed its children into the working class in the case of men (33.6 per cent) and white-collar employees in the case of women. The working class, though still composed of those from within its ranks and the peasantry, has undergone some extension of mobility. The chances of a working-class child reaching the dominant classes is slight (7.7 per cent) and almost non-existent where the liberal professions are concerned (0.2 per cent). Social mobility has been most

Table 3.2   (a) Geographical distribution of social classes, 1985

	Rural (%)	Urban centres, excluding Paris (%)			Paris metropolis (%)	Total (%)
		<20,000 pop.	20,000–200,000 pop.	>200,000 pop.		
Farmers, farm workers	84.2	10.6	3.2	2.0		100.0
Artisans, shopkeepers, employers (of over 10 persons)	29.9	21.1	17.7	16.7	14.6	100.0
Higher management and intellectual professions	12.8	11.3	17.5	21.4	37.1	100.0
Liberal professions	16.2	17.0	18.3	22.8	25.7	100.0
Administrative and commercial private sector	11.7	9.7	15.3	18.9	44.3	100.0
Intermediate professions	19.0	14.9	20.9	21.8	22.9	100.0
Employees	17.8	14.6	22.3	22.6	22.6	100.0
Workers	27.8	18.1	21.5	18.3	14.3	100.0
Unskilled	31.7	20.1	21.9	16.7	9.5	100.0

(b) Socioeconomic composition in rural areas and Paris region

	Rural (%)	Female	Paris metropolis (%)	Female
Farmers	22.7	−23.1	—	—
Artisans, etc.	9.0	8.0	6.0	4.7
Higher categories	4.4	2.4	17.5	11.1
Intermediate	14.7	14.3	23.8	24.2
Employees	17.7	35.6	30.6	50.4
Workers	31.5	16.4	22.1	9.8
Total	100.0	100.0	100.0	100.0
Total active population	5,617,759	2,159,196	4,077,294	1,827,165

Source: INSEE (1985) *Enquête sur l'Emploi.*

marked among the intermediate groups, especially the children of teachers, one-third of whom have moved upwards to the dominant classes (Gollac and Laulhé, 1986, pp. 86–7).

Women's mobility is far more restrictive given their segregation into a few groups (white-collar employees 47 per cent in 1985, intermediate professions 19.5 per cent), whatever their social origin. They tend to remain in the class of origin because of their marriage partner. Women from professional backgrounds generally married men from intermediate and higher-level professions. Conversely, two-thirds of working-class daughters married in the same class and very rarely married men in the highest category (INSEE, 1987, p. 490). Yet the role of women is crucial in the transmission of cultural capital and in the schooling of children, possibly even more so among groups with low educational attainment.

3.3   The geography of education

In a society in which the majority of the population is salaried and the lack of appropriate qualifications weighs heavily against access to employment, the educational system becomes the principal means by which cultural capital is transmitted. As the average level of educational qualification has moved upwards, so have the prized qualifications as well as the demands made on the educational system. The opening-up of opportunities for parental involvement, for example, which pathway through the secondary school their children should follow, has inevitably favoured those who are most familiar with the advantages of different pathways through the system.

It was during the Giscard years (1975 Haby reforms) that the principle of comprehensive education was finally introduced. Up to the first two years of secondary schooling, children follow a common syllabus. Nevertheless the reproduction of inequalities occurs throughout the educational system, but is most pronounced between the professional training pathways and the longer, traditional pathways, not to mention those who leave without any qualification whatsoever. The majority of pupils stay at school until the official leaving age of 16 years (92 per cent including apprentices). By 18 years, 56 per cent continue to attend an educational establishment and by 20 years one-quarter. The post-16 year presence in schools is high, due to the number of pupils repeating classes throughout their school career and to the encouragement to obtain the *baccalauréat*. Thus the number of children entering secondary school and reaching the final year has increased from 32 per cent in 1975 to 44 per cent in 1985. The *baccalauréat*, gained by almost 30 per cent of this generation, exemplifies wide social and geographical disparities, crudely dividing France into a north of lower educational achievement, with the exception of the Paris region and Brittany, and a more qualified south, excluding Aquitaine. As many educational studies have demonstrated, failure in later years can often be traced back to problems in the preschool and primary periods.

3.3.1 Preschool education

France has a relatively high level of preschool places though still an inadequate provision of child-care facilities. In 1945–6, 27.6 per cent of children aged 2–6 years attended preschool; by 1982, this figure had reached 80.8 per cent. Overall, virtually all children had attended at least one year of preschool in 1985. Most children attended school from the age of four (87.5 per cent at four years, 96.7 per cent at five years). Preschool caters for 11 per cent of children under three years, the majority being looked after by their mothers and 5 per cent in crèches. Despite the fall in fertility, there has been pressure on nursery places.

In order to understand geographical and social disparities in the use of publicly provided child-care and preschool facilities, we have to understand the various alternatives made available in different areas and how they are used (Desplanques, 1985, p. 31). Crèches tend to be heavily concentrated in the Paris region (Ile de France has 47 per cent of national crèche provision) and in large cities where almost one-third of children under three years, who are not looked after by their mother and do not attend school, are sent to a crèche. The average for the country as a whole is only one in eight. Both crèches and child nurses, also concentrated in the Ile de France, are overwelmingly utilized by educated women and higher social categories. Crèches are almost non-existent among working-class women, for these women and employees either look after their own children to a greater extent or, if they are in employment, call on their own families or send their children to nurseries, which are free.

Thus geographical disparities in preschool attendance need to take account of these alternatives (Figure 3.4c), but they cannot be ascribed to the level of women's employment. Some of the groups with extremely low rates of employment, such as Algerian and Tunisian women, send over 40 per cent of their preschool children and 80 per cent at three years to nurseries (Desplanques, 1985, p. 31), which compares favourably with the highest rates.

3.3.2 Primary and secondary education

One of the most startling statistics to emerge from the French educational system is the enormously high level of pupils repeating classes right from the beginning of their school years. It is quite characteristic of the first cycle of secondary school, where one in eight pupils repeated a class in 1985–6

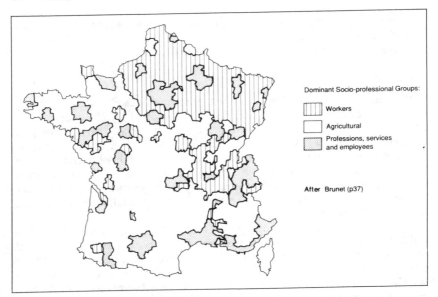

Figure 3.3   Socioeconomic composition of the population, 1982. (After Brunet, 1987, p. 37).

(INSEE, 1987, p. 550). A number of reasons have been suggested for this high rate, ranging from the implementation of a single college by the educational reform of 1977, the possibility for parents to refuse the placement of their child in a less desirable vocational stream (*lycée d'enseignement professionnel*) to, lastly, straightforward failure. Similarly, in the second cycle, whether in the short pathways (certificate of professional aptitude or the diploma of professional education) or the long pathways culminating in the *baccalauréat*, the rate of failure and repeating is high. Pupils are prepared to repeat in order to obtain the most prestigious diplomas, leading to 21 per cent of students repeating in the final year.

The most obvious explanatory factor separating those who succeed without repeating, especially in the early years, and gain the most valued qualification, and those who fall by the wayside or leave with one of the less desirable diplomas, is social class. The passage through primary school generally poses few problems for children of the higher social categories. Quite the opposite situation faces children of unskilled workers, the unemployed and immigrants. Once a child falls behind more than one year, it is extremely difficult to catch up; 92.7 per cent of children of the highest social class follow a normal and untroubled path through primary schooling, compared to only 70.7 per cent of children of employees, 60.8 per cent of children of skilled workers and as low as 36.0 per cent for children of unskilled workers. It is among the latter group that over one-quarter of children are shunted into other classes, a procedure followed once the child has fallen behind more than one year in primary school. The national average in the period 1978–83/4 was 65.7 per cent completing primary school normally, 25.5 per cent repeating one year and 9.0 per cent dropping more than one year behind (INSEE, 1987, p. 548). Social differences in types of pathway and success widen as one progresses in the system. For example, 64 per cent of the population between 17 and 19 years were either pupils or students in 1982, but for those in intermediate and higher social categories the figure reached 91 per cent as against 52 per cent of working-class children. By 20–22 years, the gap had opened up further with 65 per cent for the higher social categories, but only 13 per cent for workers. Very few of the latter pursue their studies further.

These various disparities also exhibit specific spatial patterns (Figure 3.4), reproducing the pattern discerned for preschool education of a high rate of success and attendance in the South but a low one in the North, with the exception of the educational authorities in the Paris region and Brittany. Furthermore, each educational authority (*académie*) encompasses wide variations that cannot be wholly reduced to differences in social composition. In addition to social structure, we have to take into account the strategies pursued by parents, educational provision and the policies of individual schools, all of which are situated within a local society with its specific social and historical identity. Parents, of course, deploy a number of strategies to circumvent or change the opportunities available, including, for those able to do so, moving their place of residence, demanding dispensation from the school allocated or, finally, placing their children in private schools. Two case studies will illustrate these relationships – Calvados in Basse Normandie and Paris (centre and inner suburbs).

The image of Basse Normandie as a predominantly agricultural society needs to be jettisoned, for in most rural areas the largest group consists of at least 40 per cent of workers, peaking at 50 per cent in some localities. Calvados is also interesting for its wide variations in educational achievements in a department known to have a poor educational record; for example, double the average number of children drop behind two or more years at school (20 per cent). Its population includes a high proportion of unskilled workers and large families in which women do not work, factors which have a negative effect on children's achievement and tend to retard their preschool entry (Hérin, 1987, p. 89). Like other departments in the West, the private, primarily Catholic sector is important (Figure 3.4a) but by no means dominant, comprising 25 per cent of pupils in the first cycle

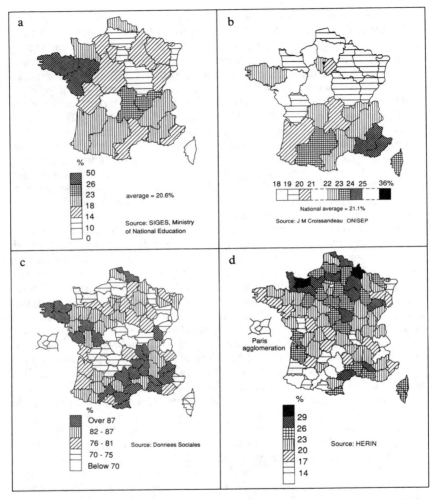

Figure 3.4 Educational provision and attainment. a, Percentage of pupils in private schools, 1981–2. b, School population in second cycle as a percentage of secondary school pupils. c, Preschool education: percentage of three-year olds attending school. d, Percentage of pupils repeating classes (6th, 5th and special classes) in state schools, 1981–4.

and 20 per cent in the second cycle of secondary schools (Crozic, Desrez and Hérin, 1987).

Three types of socioeducational establishments can be distinguished (Mary, 1987), according to size, qualification of teachers, range of options and social composition of pupils.

(1) Small colleges catering for a rural population of farmers, workers, shopkeepers and artisans. These were previously general colleges and have few highly qualified teachers.

(2) Larger colleges (500–600 pupils) in city centres (Caen, Lisieux, Bayeux) with much better qualified teachers and a far greater range of options, especially in languages. These were often originally the first cycle of *lycées* and recruit among the higher social classes – up to 40 per cent from managerial, scientific and professional classes and fewer than 10 per cent from working-class backgrounds.

(3) Mixed colleges located in small-scale industrial zones in rural areas or the periphery of urban centres. In the latter, the social composition ranges from a highly middle-class structure in inner-urban areas (Hérouville St Clair just outside Caen) to a more working-class one as one moves away from the centre, especially southwards.

Lycées exhibit even greater contrasts, for the most prestigious in Caen (Malherbe) attracts 50 per cent of its pupils from the highest social classes in the first year of the second cycle. The private sector also draws on a limited social range – over 40 per cent from middle and upper categories and less than 15 per cent from the working class. Family strategies thus operate in this hierarchy of educational provision, for the demands for dispensation from the school allocated favours colleges in the centre with their greater range of options in languages and music. However, in order to manoeuvre successfully and guide one's child, it is necessary to know and be able to formulate the type of reasons acceptable to school authorities for wanting to move a child from one school to another.

In Paris, competition for the most prestigious colleges and *lycées* is all the more fierce. The centre and middle-class suburbs of Paris are disproportionately endowed with classical *lycées* and this, in turn, attracts a middle-class population aware of the benefits of these schools, which have a high rate of success in the *baccalauréat* (Pinçon-Charlot and Rendu, 1987). The discrepancy between inner Paris and its eastern suburbs of the 'red belt' has been to some extent compensated since the 1940s, mainly in the larger left-wing municipalities. Unsurprisingly, private provision continues to be weighted in favour of the wealthy western suburbs.

The democratization of education has left intact inequalities of opportunity both in the quality and choice offered and in attainment. The working class, unemployed and immigrants live in localities with poorer provision and are eliminated disproportionately at each stage of the school process. Geographical and socioeconomic inequalities thus interact to produce very different educational horizons. In other domains where the Welfare State has extended coverage, inequalities measured in terms of access to and forms of utilization of services, also prevail, as in the field of health services.

3.4 Health: access and services

Health care is based on a mix of public and private provision. The non-hospital doctor is a private practitioner, and the patient is able to choose whom to consult. Payment is made directly by the patient and is reimbursed on a variable scale, according to type of treatment and service. Hospitals are paid directly by sickness funds. It is particularly difficult to impose financial controls on this system, since it emphasizes the individual practitioner, and different authorities act independently of each other (Collins, 1988).

During the 1970s, health expenditure rose by 16.6 per cent per annum from 6.0 per cent of GDP in 1971 to 8.4 per cent in 1981. The numbers of doctors increased by over 60 per cent during this period, as did the number of hospital personnel (INSEE, 1987, p. 427-8). In an attempt to curb expenditure and restrict large deficits in the social expenditure budget in the 1980s (1981-2, 1986, 1988), various governments have imposed maximum levels of expenditure in hospitals and lowered the indexation of reimbursement. Decentralization of health expenditure to departments and the establishment of regional observatories have also played their part in this strategy.

One of the reasons for the postwar increase in social security expenditure is that health coverage now exends to virtually the entire population, with almost two-thirds belonging to insurance schemes that make up part or all of the basic coverage. Only 1 per cent of the population is left without coverage, although lack of coverage has become a problem for the unemployed who have exhausted their benefits. On the other hand, 10 per cent of the population, often those suffering from chronic problems, come under the category of those taken in charge by the social security system. For the rest of the population health care is either reimbursed at the basic rate, itself variable according to the service provided, or topped up through supplementary schemes (*mutuelles*) which the self-employed and workers tend to join to a lesser extent.

There have been a number of notable improvements in health care. Life expectancy improved to reach 70.4 years for men and 78.5 for women in 1981. Most impressively, rates of infant mortality dropped sharply from 18.2 per thousand births in 1970 to 9.7 per thousand in 1981, a figure that compares favourably with Scandinavian levels. The wider provision of

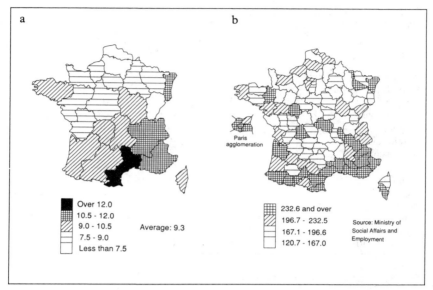

Figure 3.5 Medical provision. a, Number of doctors per 100,000 population, 1986. b, Number of hospital beds per 100,000 population.

health care has meant that geographical variations in facilities and well-being were reduced in the 1970s. Present geographical inequalities still reflect the location of university faculties of medicine and the historical legacy of health facilities, leaving the Paris region and the Mediterranean fringe better provided in terms of density of medical personnel (Figure 3.5).

At the same time, this general improvement is still accompanied by a differential utilization of the health system and concern for the prevention of ill-health. On the one hand, the health system repairs damage that has already been done among a population that tends to suffer a higher rate of illness and injuries resulting from work conditions and daily habits harmful to health (smoking, drinking). Not surprisingly, this group, largely concentrated among manual workers, has a lower life expectancy; it utilizes hospital services to a higher degree than average but makes less demand on the rarer, specialist care and the areas with a lower rate of reimbursement, for example dental care. Non-salaried categories and workers, both with above-average rural residential patterns, also tend to spend less on non-hospital care (Mormiche, 1986, p. 22). The other type of health-care user turns to specialist and expensive services, but at the same time works at avoiding illness and maintaining the body in as good a state as possible. This

Table 3.3   Utilization of health services

| | **Rural** | **Urban** | | **Paris** | |
		<20,000 pop.	>100,000 pop.	Suburbs	Centre
Annual per capita expenditure	89	95	102	102	119
Medical visits	87	97	109	108	103
Specialists	59	79	116	145	165
Generalists	101	108	101	94	82
Pharmaceutical and other medical goods	93	102	102	104	106
Medicines purchased without prescriptions	70	87	103	110	215

Source: *Enquête Santé* (1980).
The table is in terms of indices standardized for age and sex.

group is associated with the professional and management categories who, as we have already seen (p. 79) live in urban centres in proximity to the location of specialist and rare facilities (Table 3.3).

The centre of Paris demonstrates most clearly the interaction of a concentration of those groups making the greatest demands on highly technical and specialist services and the presence of these services in the centre, a medical pattern that stands out from that of the suburban zones of the Paris region (Mormiche, 1985, p. 30). As with education, so in access to and utilization of health service, where one lives matters.

As we have seen, the benefits of the Welfare State have been extended since the Second World War to all classes in French society. Levels of education and standards of health have increased, yet France remains a profoundly unequal society. While inequalities among those in employment have been reduced to some extent, especially since 1968, the gap between those in employment and those excluded from it has grown. And in addition to this group, older workers, artisans and small shopkeepers in industrially declining regions, and those without professional qualifications, have also been economically and socially marginalized (Clerc and Chaouat, 1987, pp. 40–1).

Note

1. A similar analysis based on the 1982 census has almost been completed. It includes a breakdown of socio-economic space by gender.

FOUR

Regional Patterns and Policies and Decentralization

4.1 Dimensions of regional disparity

In common with the experience in other European countries in the 1980s, regional policy and spatial planning at the national level have been in full retreat in France. Throughout Western Europe, governments have cut back regional aid, concentrated it on the worst cases, sought greater aid effectiveness and exhorted local authorities to foster indigenous growth. In France, regional grants have been cut by two-thirds since 1984, and the powers of the principal central agency, DATAR (Delegation for Territorial Development and Regional Action) have been eroded. This reflects conditions which are common throughout Europe, in addition to some which are specifically French. Decentralization to the regional level in France has been the means by which the State has withdrawn from nationally determined regional planning, with more emphasis being placed on local initiatives to promote indigenous growth. More generally, the current of economic liberalism, the lack of mobile industry and the scale of the deindustrialization problem in the industrial heartlands, as well as the increasing role of the European Commission, have all contributed to fundamental changes in the policy context. Regional policy now consists more of fire-fighting and *ad hoc* actions and has little in common with the grand spatial strategies that one associates with the spatial development characteristic of the growth years of the 1960s.

There can be little doubt that the French regional problem has changed in character, and recent policy debates reveal that the old accepted views of the Paris–provinces disparity and the industrial east–rural west dichotomy now require a far more nuanced assessment. Since the oil crisis, it has become apparent that the more backward rural areas, which benefited from industrial decentralization in the growth years, have withstood the recession better than have the industrial heartlands. Here, whether in the Nord and Lorraine, in the industrial belts of the cities or in the ports and shipyards, deindustrialization has led to the coining of the slogan 'industrial exodus' (which emphasizes the contrast with the historic 'rural exodus'). Of course, the remoter rural and mountain areas have continued their decline and, from a demographic point of view, may have passed the point beyond which regeneration is impossible (see Chapter 7). But this emphasizes the more varied evolution since the oil crisis. Economic and demographic dynamism has tended to shift more to the South, and about fifteen French cities can be seen as dynamic performers in the newer industries. The main foci of concern are the old industrial regions and the remoter rural areas. It is, then, hardly surprising that we can no longer speak of 'Paris and the French desert'; indeed, even as an interpretation of the historic French regional disparities, this view is now coming under attack. Symbolic of the changed regional context was the lifting in 1985 of dissuasive development controls in the Paris region.

In later paragraphs, we will be sketching the stages in the evolution of the policy of spatial management, emphasizing its threefold aspects of distribution of industry, national spatial strategies and regional planning. It has long been a matter of debate whether these policy orientations, so impressive in their range and ambitions, have in fact acted as fundamental stimuli, or merely channelled and modified at the margins what were strong, autonomous economic and urbanization processes. As will be seen in the discussion of industrial movement, regional assistance was merely an added incentive when the economic pressures were for a decentralization of industrial capacity to less-developed areas. This has led French critics to pose the question whether regional planning policy really established the bases for indigenous regional growth, or whether it was in fact a buttress to the strategies of industrialists themselves.

4.1.1 *The regional evolution in periods of growth and recession*

The question we must address is whether the long, secular demographic and economic processes, which led to such fundamental regional disequilibria in France, have been modified sufficiently since 1945 to produce a rather different contemporary picture of disparities, from that to which we are accustomed. The traditional, geographical Paris–provinces dichotomy is graphically encapsulated in the notion of 'Paris and the French desert'. Here, the primacy of the urban structure, the historic migration pattern and the marked gap in productivity levels, material standards of welfare and levels of professional qualification combine to reinforce the picture of centralized political and economic power. This picture is amplified by a classic east–west division from the Seine estuary to the Rhône delta, separating an industrial east from an agricultural west. Finally, there is the traditional low fecundity of the southern departments (Noin, 1974; House, 1978). These considerable disequilibria are, of course, the result of the pattern of industrialization, urbanization and loss of demographic vitality, which began to emerge in the 1840s and which continued until 1945. This resulted in a haemorrhage of rural population (particularly from the Massif Central and the South-west), a sapping of the demographic vitality of the rural West, and the ever-growing primacy of Paris, which stunted the growth of the regional capitals. The steady growth of basic industries in Nord-Pas de Calais and in Lorraine, together with the growth of engineering and consumer goods industries in the capital and, to a lesser extent, in Lyons–St Etienne–Grenoble, meant that the South and West were starved of industry before 1945, other than of port-refining industries and of strategic industries moved to the South-west in the 1930s.

This pattern was reinforced in the postwar reconstruction years, but was it modified in the periods of high growth and recession? By 1981, the socioeconomic composition of the population (Figure 3.3) shows a more nuanced picture: parts of the West, South-west and Massif Central still reveal a predominantly agricultural economy and society, but what is apparent is the presence of industrial and tertiary activities within this western half and the dominance of a manufacturing/agricultural combination in most of the Paris basin, the Centre and the eastern Massif. One may note the predominance of manufacturing in the outer Paris region and in adjacent departments. The prominence of tertiary activity (tourism, research establishments and head offices) in the Côte d'Azur is clear.

We may conclude then that industrial movement and the growth of the tertiary sector have led to a substantial moderation of the traditional disparities, though the historic pattern remains quite discernible. In practice, certain regions show a strong reliance on one or two branches of industry – Franche-Comté on vehicles and mechanical engineering, Auvergne on rubber and plastics, Lorraine on metal manufacture and the Nord-Pas de Calais on coal, steel, textiles and clothing, and metal manufacture. In terms of productivity differences (Table 4.1), the prominence of the Ile de France compared with all others is apparent, and the more rural regions show a productivity per capita less than 80 per cent of the average. The dispersion in the recent period is, however, less than in 1970–2. This arises from the fact that per capita GDP since 1973 has risen at less than average rates in the industrial heartlands, and has grown quite strongly in the West, South-west and southern littoral. Before looking in detail at the regional employment evolution, let us first consider population change and its migration component.

Demographic change   The post-1945 period has seen very substantial changes in the demographic evolution, which have favoured the less-developed regions and rural communes. Decentralization of activity and

Table 4.1   Regional disparities in gross domestic product per capita

	Average gross domestic product per capita		
	1970–2	1979–81	1984 (FF)
Alsace	101	103	69,254
Aquitaine	86	89	72,139
Auvergne	78	81	62,300
Basse Normandie	77	84	65,020
Burgundy	88	88	68,243
Brittany	71	79	62,560
Centre	89	93	69,683
Champagne-Ardenne	100	99	74,121
Corsica	N/A	51	51,594
Franche-Comté	89	95	69,254
Haute Normandie	108	111	82,432
Ile de France	153	146	112,423
Languedoc-Roussillon	69	77	58,770
Limousin	71	77	65,555
Lorraine	96	92	70,352
Midi-Pyrénées	72	77	65,924
Nord-Pas de Calais	93	86	65,760
Pays de la Loire	83	87	67,386
Picardy	90	91	68,109
Poitou-Charentes	72	79	59,861
Provence-Alpes-Côte d'Azur	88	93	72,865
Rhône-Alpes	103	98	82,148

Source: INSEE.

'counter-urbanization' account for this favourable trend, but have been insufficient to reverse the continuing demographic exodus from the more isolated areas. In broad outline, the traditional migration flow to the Paris region from the more rural regions has been stemmed, particularly since 1962, and this has meant some shifts in the relative shares of the most populous and less populous regions. Overall, in the period from 1954 to 1982, only the Limousin and Corsica lost population, while once typically backward rural regions such as Brittany, Auvergne and Poitou-Charentes have made gains. Over the whole period, the strongest growth has, however, been in the north–south axis from Haute Normandie and the Paris region to Rhône-Alpes and Provence-Alpes-Côte d'Azur (PACA); the strength of this axis, and latterly of its southern extension, is a feature of the postwar evolution.

The Paris region has shown a marked slowdown, and is now growing only

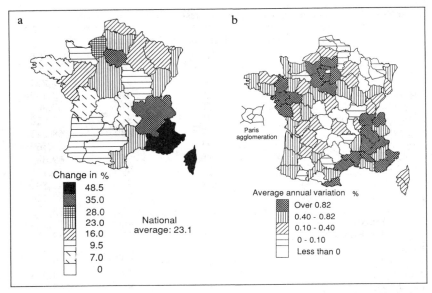

Figure 4.1   Population change. a, Variation in population, 1954–75. b, Variation in population, 1975–82.

by natural increase; since 1975, the growth rate has been slightly slower than the national average (Figure 4.1). Many regions of the West have a healthier demographic picture, with net in-migration. The crisis regions of Nord-Pas de Calais and Lorraine have seen heavy out-migration, with Lorraine losing population since 1975. Thinly populated regions remain in a critical position, though with some in-migration. Of course these global population movements disguise qualitative changes concerning age and social class characteristics. Broadly speaking, in-migration to the Paris region concerns younger, unattached workers, while those leaving may be retired or workers with families. Equally, rural regions can benefit from the in-migration of those of retirement age.

In a subregional analysis, a 'counter-urbanization' movement is under way, as in other West European countries. This does not necessarily mean that the rural exodus is at an end. If, by 'counter-urbanization', we signify urban deconcentration, involving net population loss in the inner areas and strong in-migration on the outer metropolitan and urban fringe, then the recent two census periods support the case for France. For example, for the census period 1975–82, the population of rural communes grew by 1.1 per cent per year (urban, 0.2 per cent; see Figure 1.3). The strongest growth of

1.9 per cent per year was found in the rural communes of the *Zones de peuplement industriel et urbain* (ZPIU, zones of industrial and urban settlement), which embrace urban areas and their associated commuting zones. From 1968 to 1975, the fastest growth was in the suburbs of ZPIUs. This centrifugal tendency is also found in the agglomerations proper, where very slow growth occurred in the urban centres from 1968 to 1975, and more recently in almost all central communes of cities of more than 100,000 inhabitants which have been losing population (excluding cities in the South and on the coast). This counter-urbanization has not, however, led to a revitalization of rural communes outside the ZPIUs, more than half of which continue to lose population (see p. 173).

Regional employment change Clearly these population movements reflect in a very generalized way the underlying shifts in employment. In practice, the decisive influence on the employment evolution in less-developed regions has not been the decentralization of industry or the growth of services, but the continuing loss of farm employment. The ranking of regions according to their degree of rurality scarcely changed between 1954 and 1982; the point is that farm employment as a proportion of total employment has fallen by well over two-thirds. And so this tends to be the predominant factor in the evolution of total employment. In spite of the evidence of widespread decentralization of industry to the Paris basin and to the West, from 1954 to 1975, the evolution of employment shows how the more rural regions have nevertheless lost employment overall. From 1954 to 1975, when total national employment grew by 11 per cent, the loss in Brittany and the South-west was over 4 per cent and in the Limousin 20 per cent. The previously developed regions grew strongly (Ile de France, 30 per cent; PACA, 36 per cent; East, 10 per cent), while Haute Normandie and Picardy (20 per cent) reveal the strength of decentralization pressures from the Paris region. The coalfield crisis shows in the employment stagnation in the Nord-Pas de Calais.

The effects of the economic crisis in helping to reduce disparities by hitting hard the most developed regions is fully apparent for the two census periods 1968–75 and 1975–end 1981. Total employment evolution (Figure 4.2a,b) shows a singular reversal, from East to West, reflecting the crisis in mining and manufacturing. In the latter period one may say that the western half has experienced employment stagnation or some slight growth. For industrial employment, the 1968–75 picture shows with great clarity the decentralization trend of the time: the later period reveals just how the western half has survived relatively unscathed during a time of severe industrial employment cutbacks in the industrial centres. If one turns to the regional pattern of growth in tertiary employment, then a small differential

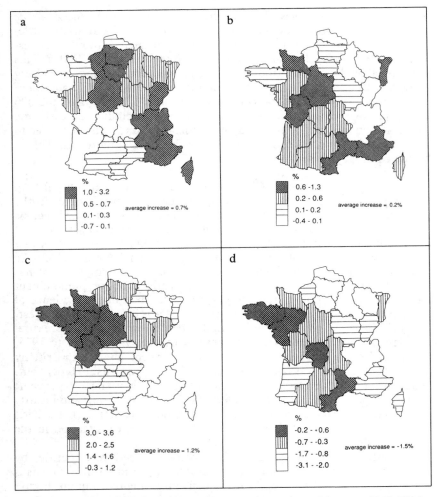

Figure 4.2   Employment change. a, Increase in total employment, 1968–75. b, Increase in total employment, 1977–81. c, Variation in industrial employment, 1968–75. d, Variation in industrial employment, 1975–81.

growth in favour of the West and Centre can be detected; in retailing and wholesaling, transport and telecommunications, it was the Paris region, Haute Normandie and the East which grew at less than average rates. The

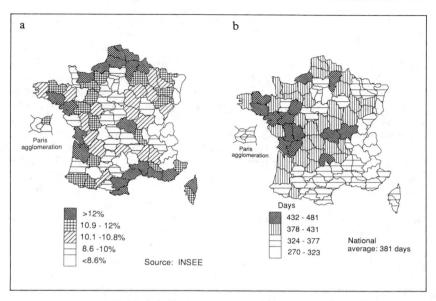

Figure 4.3 Unemployment. a, Level of unemployment, 1987. b, Duration of unemployment (days).

remaining parts of the tertiary sector grew at less than national average rates in the Paris region, Haute Normandie and Lorraine. The scope for a substantial reduction in disparities through the distribution of service employment is less, and, of course, these small relative shifts do little to redress the overwhelming strength of the Paris region and of the subsidiary centres in Rhône-Alpes, PACA and the Nord-Pas de Calais.

As a final point, unemployment rates (Figure 4.3a) reveal that, in general, the more rural departments (outside of Brittany) have lower than average unemployment. The heaviest unemployment is to be found in the coal, steel and textiles areas as well as in ports with shipbuilding and refining activities. In addition to the port industry difficulties in the Bouches du Rhône (Marseilles), the whole Mediterranean fringe shows higher unemployment rates, which reflect the strong international and domestic migration into this area and the youthful population.

4.2 Industrial movement and locational factors

Regional disparities have, therefore, narrowed, though the old pattern remains in outline. This narrowing is due to a number of factors, of which the 'decentralization' of industry and services plays an important, but subsidiary, role. It is other economic factors which have played the prime role in employment growth and decline. Thus, for example, industrial jobs created with regional assistance represent only 10 per cent of the total industrial employment in the provinces, and these are located in a relatively contained area. It is in the Paris basin and the West that decentralizations have fundamentally changed the local employment structure. Perhaps the greatest impacts have been those resulting from the collapse of farm employment and the sharp shrinkage of industrial employment since 1974.

Industrial output rose by 5 per cent per year from 1949 to 1973 and subsequently it fluctuated sharply. In the period 1954–75, one million jobs were created in manufacturing and an additional 500,000 in construction. Subsequently, from 1975 to 1984 the effects of the crisis can be seen in the loss of one million, or one-fifth, of manufacturing jobs. Broadly speaking, during the reconstruction period, rebuilding took place in the traditional locations and so historic disparities were reproduced. From the mid-1950s, however, growth and competitive demands began to exert pressures for a geographical dispersal of capacity. The rapid rise in industrial investment favoured sectors such as electrical and mechanical engineering, vehicles, steel and chemicals; certain of these sectors began to feel the rivalry of US investments in Europe and the beginnings of the Customs Union exerted strong competitive pressures (Laborie *et al.*, 1986). Capacity expansion and the required reduction of unit production costs forced firms to consider areas of plentiful, lower-cost (and, therefore, less-qualified) labour, notably those with large agricultural or immigrant populations. During the phase of the 'industrial imperative' (1965–73), the rapid concentration of manufacturing firms into a more oligopolistic structure involved restructuring and diversification, within an expansionary strategy, and, once again, decentralization was favoured.

Finally, since the oil crisis, the shake-out of industrial employment, which has been concentrated in certain sectors, and in large establishments, has clearly had major geographical consequences: the heavy energy-consuming industries (steel, bulk chemicals), those facing severe competition from newly industrialized countries (NIC) (shipbuilding, cars), and those subject to rapid innovation in automative technology (cars) have experienced heavy output and employment losses. Given that such industries are highly concentrated, these losses are reflected in the fact that establishments employing 500 persons or more lost one-quarter of their workforce from 1975 to 1984 and their share of total industrial employment fell from 45 per cent (1974) to 38 per cent (1983) (Gloaguen, 1986). These sectoral and size characteristics explain why it is the industrial heartlands which have experienced a haemorrhage of manufacturing employment, whereas the regions of recent industrialization have proven more resilient to the economic crisis. Very recently, however, regions such as Basse Normandie have suffered closures.

In relation to the geographical pattern of industrial movement, it appears that only one-half of decentralization operations (i.e. those receiving industrial assistance) represented a true transfer from Paris to the provinces. Other cases concerned subsidiaries, branch plants or extensions. The 500,000 or so new industrial jobs concerned represented only one-half of the total industrial jobs created in the period, and compare with 3.1 million new provincial jobs in the service industry. This huge wave of industrial job creation in the provinces shows a clear temporal and spatial pattern. Eighty per cent of decentralized industrial job creation took place between 1955 and 1968, with a peak of transfers in 1962. By 1974, most of the operations had taken place. Decentralizations tended to favour the Paris basin, and then the West (Aydalot, 1983; see Chapter 1).

There have been clear waves of new investment: in the early period up to 1962, decentralization favoured the Paris basin (close to the Paris region), when most of its 400,000 new manufacturing jobs were created. The industrialization of the West brought 200,000 new manufacturing jobs between 1962 and 1975, or 31 per cent of the national total. After 1966, due to a shift of policy emphasis, one-third of regionally assisted manufacturing employment was located in the 'conversion' zones of Lorraine and Nord-Pas de Calais.

The decentralization of service employment has had a far smaller impact. The Paris region has continued to take by far the largest share of all new office construction. During the 1970s, Lyons, Lille and Marseilles shared one-quarter of new office space, while all other towns (outside the Paris region) of more than 150,000 inhabitants took a further 25 per cent. From 1970 to 1980, the decentralization of state tertiary employment created only 16,800 jobs, and the banks and insurance companies have created an equal number by the transfer of operations (Aydalot, 1983).

Critical commentators point to the high degree of concentration, by firm and by sector, which has characterized this movement: the clear implication is that regional development is dependent on the fortunes of a few firms and a few branches. Hannoun and Templé (1975) show, for example, that 38 per cent (14,000) of the new industrial jobs created in Brittany from 1961 to 1970 were provided by seventeen plants, while in Basse-Normandie, 50 per cent of such jobs were in thirty-one plants. In total, 95 per cent of the new jobs created in French industry from 1961 to 1970 were in plants of more than 100 employees. In terms of sectoral composition, it is clear that regional specialization has been taking place. The electrical and electronics industries and vehicle manufacturing have shown a remarkable capacity for decentralization. One-half of new employment in the electrical and electronics industries has gone to the West and to the Paris basin. Automobile plants have been established on greenfield sites in the Paris basin, Nord and Alsace, though Citroën were established quite early at Rennes in Brittany. However, it is not surprising that industrializing regions should become quite dependent on such a narrow range of branches, given that most net industrial employment creation has been in these sectors.

We should, of course, complete the picture by considering the regional employment consequences of the crisis and recession years since 1974. As we have noted, it is the industrial heartlands which have suffered severely, while the regions of recent industrialization have emerged relatively unscathed. During the ten years 1975–84, Lorraine and the Nord-Pas de Calais lost one-third of their industrial employment: Champagne-Ardennes, Picardy and the Paris and Lyons regions were also badly hit. From 1975 to 1980 alone, the eleven eastern regions accounted for 94 per cent of the total jobs lost in industry. Here, then, was a prime factor in regional equalization. Meanwhile, for the regions of recent industrialization, Pottier (1984) shows the resilience of decentralized plants. Their survival rates are high, even in sectors exposed to NIC competition. Those establishments decentralized before 1974 have maintained their employment levels, while the relatively few establishments decentralized since then have raised their total employment slightly. This points, then, to a certain resilience, rather than fragility, in the decentralization process. The other factors which seem to have played a part in this resilience are the smaller size of establishments (predominance of small- and medium-sized industry) and the higher proportion of less-exposed sectors in these less-developed regions (Pottier, 1984).

Industrial movement studies all point to the fact that industrial mobility is determined principally by a firm's growth strategy and its labour requirements, rather than by regional policy (Hannoun and Templé, 1975). It is not often a regional specialization which attracts the investor, but principally the labour market characteristics – availability of unskilled labour, sometimes female or immigrant, low degree of unionization and lower prevailing wage rates. Firms in expanding sectors have been able to embrace new technologies, adopting standardized processes, which can be operated by unskilled workers. Hence traditional location factors such as transport costs, supplier–customer relationships, raw material availability and skilled workforce, count for little (Hannoun and Templé, 1975). The consequence is, of course, that links with the regional economy are poor, and multiplier effects weak.

Further evidence of the primacy of the labour factor is given by studies of the local labour markets associated with different sizes of settlement. We know that, from 1960 to 1975, 43 per cent of decentralization operations were made to towns of 20,000–100,000 inhabitants and 42.5 per cent to towns of fewer than 20,000 inhabitants (Bouchet and Savy, 1982). Saint Julien (1982), in a study of the effects of decentralization on the urban hierarchy in the West, found that the more slowly the branch of manufacture grows, the more a firm seeks the interstitial labour markets not dominated by a large firm. Aydalot (1983) stresses that firms consciously locate in very small towns since it is here that unskilled female employees are easiest to organize. Hence a polarized pattern emerges of the dequalification/overqualification of work, as key management and research and development functions are retained at the centre (in the Paris region) and deskilled work is decentralized. Over time this leads to a notable reduction of wage disparities. The manual worker wage gap between the less-industrialized regions and the Paris region has since 1954 been reduced by one-half, in spite of this deskilling (Pottier, 1984).

This path of development has naturally attracted a range of criticisms, of which two strands seem the most significant. A form of regional development which is dependent on a small number of sectors and firms is inherently fragile, especially when the regional advantage is that of low-skilled, cheap labour. Subject to the rigours of the international division of labour, such regions are in competition with low-wage countries. Matteaccioli (1981) claims that this is not development in the sense of an increasingly complex and interrelated process: she argues for 'autocentric' not 'dependent' development, based on the existing, local small- and medium-sized firms.

The Marxist current of thought is represented by Lipietz (1980), who places theories of international capitalism in a spatial context, and analyses the evolution in terms of the 'spatial division of labour'. Here, regions have no individual 'vocation', they are allotted roles. Regions of archaic industrial and agricultural structure may be exploited by monopoly capital from the dominant regions by relations of unequal exchange, or by having them perform routine, discrete activities in the manufacturing chain. In contrast, there will be an increasing trend towards centralization of key functions in the most developed region. Thus a marked spatial hierarchy of regions emerges, characterized by dependence and by the recuperation of surplus value by the metropolitan region.

4.3   Spatial management and industrial distribution policies

Regional development policy has evolved incrementally in the postwar period, often in an *ad hoc* manner. One is tempted to interpret the responsibilities of the *Commissariat Général du Plan* (CGP, government planning authority, the) as being concerned with the policy of industrial distribution and those of DATAR, as being concerned with spatial management policy; unfortunately, the considerable overlap in their competences complicates the picture.

Regional development policy then had a number of strands (see Chapter 1): decentralization of industrial and service employment, rural modernization, an urban policy to accommodate urban pressures and to produce a less primate structure, and an infrastructural policy which established the essential industrial and tertiary sector operating environments. It did, of course, also incorporate the remaining backward areas into the market economy. Administratively, we can say that the main tasks of the CGP have been to assess and plan for medium-term regional employment needs, and for the corresponding infrastructural and urban investments. DATAR curiously takes both long- and short-term action. It undertakes the longer-term studies and prepares the associated physical strategies, but also, as an interministerial body (attached at various times to the Prime Minister and to the housing and environment ministries) it regionalizes the Five-Year Plan, co-ordinates ministerial action in pursuit of planning targets, and is directly responsible for attracting industrial investment and granting regional aid (from the FDES). DATAR has two funds at its disposal – the FIAT for pump priming the major spatial management schemes, and the FAD for decentralization operations. An important advisory committee, CNAT, brings together government, industry, trade unions, academics and credit institutions, to discuss the long-term spatial management objectives and targets. Spatial planning comprises three interlinked policy areas of distribution of industry, strategic physical planning and regional planning.

4.3.1   Industrial distribution policy

'Decentralization' refers to all types of new capacity investment, including *in situ* extensions and branch plants, as well as complete transfers. A series of decrees issued in 1954–5 designated the development areas, established the FDES to offer regional development grants and incentives and instituted dissuasive controls in the Paris region comparable to the British industrial development certificates. We should perhaps not forget that this policy of distribution formed part of the wider framework of the national plan and was an instrument at the disposal of the DATAR Commissioners for Industrial Conversion and Rural Reform, who were responsible for certain declining industrial and backward rural areas respectively.

Turning first to the regional incentives, we can see an extension of the initial concern with areas of declining basic industry to the much broader areas of rural backwardness, and finally to include cities capable of

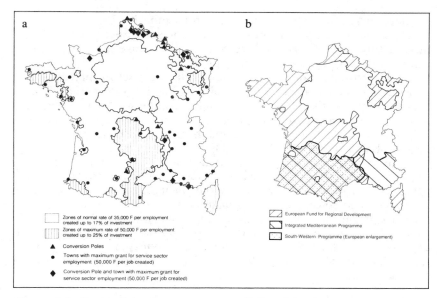

Figure 4.4 Regional development grants. a, Industrial and service sector priority zones, 1982; conversion poles. b, Zones of European Community grants.

attracting high value-added services. Thus, in 1960, an earlier policy addressing zones in structural decline was extended to rural regions, and was modified again in 1966–7 to include the reconversion plans for Lorraine and Nord-Pas de Calais. Services decentralization from Paris was aided from 1967, and research activities after 1976. House (1978) details the various levels and conditions of assistance, and for much of this period a fivefold graduation of aid applied, reflecting the degree of severity of difficulty. A simpler system for the attraction of industry has operated during recent years (Figure 4.4a) and the areas benefiting from EC regional aid are shown in Figure 4.4b.

The dissuasive policies of a development control certificate and fee for the granting of planning permission were a necessary accompaniment of the incentives policy. For the period 1955–85 (when it was substantially relaxed), this policy applied to industrial and office growth in the Paris region and, for the period 1966–70, it applied to industrial floorspace in the Lyons metropolis. Over time the size limits for permitted developments were raised somewhat, and the Committee for Decentralization, which supervised the policy, often faced great difficulties in restraining office development in the centre of Paris and in its suburbs. Until 1973, office development control in Paris proved lax, and in some cases, the transfer of manufacturing out of Paris was accompanied by a change of use of the site to a head office development (Doublet, 1976).

These instruments of the 'stick and carrot' were set in the context of medium-term employment location policies. The Fifth Plan (1966–70) set itself the key objective of the industrialization of the West (comprising ten regions). The target was to raise the proportion (to 35–40 per cent) of all new industrial jobs which were to be located there. For the reconversion of the industrial economies of the North and East, infrastructral investments were to be given priority. Similarly, the Sixth Plan (1971–5) set as a target the creation of 250,000 new industrial jobs in the provinces, and so raising to 80 per cent the proportion of non-farm employment (out of total employment) in the West and South-west. It postulated a stabilization of employment in the Paris region and a reversal of the falls in the North and East.

It is clear that the policy had only a weak incentive effect. The actual distribution of industry in no sense matched the map of graduated assistance (Hannoun and Templé, 1975; Aydalot, 1978), while the decentralization of industry was a strong autonomous force.

4.3.2 National spatial strategies

The grand physical planning strategies of the 1960s, drawn up by DATAR, have already been elucidated (see Chapter 1). While the infrastructural plans were designed expressly to open up areas not fully integrated into the national productive space and help them contribute to fast French economic growth (and promote a certain regional equity), the urban policy addressed the problem of the primacy of Paris. A series of strategic plans for the Paris region were designed, under which its rate of growth would be slower than existing trends (House, 1978), and provincial cities would form a counterbalancing urban hierarchy (see p. 14).

DATAR was able to act through other agencies in two ways in order to implement its strategies. The urban strategy rested on a hierarchy of physical plans first established by the 1967 *Loi d'orientation foncière* (Land Law). This ensured that a physical strategy, once approved by the *Comité interministériel d'aménagement du territoire* (CIAT, the Interministerial Committee for Territorial Development), would, in theory at least, be binding on subordinate planning authorities. In the case of the infrastructure plans, once these had been approved by the CIAT, they were given budgetary support both by the FIAT and in national plans. Since 20 per cent of state investment credits made under the Plan were available for distribution according to spatial management criteria, this strengthened DATAR's ability to push through its ambitious schemes. Most state investments in the Plan concerned heavy transport, energy and telecommunications infrastructures, and so, incorporating these in its spatial strategies, DATAR was able to strengthen the north–south axis, develop the industrial port complexes at Fos, Dunkirk and Le Havre, embark on giant tourist developments and pursue rural renovation and industrial reconversion.

4.3.3 A policy criticized by Right and Left alike

This spatial management came under attack during the 1970s from different quarters. The neo-liberals disliked its controls on market forces and its resolutely 'hexagonal' framework, while those on the Left saw in it a policy favouring firms rather than one seeking spatial equity. Already in 1970 those of neo-liberal ideological persuasion directed their fire at the assumptions of the policy. President Pompidou, who was suspicious of the ambitions of the national planners to 'correct' market forces, also found the locational controls and purely French context of planning an unnecessary constraint on the industrial imperative of achieving European competitiveness. This criticism was reflected in the 1970 *Report on the Options of the Sixth Plan*, and only the commitment of Prime Minister Chaban-Delmas and parliamentary opinion led to the retention of the policy (Lajugie, 1979). President Giscard, who was instrumental in emasculating the CGP, also opposed the pretensions of DATAR. In 1975, Giscard demanded a fundamental revision of this policy, so that France could adjust to the post-oil shock conditions by a redeployment of investment and employment towards those sectors enjoying a comparative advantage. From this time, the policy was shorn of its linkage with the CGP. However, as the crisis of the 1970s developed, so the policy offered a 'fire-fighting' apparatus to deal with the lame ducks and bankruptcies, though it had lost its strategic pretensions.

More radical critiques were voiced by observers of the Centre and Left. It had long been clear that the beneficiaries of regional aid had been principally the large French groups in the automobile, chemical, steel and capital goods industries. The Hannoun Report of 1979 showed that in 1976, six firms received over one-half of the total industrial assistance, and the capital goods sector received three-quarters. As Matteaccioli (1981) points out, these oligopolistic firms had not had a good record in employment creation, and the nature of the assistance (until 1976, designed primarily to promote capital-intensive investments) necessarily favoured large firms in the intermediate goods and capital goods sectors. Frémont (1978), therefore, claimed that the true planners were the steel, automobile, refining and construction firms and the banking interests behind the office construction boom in the Paris region, Lyons and Marseilles.

The geographic outcome in this case was a strengthening of the north–south axis to compete with the Rhine, while the decentralization to the West of unskilled, labour-intensive work was just sufficient to give the appearance of even-handedness. The dependent nature of development, the branch-plant regional economy and the substitution of a tissue of local economic interlinkages by interregional or international dependency can be interpreted as a manifestation of the spatial division of labour (Lipietz, 1980). French policy has not, in the view of Matteaccioli (1981), created development, if this is construed as a process of ever-increasing complexity and diversity. Pascallon (1981) stresses that autonomous, autocentric growth, which develops the present tissue of local economic relationships, built on local resources, would avoid a specialization dictated from outside (see p. 109).

4.4   Regional policy under changed conditions

There was a delayed recognition in the late 1970s that the context in which regional policy operated had changed, and that the structural adjustment of industry posed new difficulties. From about 1978 the policy changed focus; it accepted that there was little mobile industry and that older industrial regions now presented the greatest problem. The Committee for Spatial Management and Planning, in its preparatory report for the Eighth Plan in 1980, posed the question of whether the geographical redistribution of employment had any meaning in the economic conditions of the time. The new policy concentrated aid in the worst-hit areas, was more selective and relied on indigenous sources of growth elsewhere.

Although the Giscard–Barre government never ceased to stress the importance of redeployment in the post-oil shock world, in practice previously unimaginable sums were spent to keep ailing sectors afloat. Apart from the quasi-nationalization of steel in 1978 and the plan for shipyard rationalization, a number of organizations intervened to alleviate the consequences for local employment of restructuring by channelling vast sums into reconversion areas, allocating credits to save firms from bankruptcy and lending to firms in difficulty (Laborie, 1986).

Regions of recent industrialization were exhorted to build on indigenous sources of growth. Adopting the practice of the recent regional development plans for the Greater South-west, Brittany and the Massif Central, the emphasis was placed on developing artisan and medium-sized industry using local resources, developing services to industry (especially computing, research and consultancy), and establishing a dialogue between local and regional authorities and the State through the medium of planning contracts.

However, the State remained adamant, and in fact tightened legislation, preventing municipalities and regions intervening economically so as to thwart market forces. Left-wing municipalities, in particular, were prevented from rescuing firms. For example, the prefect made it very difficult for Besançon to aid the establishment of a co-operative by Lip workers, while the attempt by Marseilles to rescue the shipbuilding firm Terrin in the mid-1970s was vetoed (Keating and Hainsworth, 1985, p. 114). The regional public establishments, (p. 22) mostly, but not exclusively those on the Left, were also beginning to want to flex their economic muscle by the end of the 1970s, but legislation was passed in February 1981 to counter this trend (Kofman, 1985, p. 16).

The accession to power of the Left brought to the fore local development initiatives as a means of combating the crisis through a model of development from below. Strategies of this kind had originated in the mid-1960s in Brittany among modernizers who were keen to bypass established administrative channels. The rural action plans (PAR) and local planning contracts, introduced in the early 1970s, were official versions of more supple administrative entities. Regionalist movements, with their desire to live and work in the locality and achieve a more autonomous form of development (Kofman, 1981), also contributed to this current of development thinking.

The early days of the new government witnessed a lively social mobilization of those involved in local initiatives, for example the meeting of the *Etats Généraux des Pays* (States General of Rural Localities) in Macon in 1982, where there was a large representation of delegates from the Southeast from localities with a strong sense of identity and/or concern for their survival (Coulmin, 1986). It was then that the social and cultural preoccupations of earlier years were complemented by more economic considerations of employment creation based on local solidarity and the potential of small- and medium-sized firms. The latter was also a priority of the Socialist government in its national development strategy (Ninth Plan). In a period of economic crisis, the great plan for regional autonomy in opposition to the State seems to be excessively Utopian (Touraine, 1983, p. 182). Local development is vaunted as an appropriate form of alternative development, integrating economic, social and political forces in a given territory and based on local solidarity. The state now becomes a partner, and no longer a foe whose legitimacy is challenged.

Second, the new Socialist government demonstrated a greater commitment to regional policy by a 60 per cent increase in the regional aid budget in 1981–2 and by giving priority to decentralization at all levels. However, the hopes of vastly extended regional powers and redrawn boundaries (a new

Table 4.2   Regional budgets and contract plans

Region	1985 budget millions of FF	1987 budget millions of FF	Ratio of state/region contribution to regional plan (1984–8)
Alsace	397.8	643.8	1.6
Aquitaine	822.3	1,191.0	1.6
Auvergne	443.3	711.9	1.7
Burgandy	462.8	739.6	1.4
Brittany	702.6	1,148.0	2.2
Centre	490.0	10,469.4	1.4
Champagne-Ardenne	350.7	621.5	1.9
Corsica	241.3[1]	329.4	3.7
Franche-Comté	303.1	411.1	1.5
Languedoc-Roussillon	592.8	1,045.2	1.8
Limousin	257.9	436.0	2.5
Lorraine	525.9	1,058.9	3.2
Midi-Pyrénées	665.9	832.5	1.8
Nord-Pas de Calais	1,252.3	2,031.9	1.6
Basse Normandie	300.0	494.9	1.7
Haute Normandie	371.9	641.3	1.7
Pays de la Loire	823.7	1,277.6	1.3
Picardy	543.3	1,042.9	2.1
Poitou-Charentes	502.6	769.6	2.0
Provence-Alpes-Côte d'Azur	1,442.5	1,935.0	1.5
Rhône-Alpes	1,196.6	1,851.1	2.0
Ile de France	4,331.0	5,513.0	0.8
France[2]	16,758	25,797	1.5

Source: DATAR and INSEE.
[1] Figure for 1984.
[2] Excluding overseas departments and territories.

Basque region and a five-department Brittany), sought by autonomist movements, were dashed. The major beneficiaries of the decentralized responsibilities were those departments to which were attributed social services and health, the key areas of welfare spending. Regions gained economic functions and responsibility for regional planning and professional training, which now took on a more contractual form through plans negotiated between them and the State. By June 1984 all regions, except Corsica, had signed planning contracts. For 1984–8, the State gave

FF 35,000 million to the twenty-two regions, while regional budgets increased markedly by 53.4 per cent to reach FF 25,797 million in 1987 (*Le Monde*, 1988a, p. 64; Table 4.2). Although all three levels (communes, departments and regions) were permitted to give direct assistance to firms, this had to be undertaken within a framework determined by the regions and rules laid down by the Plan. Private equity in firms could only be introduced through the creation of mixed-economy societies bringing together private and public capital (Keating and Hainsworth, 1985, p. 117).

Despite the previous hostility towards regionalism of many on the Right the new regional functions and assemblies were not called into question after the Right's victory in March 1986. The traditional Right, with a little help in five regions from the National Front, had swept up twenty of the twenty-two presidencies in the regional elections held at the same time as the legislative ones. Only Limousin and the Nord remained in the hands of the Left. A new round of regional planning contracts for 1989–92 was signed in February 1988 (*Le Monde*, 1988a, p. 65). More generally, the reasons for leaving decentralization largely intact reside in the underlying rationale of the process, and in the way that power has, in effect, been transferred.

The reorganization of territorial structures was intended to give more power, increase the control of resources, encourage a 'new form of citizenship' and refashion the relationship between State and civil society. In reality the legislation (over 20 laws and 200 decrees since 1982) served to reinforce the power of the executive, especially the presidents of departments and regions. Thus devolution was an institutional affair and not one that increased public participation.

One of the fiscal reforms, already initiated in 1979, was the consolidation of specific grants and loans into a block grant. Greater autonomy has been gained to allocate resources within a fixed budget so that the lower levels are now more directly implicated in the management of austerity. No longer can demands be channelled directly to the State. Thus social expenditure and fiscal resources have been brought closer together (Preteceille, 1988, p. 413). Furthermore, the decentralization of major areas of social expenditure to departments, which principally represent rural interests, is an additional constraint on social spending, for the greatest pressure emanates from urban municipalities.

More specifically at the regional level, it is difficult to generate increased resources since regional investment banks, promised originally by the Socialists, were never set up. Regions found it easier to slot into nationally defined priorities so that many simply drew up a shopping list as part of their planning contracts. Somewhat surprisingly, no provision was made for links between regional economic planning and nationalized industries,

Table 4.3   Nationalized industries by region

	% of value added of industrial production, 1982	% industrial employment Before nationalization	% industrial employment After nationalization
Alsace	16.0	6.6	14.7
Aquitaine	42.2	14.7	26.3
Auvergne	17.6	3.7	12.3
Basse Normandie	24.5	10.3	17.2
Burgundy	17.3	4.7	16.9
Brittany	25.1	3.0	15.2
Centre	23.4	6.4	13.9
Champagne-Ardenne	11.5	2.2	9.7
Corsica	52.4	37.7	39.6
Franche-Comté	14.1	1.4	9.1
Haute Normandie	29.3	10.5	26.8
Ile de France	33.7	18.6	25.8
Languedoc-Roussillon	27.8	14.0	23.0
Limousin	35.4	21.1	15.5
Lorraine	37.5	14.1	40.6
Midi-Pyrénées	38.4	20.8	26.8
Nord-Pas de Calais	25.1	18.5	23.0
Pays de la Loire	34.6	11.6	23.5
Picardy	18.3	3.4	15.7
Poitou-Charentes	17.2	4.1	12.7
Provence-Alpes-Côte d'Azur	30.4	15.2	29.7
Rhône-Alpes	30.2		23.5

Source: DATAR.

which have been deemed to be the domain of national policies (Keating and Hainsworth, 1985, p. 125). The enlarged nationalized sector after 1982 contributed 28.7 per cent of value-added in the industrial sector and is particularly strong in several South-western regions and, in terms of employment, in the Lorraine (Table 4.3).

Before 1986, it tended to be the Left-controlled regions, for example Provence-Alpes-Côte d'Azur and Nord-Pas de Calais, which had most fully developed their planning services and were prepared to intervene economically. It is likely, therefore, given the current political composition of the regional assemblies and the keenness of some to pursue economic liberalism, that investment in infrastructure and research will be chosen in preference to economic intervention.

In the final section of this chapter we turn to two case studies of regional societies with different development strategies and State involvement. The first case, that of the Lorraine, is a region where paternalistic capitalism, which provided amenities (housing, schools, leisure activities) for the worker from the cradle to the grave, has collapsed along with the weakening of traditional dominant institutions such as the Army and the Church (Gehring and Saint Dizier, 1986). In its place, the State has taken over the regulation of production and provision of social welfare in the postwar years, especially since the 1960s. The role of the State was reinforced by the 1982 nationalizations (see Table 4.3), preceding another round of regional industrial restructuring.

Our second case study, Corsica, exemplifies a region where traditional political forces have managed to remain dominant, though contested by those groups that have not partaken of the fruits of the considerable transfer of State expenditure. Unlike Brittany, where socioeconomic and political elites attempted to manage and direct the transformation of the region (see p. 7), the clientelist political system had not attempted to mediate or control the regional development proposed by the State and national and multinational capital.

4.5   Reconversion in the steelmaking area of northern Lorraine

Lorraine exemplifies the decline of basic industry in its most acute form in a region where local labour markets are primarily dependent upon a single branch of industry. The four largest employing sectors – coal, steel, textiles and woodworking – all face grave difficulties. The Lorraine steel industry has borne by far the largest cutbacks in the national closure programme, such that regional steel-industry employment fell by two-thirds, compared with one-half nationally, in the period from 1964 to 1985. In the ten years to 1987, 50,000 jobs were lost in Lorraine steelmaking, 19,000 in textiles and 7000 in the coalfield. A further loss of 25,000–30,000 jobs is forecast by the end of 1990. While the job losses in textiles have been more widely spread throughout the valleys of the Vosges, the impact of steel closures has been highly concentrated, having a particularly devastating effect in the northern steel zone focused on Longwy and Thionville. Here, total employment has fallen by one-quarter since the mid-1970s. These grave difficulties are scarcely reflected in the regional unemployment rate, since many workers affected are in pre-retirement. They are more clearly shown in the demographic statistics, where substantial net out-migration, accelerating throughout the 1970s and 1980s, reflects the poor labour market prospects, especially for the young. An INSEE report (quoted in *Le Monde*, 24 April 1987) estimates that a net 20,000 new jobs would have to be created annually to absorb the unemployed and labour-market entrants.

The origins of this crisis are to be found both in national steelmaking policy and in the changing locational requirements of iron and steelmaking. When the world crisis in steel production occurred at the end of 1974, as Japan forced down prices through its efforts to sell surplus output, the French industry was in a poor state to meet price-cutting competition. Its unsatisfactory productivity and high indebtedness arose from slow modernization, political restrictions on plant closures and the effects of longstanding price controls. Nationally, in 1974, 30 per cent of steel output still emanated from the outdated Thomas and Martin processes; given that the newer coastal investments at Dunkirk and Fos were still coming on stream, severe retrenchments elsewhere were unavoidable in the new world situation of overcapacity. It is in this context that the Lorraine steelmakers fell from their pre-eminent position. Using the low-grade Briey field ores, Lorraine accounted for 70 per cent of French iron production and 65 per cent of steel output in 1966. Northern Lorraine seemed a self-contained, integrated steel-producing area, with a 'core' location in the European Community and benefiting from low transport tariffs (due to rail–Moselle waterway competition). However, the industry was technically backward and had higher unit costs. Much of the capacity was inherited from pre-1914 German Lorraine, and there had been low levels of interwar investment, partly because of the military 'glacis' (buffer zone) policy. Little thought had been given to restructuring, and company rivalries ensured that vertical integration and scale economies would remain under-exploited. Specialization and adoption of the new technologies (electrical steels, basic oxygen) remained inadeqaute (*Economie lorraine*, 1986).

The first sign of crisis appeared in 1964, when cheap, imported enriched ores began to render the Lorraine ores uncompetitive. However, it was the opening of the Dunkirk coastal works in the late 1960s and the decision in 1970 to build the Fos integrated coastal works that ensured the dismemberment of the Lorraine industry (see p. 14). From 1974 to 1978, Lorraine steel output fell by 36 per cent and its share of national output fell to 40 per cent. Since then, the continuing crisis has led to the closure of much of its crude steelmaking. Lorraine has suffered from its poorer productivity, its relative lack of process integration and its product composition. Its steelmaking productivity is 2.25 times lower than that of the coastal plants, and the very marked concentration on long products (beams, rods, wire) renders it vulnerable, given the depressed state of these markets.

The successive national plans for steel proved to be badly misconceived. France suffered a brutal loss of external markets after 1974, and the industry was virtually bankrupt in 1978, with debts of FF 38 bn. The rescue package of that year, leading to the quasi-nationalization of Usinor and Sacilor, reorganized the industry into these two main national groups. This reorganization took place at the expense of the operational cohesion of the

Lorraine industry, and showed a general disposition in favour of flat products. Any hope of achieving production economies by better integration within the Lorraine industry was dashed by the 1984 Davignon Plan, which paid little heed to intraregional linkage. The congenital overoptimism of successive plans was evidenced once again in the 1982 Judet Report for the new Socialist goverment; only the steel plan of 1984 showed realism, reflecting EC pressures for the ending of state steel subsidies, but the dismemberment of the Lorraine steel industry was already under way. The 1978 steel plan had led to large-scale iron- and steelmaking closures at Longwy (5500 job losses) and Pompey (2500 job losses). The attendant violent unrest and political disaffection, that spilled well beyond the trade unions and included a whole range of local groups (Zukin, 1985), led the presidential candidate Mitterrand to promise that no further closures would take place in Lorraine without the provision of alternative employment. Already by 1982, however, the mounting losses forced further cuts in north Lorraine (Longwy, 2300 job losses); at the end of 1983 further steelmaking and plate- and wire-mill closures were announced. Finally, the 1984 plan signalled the end of all steelmaking which used Lorraine ores. Job losses in the industry in Lorraine have totalled 65,000 since the mid-1960s.

From the earlier discussion it will be clear that regional policy has been active in the steelmaking areas for many years and has specifically addressed their reconversion needs since 1966–7. Early policy quite clearly sought to diversify the economic base, but contained no realistic assessment of the scale of the task. The key agent is the State in its various guises: as employer of 41 per cent of the Lorraine workforce; as the largest single industrial investor (coal, steel, chemicals, nuclear power); as the source of social and regional assistance especially through its two main agents – the DATAR Commissioner for the Industrial Reconversion of Lorraine and the Prefect-Delegate responsible for industrial redeployment in Lorraine. The regional council has taken an increasingly active role as its powers have grown, and the so-called reconversion companies owned by the nationalized coal industry (CDF) and Usinor–Sacilor promote reindustrialization and retraining. As the policy has developed in recent years, the respective roles of each have become clearer. The State has borne the main social and regional assistance costs and, in agreement with the regional council, it has borne a substantial part of the cost of infrastructural projects specified in the regional plan (through the channels of the planning contract and a 'parallel plan'). The task of attracting industry falls to the DATAR Commissioner, the Prefect-Delegate and the region, while the strategic regional plan and its assistance to small- and medium-sized firms lie within the competence of the regional authorities.

In setting up the growth pole of north Lorraine in spring 1984, the Mauroy government announced major policy departures in recognition of the grave employment situation in the area:

(1) A three-year labour cost subsidy payable to local firms creating new jobs for redundant steelworkers was instituted (and led to the creation of 1800 jobs).

(2) The *Convention générale de protection sociale de la sidérurgie* (CGPS, General Agreement on the Social Protection for the Steel Industry) was agreed on the lines of the longstanding European Coal and Steel Community readaptation, retraining and redeployment aid for steelworkers. Special measures were taken for the retraining of 5000 Lorraine workers for jobs in the gas and electricity utilities.

(3) Two special industrialization funds were established.

(4) State infrastructural expenditure of FF 6 bn over two years was agreed, channelled through the State-region contract of 11 July 1984 and through a 'parallel plan'.

The regional plan of 1984–8 set itself three prime objectives: reconversion of the worst-hit zones, especially by promoting high-technology activities and building on Lorraine's geographical position with its excellent communications; environmental improvement; and, finally, aid to small firms, aid for retraining and R&D. These objectives are encapsulated in eleven regional priority programmes. To maximize the co-ordination of aid from Brussels and Paris, zones of 'integrated development operations' have been designated (as, for example, in the northern steelmaking basin of Longwy–Briey–Thionville), which concentrate assistance, recognizing the intrinsic inter-relatedness of the reconversion problems. The most publicized of the actions mirror the regional objectives of concentrating on the worst-hit areas and of developing high-technology industries:

(1) The European Development Pole (PED) at Longwy was announced as a collaborative French, Belgian and Luxembourg governmental venture in mid-1985, at a total cost of FF 2bn, including substantial European Regional Development Fund assistance. Apart from an international industrial estate, there will be a free zone offering incentives of up to 37.5 per cent of investment cost. At Longwy, 200 ha have been set aside, and the objective is to create 5500 jobs over ten years.

(2) On the old blast furnace site at Hagondange, a huge theme park is near completion.

(3) Two 'technopoles' (research parks) are under construction. The Metz–Queuleu 2000 park will focus on telecommunications, while the

Nancy–Brabois innovation park combines higher-education engineering institutes with private firms in the new technology branches.

As if to emphasize once more the European context for these endeavours, the Lorraine regional council took the initiative to breathe new life into the Saar–Lor–Lux triangular agreements. This resulted in the creation in 1986 of an inter-regional parliamentary council bringing together elected representatives from the nine frontier regions.

The more mundane development activities of the State and region do nevertheless deserve mention, as they may have a more fundamental influence. Infrastructural projects contained in the regional plan, which stresses accessibility improvements (including preparatory studies for the eastern high-speed train route, and a new regional airport), are jointly financed. The region has chosen to focus its own economic development assistance principally on the medium- and small-sized firms. This will take the form of investments in industrial estate projects, in the rehabilitation of factory buildings, grants for training, exporting and technology transfer (especially in electronics, information technology and robotics) and through capital injections by a Lorraine industrial investment agency (*Institut lorrain de participation*).

An assessment of the achievements to date reveals somewhat mixed results. Over a four-year period, 15,000 new jobs have been created, largely with the assistance of the Lorraine Industrialization Fund. The attraction of foreign investment has been disappointing and the promised new job creation by nationalized industries and the administration has in practice been on a much smaller scale than was forecast. The work of the CGPS in readaptation assistance for displaced steelworkers reveals that, in practice, cultural factors exert a profound influence on the placement of retrained workers, which needs to be set in the context of the nature of the new employment on offer. Workers have been unwilling to move and reluctant to accept employment terms less favourable than those to which they were accustomed. New employment has often tended to seek out locations with inexperienced and cheap, frequently female labour. On the other hand, research and development and higher-level services employment have gravitated to the major cities, thereby demanding long commuting distances (Zukin, 1985, pp. 357–8).

4.6 Corsica and the 'special statute'

The development schemes for Corsica starting with the first regional action plan in 1957 and the later 1970 proposal, envisaged an agricultural and tourist future for the island. Over the next two decades, Corsica was opened up to French capital and attracted an influx of *pieds-noirs* (17,000 in all) and

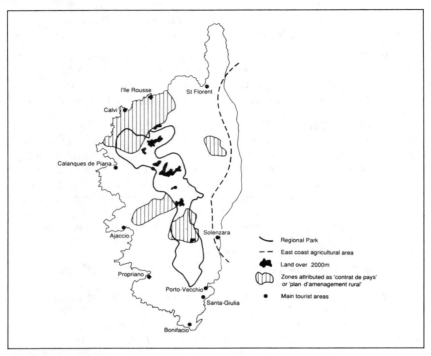

Figure 4.5   Corsica

metropolitan French. The coastal regions saw their economies change and their population increase; the interior, symbol of Corsican communitarian values, continued to depopulate and die economically (Kofman, 1982). While the total population has grown from 176,000 in 1962 to reach 230,000 in 1982, only 85,000 live in the interior. Almost 80 per cent of agricultural production comes from the modernized sector, especially the east coast. Tourism is also concentrated on the coast (Figure 4.5). Seventy-five per cent of part-time jobs (6000) but only 50 per cent of full-time (250 jobs) are held by Corsicans. This pattern of stark contrasts is not unusual in peripheral regions undergoing a profound economic and social change, but in Corsica it was not mediated by modernizing élites, as had happened in Brittany.

Two hereditary clientelistic systems, with origins dating back to the nineteenth century (Tafani, 1986), had adopted the trappings of modern political formations and reinforced their power through their ability to distribute the increasingly large transfers from the State. Rocca Serra

(RPR) dominated in the South (Corse du Sud), and Giacobbi (MRG, Radical Party) in the north (Haute Corse). The rapidity of the transformation and the rigidity of the traditional political system left little room for the incorporation of modernizing and intellectual élites (fractions of the liberal bourgeoisie), or those excluded from the development process (farmers and pastoralists in the interior, small shopkeepers, hoteliers). Thus a wide range of groups gave support to regionalist, and later autonomist and nationalist movements, which challenged the State and attempted to combat the closed political system.

Each wave of autonomist and nationalist activity in the 1970s led to the injection of more resources. For example, the series of events around the illegal addition of sugar to wine, which culminated in the shoot-out between autonomists in Corsican Regionalist Action (ARC) and the police in Algeria in 1975, brought in extra resources. In addition the region was carved up into two departments that simply demarcated more clearly the territorial hold of the two clans. By 1980, Corsica had by far the largest per capita expenditure of all regional establishments (FF 234.27 per capita in Corsica compared to an average of FF 84.35) (Nivollet, 1982, p. 32). The tense situation after the confrontation in 1980 between autonomists – the Union of Corsican People (UPC) – and those in favour of remaining an integral part of France was probably only brought to an end by the promise of future reforms following the election of the Left.

The need to find a solution to what some felt was almost a state of civil war, prompted the government to grant Corsica, ahead of all other regions, a special statute with economic and cultural functions. The first elections to the regional assembly (August 1982), in which the UPC won seven seats and non-aligned lists favourable to the new institutional arrangements won four, kindled some hope that more appropriate development programmes would be a possibility. There seemed to be some opening up of political space for a short time after the regional elections, despite the fact that the Socialists had ceded on a number of demands for electoral reform and institutional change (Dressler-Holohan, 1985).

However, the traditional clans, though for the present slightly split, opposed the statute and demanded more of the same, namely a transfer of resources from the State. The Communist Party had probably the most coherent development programme, but this was based on industrialization, which many groups considered to be unrealistic and undesirable. Socialists (two lists), the UPC and the Radicals in the South, who supported the statute, favoured a more autonomous development, additional resources and diversified productive structures, especially the encouragement of artisan activity and the revitalization of the interior as part of a global concept of development for the island. Nationalist discourse, for example, that of the Corsican Movement for Self-determination (MCA) and the clandestine Movement for the Liberation of Corsica (FLNC), tended to concentrate on themes of exploitation and appropriation of land and resources and to see a solution in the expulsion of all non-Corsicans, exemplified in the commonly daubed '*I francesi fora*' (French Out). In general, autonomist and nationalist movements paid relatively little attention to economic and social developments and participation in local associations.

In the short life of the first Assembly (1982–4), Corsica began to catch up on strategies for local development, common elsewhere in France (see p. 109). In the 1970s only four rural action plans and local planning contracts had got off the ground (Balagne, Gravona, Haut Taravo and Castagniccia). The Regional Natural Park had also set up, as from 1977, five local development schemes. However, when these plans came under the jurisdiction of the regional establishment in 1980, Corsica failed to put forward any proposals. The first Assembly, under the presidency of Prosper Alfonsi (Radical from the Haute Corse), financed studies on micro-regional development and local development associations. The idea was to bring together politicians, professionals and development associations within a reasonably manageable territory and to link this in with the regional plan.

The collapse of the first Asssembly and the new elections in August 1984 led to Rocca Serra becoming the president with the support of the National Front, now with six seats. The clans had returned in full force. The moderate autonomists had only gained three seats to add to the nationalists' three. It was, of course, the end of any idea of micro-regional or local development scheme, for the new Assembly proceeded to withdraw financial aid on the pretext that these local associations and development committees had been infiltrated by nationalists. In its stead, a project for a free enterprise zone was preferred.[1]

Elsewhere in France, autonomist and nationalist movements have been in decline, unable to sustain a challenge to the State in a period of economic crisis and decentralization. The exceptions are the revival of such movements in the Basque region in the 1980s and their continuing activity in Corsica. The penetration of these formerly closed societies by outside influences and conflicts over the pace and nature of economic and social change are unlikely to produce an easy solution.

Note

(1) The section on Corsican development is based primarily on unpublished documents, provided by Wanda Dressler-Holohan and the Institute for the Development of the Mediterranean Islands (IDIM), and on interviews.

FIVE

The Urban Environment: Policy and Conflicts

5.1 The pressures of urbanization

The successive waves of urbanization, suburbanization and counter-urbanization, which France has experienced since 1945, were bound to create great tensions in the urban fabric, in urban communities and in policy, particularly as they caught a France so ill equipped after the stagnation of the interwar years. Lack of investment had left France with an aging housing stock and with a majority of dwellings lacking what are now considered to be basic amenities. Policies for housing and urban planning, such as they were, reflected the low level of activity and conservative attitudes of the prewar era. And further, the unbalanced urban structure of the country, with the dominance of Paris and a poorly developed network of provincial capitals, was ill-suited to meet a wave of in-migration.

French cities experienced a very rapid, at times almost anarchic growth in the postwar period, which produced great social and economic strains. Adopting the definition of 'urban' as the population living in urban agglomerations, then the urban proportion of the total population, which had more than doubled to 53 per cent from 1850 to 1946, rose again to 72.9 per cent by 1975. Roughly speaking, it had risen from one-half to three-quarters in thirty postwar years, representing an additional 16 million urban residents (Scargill, 1983). There were, of course, three components to this increase: the remarkable demographic growth represented by the postwar 'baby boom'; foreign immigration (including '*pieds-noirs*' from Algeria); and rural/urban migration which involved 3 million farmers and farmworkers during the period 1955–75. Of course, by the mid-1970s the rural exodus was reversed to produce the phenomenon of so-called 'counter-urbanization'.

The favoured regions and cities of in-migration varied significantly over the period, reflecting economic and housing opportunities and changing social values. Until 1962, the Paris region, the Lyons metropolis and the Provence-Alpes-Côte d'Azur (PACA) region grew most strongly. During the 1960s, the wave of foreign immigrants swelled the most urbanized regions. This period brought other changes: the Paris region began to grow more slowly than the rest of urban France, and then after 1968, slower than the French population as a whole. At the same time, the industrial cities of Lorraine and the Nord manifested their structural problems in net out-migration. During 1968–75, the fastest growth was in the small- and medium-sized towns (20,000–50,000 inhabitants) and, subsequently, growth favoured the smallest towns and the rural hinterland (rural communes of the zones of industrial and urban settlement, the ZPIU) (Findlay and White, 1986; see Figure 1.3). The exodus from the city centres and the deconcentration of population to the small settlements within commuting distance are the most obvious signs of counter-urbanization after 1975. It is the foreign immigrants who are concentrated in cities of greater than 100,000 inhabitants, and they show a marked concentration in the Paris and Lyons metropolises and Marseilles–Côte d'Azur, particularly the North and Central African immigrants.

It is not surprising that this wave of urbanization posed great difficulties for the existing urban areas, considering the poor quality of housing and the lack of new construction which typified the early postwar period. Even if we take the census statistics of 1962, 62 per cent of principal dwellings were constructed pre-1914, 39 per cent were in a state of moderate or acute overoccupation, 60 per cent had no WC and 70 per cent no bath or shower (Table 5.2). The pressures were, of course, magnified because of the concentration of new urban residents in the larger metropolises and especially in Paris, Lyons and Marseilles. In the following discussion we seek to show broadly how the urban situation evolved, and subsequently to give detailed policy assessments, illustrated by several case studies.

To begin to understand the ensuing problems in the urban fabric requires some sense of the interplay between a range of factors – the demographic pressures, the existing housing stock, urban policy, the changing economic base of the city. All these forces are operating within an environment in which rent and planning controls, tax reliefs and the site monopoly of the landowner all lead to a large-scale distortion of the market.

Before focusing in particular on the inner-city problem and the difficulties of the high-density surburban housing estates, let us mention briefly the urban policy of the time. The low priority given to house-building and the imposition of rent control under the 1948 Act meant that the reconstruction period had greatly exacerbated the problem of housing supply, resulting in the 1953 housing riots in the Paris region. The government reacted by a rapid expansion of residential construction and, to ease the difficulties of operational planning (given the wholly unadapted structure of local authorities), it adopted a policy of zones of urban development in 1958. On the urban periphery, ZUP (urbanization priority zones) were designated on huge sites bought at agricultural use price, and the housing estates were concentrated here, permitting a rapid expansion in the numbers of lower-cost, system-built apartment blocks. In the inner city, the ZRU (urban renovation zones) were earmarked for comprehensive redevelopment of a 'balanced' nature. In practice, the ZRU encountered serious policy failures, notably as a result of an inability to control the land market. So a number of inadequate, disparate measures were taken until a redirection of policy in 1967, when the ZAC (joint planning zones) system was implemented. In sum, comprehensive redevelopment came to be anything but balanced; displacement of the poor, land speculation and huge central business district (CBD) expansion schemes marked an abrupt change with the human scale and diversity of the traditional cityscape.

Cities in France, as elsewhere in Continental Europe, displayed high densities of occupation and different social classes lived in quite close proximity. In part, this reflects the continuing desire of the middle and upper classes to reside in the central city. The inner-city evolution in the postwar period has modified this picture in the sense that overall densities have fallen, but the social composition has become more polarized with a stronger middle-class representation together with more single people and a greater proportion of the old, the poor and immigrants. Clearly, processes of gentrification and of physical decay have been at work, while generally, the French working-class family has been 'decanted' to the peripheral estates, and their somewhat wealthier counterparts have acquired suburban, single-family homes.

This process of relative loss of central residential function and of suburban spread exhibits certain distinctively French features which will become apparent. It is evident that, during the early 1950s and 1960s, many inner-city areas of rented housing for the working class played a role of reception and socialization for French rural migrants. They had always done so but the wave of urban in-migration was greater during these years. Typically, inner-city housing for the working and middle classes was rented from private landlords, and poorer housing was often subtenanted and subdivided, with few amenities. Even in 1975, 40 per cent of dwellings in the Paris city lacked at least one minimum amenity, and in the inner ring of Parisian departments the figure was 25 per cent. Of these, two-thirds were privately rented and a high proportion were occupied by the retired or the inactive, with all these residents having a lower income than social housing tenants; 42 per cent of these dwellings were subject to the 1948 Rent Act control. This sector had served the huge influx of rural migrants: as these young people prospered and started families, so they found social housing perhaps in a peripheral housing estate and were replaced by new immigrants.

The influx of French-born in-migrants slackened in the 1960s and the dominant migratory movement became one of net out-migration. In part, this was offset by the middle class, the young and the single and, progressively during the 1960s, by immigrants of North and Central African origin, often of Muslim background. In the poorer, rent-controlled sector, these shifts in social composition brought accelerated decay. White (1984) notes the change in the Belleville district of inner Paris; from having a century-long traditional working-class character it became the most cosmopolitan district in Paris during the 1950s and 1960s, with a notable Indo-Chinese minority. The central area of Marseilles, in particular the dilapidated Belsunce district, has all the character of an Arab 'souk'.

A number of French writers speak of the crisis of the inner-city during this period. Aballéa (1986) makes clear that many older districts in French cities had lost much of their residential and economic function by 1975. Central Clermont-Ferrand lost 20–40 per cent of its main residences from 1962 to 1972, and even the city of Paris lost 300,000 residents in the years from 1968 to 1975. As for economic decay, central Bordeaux lost 17 per cent of its commercial business between 1962 and 1972. Barrère and Casson-Mounat (1980) speak of a serious crisis, which was evident in dilapidation and abandonment. These assessments are doubtless too all-embracing; closely linked are the forces of gentrification and new commercial expansion, both in favour of change. The increasing middle-class presence in the inner city encouraged the cleaning of façades and the restoration of historic properties in the conservation areas (of which sixty had been designated by 1979 including the Marais and Old Lyons) under the 1962 Malraux Law. Rehabilitation of older property resulted in release from the 1948 rent control, and thus stimulated change in the historic cores of many French cities.

Accompanying this suburbanization of population has been a suburbanization of manufacturing, retailing and wholesaling, as well as the death of many small- and medium-sized firms in the traditional branches of engineering, clothing and woodworking. This deindustrialization of the inner city, even the establishment of peripheral shopping centres, can be explained by the poor operating environment of the inner city, physical constraints and planning controls, poor access and the associated high operating costs, including those of labour. The deindustrialization of the centre of Paris and the inner ring of departments is now well advanced and has been viewed with mounting alarm in the 1980s. Tuppen (1983) notes that, while the level of manufacturing employment in Paris was stable in the 1960s, it dropped by 3.5 per cent per year up to 1975. From 1975 to 1981, 40,000 jobs per year were lost. In the recession years, closures and transfers accounted equally for these losses. Very badly hit by closures in the engineering and vehicles industries were communes in the manufacturing belt, such as Saint Denis, Genevilliers, Montrouge and Boulogne-Billan-court. Lastly, we can cite Marseilles, where industrial employment fell by one-quarter, between 1975 and 1982, and where substantial employment losses in port-based industries are now to be expected.

The marked shift towards the service industries in employment structure and in value-added has presented both opportunities and new pressures. The office boom, the expansion in financial and management services (legal, computing, advertising, marketing) and the provision of both specialist and multiple retailing services, all lead to an extension of the central urban area. Floorspace, transport accessibility, proximity to related services and the prestige image of the central area are among the key locational factors. The adaptability of the existing urban fabric to these new requirements, in particular large floorspaces and public transport access, can determine whether a city centre attracts such new functions to replace those in decline, though the matter is scarcely so simple. Tuppen (1983) reports that the office-building boom accelerated from 1965 and reached its most rapid growth in the first half of the 1970s. Office employment expanded by 27 per cent from 1968 to 1981, with the most rapid expansion in finance and management services. Nevertheless, public administration still represents 60 per cent of total office employment. In terms of location, Paris continued to exert an overwelming dominance in terms of both employment and floorspace constructed, but the four largest regional capitals (Lyons, Lille, Marseilles, Strasbourg) all saw a vast expansion of speculative office construction in the 1970s.

In part, these large commercial expansion schemes were promoted by the State itself. An important element in the policy of spatial management was that of strategic spatial planning, and particularly urban policy. Regional capitals were designated as counter-magnet cities to the growth of Paris; later the policy focused on promoting the growth of medium-sized provincial towns. In Paris (notably La Défense), in Lyons (La Part-Dieu), and in Marseilles (Centre commercial de la Mediterranée), so-called '*centres directionnels*' were developed as huge central business district expansion schemes with the express intention of attracting the headquarters of national and multinational companies. Each of these outsize developments grew out of much more modest comprehensive redevelopment plans on the ZRU model, but came to lose any pretence at social balance, as we see later. In medium-sized towns, the policy also came to be associated with expansion of the central area.

These massive comprehensive redevelopment schemes began to take shape in the late 1960s and early 1970s. They provoked adverse reaction, sometimes in the form of organized social movements (Castells, 1978), to their gigantic size, bulldozer renovation, displacement of poorer social groups and land speculation, which seemed to go hand in hand. And so we find a link between commercial expansion, public renewal policy, urban decay and the displacement of social groups. Perhaps the most important transmission mechanism here is that of the land market, which we have already described as being highly imperfect. Expected or real land-price changes can generate spirals of renewal or decay. If a site could support a higher-yielding use, then a change of use could sooner or later take place, with eviction of the existing user. It is easy to see, for example, how an inner-city manufacturing firm may close and sell its site for office development, or how poor tenants with no security are evicted in favour of 'improvement' or conversion of space to offices. Here there is a development gain, namely a realized increase in site value.

However, for upward and downward spirals to set in, we must introduce the concept of externalities. An improvement carried out by another, such as, for example, local authority investments in transport or facilities, will lead to betterment, namely an unearned increment in the site value of the property. But in a deteriorating area, why make private investments? Either these lead to no increase in value, or the effect is dispersed as neighbours also benefit from the improvements. In France, the city centre is primarily characterized by a multitude of small parcels of land, either individually owned or with complex and varied leasing arrangements. Certainly until the past decade, in the absence of development, the parcels rarely changed hands. The actions of the public authorities then served to stimulate and create a land market.

All this makes public land acquisition and assembly for redevelopment slow and costly, but all the more so because the public investment can set in train a land-price spiral, as the expropriating authority struggles to acquire the land. Betterment is appropriated privately as the land changes hands. And so, as in the ZRU or even the ZAC, initial comprehensive redevelopment plans were stymied by poor public control over land prices, plans were drastically pruned and public finances fell heavily into deficit. A much more commercial development, with little social housing, then had to be adopted to recover the situation. Marxists, such as Castells (1978), see this as the reconquest of former working-class areas by the dominant class interest and finance capital, hence the slogan 'renovation–deportation'. Working-class voters in key city centres are displaced by the middle class who support 'bourgeois' political parties and entrench the dominant class interest. Monopoly profits from a central redevelopment are then reaped. This analysis overlooks the fact that, prior to development, a multiplicity of landowners were involved, although ownership becomes more concentrated after development.

Finally, the peripheral housing estates rarely had a good reputation –they

Table 5.1   Housing construction

	No. of house completions
1952	90,000
1958	292,000
1964	369,000
1970	456,000
1972	546,000
1974	500,000
1976	449,000
1978	445,000
1980	379,000
1982	336,000
1984	271,000
1986	296,000
1988	310,000

Source: Ministère de l'Equipement, *Annuaire statistique de l'équipement*; Ministère de l'Urbanisme, du Logement et des Transports, *Statistiques de la construction*.

were tower-block estates with poor transport and service provision and were suffering from all the quality and noise insulation defects of prefabricated constructions. The disaffected French left in large numbers from the early 1970s, to live in single-family housing. High vacancy rates led to disastrous housing finances, and vacancies were often filled by immigrants, with large families and different cultural and religious values. Riots in 1981 and 1983 by disaffected black and Arab youths led to a number of public measures (see below), and it is recognized that the problem is one of deprivation and blocked opportunities, as well as of the physical environment. Many of the social problems normally associated with British inner cities, are actually found in these suburban housing estates. France's inner-city problem is much less intense and also differs from the British one in that the inner areas remain a prized residential location for the bourgeoisie.

It would be unfair to close this introduction without stressing just how much has been achieved. Pearsall (1983) sees the housing construction effort as certainly a success in quantitative terms, and the rising aspirations for a better quality of housing have broadly been met (Tables 5.1, 5.2). In the remainder of this chapter we examine in more detail public policy in urban planning, housing and land, before giving case studies of renewal, peripheral estates and metropolitan planning.

Table 5.2   Housing tenure and amenities

	% of total housing				
	1954	1962	1968	1975	1982
Individual housing	42.2	48.4	47.4	49.3	52.4
Owner-occupiers	35.5	41.3	43.2	46.6	50.7
Overcrowding	—	38.7	31.6	22.7	15.8
Running water	61.9	78.4	90.8	97.2	99.2
Inside toilet	26.6	40.5	54.8	73.8	85.0
Bath or shower	10.4	28.9	47.5	70.5	84.7
Central heating	—	—	34.9	53.1	67.0
All comforts	—	—	—	47.6	62.0

Source: INSEE census.

5.2   Urban planning, housing and land policies

5.2.1   The urban planning system

To the outside observer, France's local government structure seems singularly ill-suited to the task of physical planning. With 32,400 communes of fewer than 2000 inhabitants, out of a total of 36,400, and with superimposed departments and regions, the questions of the division of competences and of technical and financial capacity of the communes spring to mind immediately. Even after the Socialist government's decentralization project of 1981, most mayors of communes remain ill-equipped for the task (Flockton, 1983). Before 1981, the centralized system meant that although the mayors granted planning permission, they were nevertheless subject to the tutelage of the prefect and to the technical approval of plans by the *Direction départementale d'équipment* (DDE, Departmental Direction of Public Works).

In practice, the system was far from rigid, since larger towns had their own planning staffs and mayors of national political standing were always heard favourably in Parisian ministries. But typically, because of their weakness and the strict legal limits on their borrowing, municipalities would set up an agent at arm's length to conduct their planning and operational development. This would be a mixed-economy agency (SEM), which included private capital and which grouped together the different public authorities and the powerful subsidiaries of the *Caissé des dépôts et consignations* (CDC, Deposit and Consignment Office), namely the SCET and the SCIC. The former is responsible for land acquisition, assembly and site preparation, and the latter for financing building construction. The

SEM would often be granted compulsory purchase powers. We emphasize this multiplicity of agents acting in urban development, because it has tended to produce a considerable confusion of roles, and sometimes an abnegation of responsibility by elected municipal councillors. It is hardly surprising that technocratic, insensitive and more market-based solutions have prevailed (in the peripheral estates and inner-city renewal) when municipalities adopt an arm's length approach. Of course there are many exceptions, and muncipalities can choose the direct control method, as some Communist municipalities have done.

The present planning system dates substantially from the major legislation of 1967, the *Loi d'orientation foncière* (LOF, Land Law), which introduced structure planning. Building permission and regulations – the *Règles nationales d'urbanisme* (RNU, National Town Planning Regulations) – date from 1955 and compulsory purchase has a long history. However, it is noteworthy that social housing organizations could be given these powers as far back as 1953, and the SEMs from 1958. Earlier physical planning regimes afforded only poor development control (often breached) and were ill-adapted to regulatory needs (Dauphin and Jacotey, 1974). All that remain of interest from the 1958 legislation are the provisions for operational development by zone (ZUP and ZRU).

The ZUP was to be the key public instrument for urban extension, whether for housing estates or industrial areas. All housing projects of more than 100 dwellings had to be located in a ZUP. Here was the instrument for the peripheral tower-block developments, where, promoted by the DDE, the SCIC and SCET, large-scale urban extensions were added to communes in developments over which the municipality exercised little influence; in addition, the municipality found itself financially pressed as a result of the project. Small wonder that these insensitive developments suffered from poor transport, educational and service provision. Of key interest are the land-policy powers in a ZUP. The developing agent exercised a pre-emption right in a ZUP to buy land coming on to the market at existing use price. Swathes of peripheral land were bought for housing at a non-speculative price. In the ZRU, in contrast, the market price of the land had to be paid. The public purse bore the burden of this policy.

The 1967 LOF sought to correct a number of shortcomings. As we have seen, it embraced the vogue for structure planning, and so two-tier plans were required – a *Schéma directeur d'aménagement et d'urbanisme* (SDAU, Strategic Plan for Development and Urbanization) was the overall structure plan in urban centres of over 10,000 inhabitants. This was to set the main lines for longer-term developments, and was legally binding only on public authorities. At the commune level, a land-use plan (POS) was required, which was legally binding on all and specified zones, densities, servitudes, building regulation requirements and so on. The POS was to implement the aims of the SDAU and was intended to be renewed every five years. The land-policy aspects of the ZUP and ZRU were replaced by the introduction of a new type of zone (ZAC), but this reflected new concerns. The previous system suffered in two ways from the dominant position it afforded public authorities: public finances, it was argued, could no longer bear the burden, and the insensitivity of developments reflected the technocratic centralism of the procedure. In a ZAC, then, a partnership with private capital would be sought, to produce a more balanced development and to share the costs. For land acquired through compulsory purchase, private developers in the ZAC would make payments in cash or in kind (provision of public buildings, for example). In the ZAC, there was derogation from the constraints of the prevailing land-use plan, which provided a major loophole.

Later legislation and policy have tended to focus primarily on land policy and on inner-city renewal as, for example, the 1975 land law and the 1977 creation of the Fund for Urban Development (FAU) to co-ordinate action in inner areas. However, two important aspects of the 1967 LOF required subsequent correction. First, in common with experience elsewhere, there was disappointment with the results of structure planning. Its general nature and long-term perspective became perceived as disadvantageous, especially with the coming of the economic crises of the 1970s. Few SDAU were completed in France and many POS were prepared in the absence of such a guiding structure plan. To provide some statement of future development intentions, the simpler reference plans were introduced in 1977, especially for built-up areas. A second shortcoming concerned the ZAC, which had been exempt from the controls of the POS. This naturally gave rise to developments in conflict with the POS and to unscrupulous behaviour by developers. Later a 'plan for the zone' (PAZ) was required, which set out clear objectives and responsibilities.

It will be apparent, then, that development control was not as effective as might have been desired; before the early 1970s derogation was not uncommon, or a plan was circumvented, as happened originally in the ZAC. (Now planning permission can only be granted when there is a POS in existence.) And structure planning for conurbations was only partially implemented; it was to some extent merely a set of pious hopes.

5.2.2   Land policy

As we have seen, the land question poses perennial problems for urban development, not least because inadequate land-price control can thwart the aims of the public authority. Its very intervention often leads to the creation of betterment and can set in motion a price spiral, which puts the very project at risk. Granelle (1975, 1976) shows how urban land prices have risen, though they have followed a very fluctuating course: in real terms, building land prices trebled from 1955 to 1967, but subsequently only rose by 40 per cent between 1968 and 1975. In Paris, costs are very high but show marked fluctuations in response to demand and borrowing conditions. Given these various types of capital gain, pressure has mounted for a reform of land taxation.

The most original aspect of French land policy concerns the use of the pre-emption right in designated zones (Derycke, 1979; Renard, 1980). Here the authority may step in to acquire land coming on to the market. In the ZUP and ZAD, the latter instituted in 1962, land is acquired at near agricultural-use price, at a non-speculative price. This zoning legislation has been used very widely for housing land and the major national infrastructural developments. In built-up areas, in a ZAC, land had to be acquired at the market price. A new zone, the ZIF, was created in 1975 to cover the built-up areas of centres of over 10,000 inhabitants; finally, the pre-emption right was extended in 1986 to all urban areas covered by a valid land-use plan. This right tends to be exercised in urban areas to make purchases when favourable conditions arise in the local land market. In the case of greenfield developments, it can also be used to dissuasive effect against land speculation. The huge speculative land-price increases of the early 1970s led to mounting pressure for land tax reforms (ADEF, 1983). A form of development gains tax was introduced in 1975, but it proved highly dissuasive. The Socialist government's plans of 1984 for a site value tax also came to nothing, like so many earlier proposals, in the face of political opposition and strong technical objections.

5.2.3 Housing policy

A study of the evolution of postwar French housing policy reveals quite marked shifts and changes; housing finance has been reorganized three times and there have been notable changes in the respective roles of the State, the social housing organizations and private investors. And of course the process of urbanization itself has conditioned housing policy.

Housing policy omissions and commissions during the reconstruction period (1945–50) proved to be the origin of a number of later difficulties. The low priority given to house construction meant that only 200,000 dwellings were built, in spite of the manifestly degraded state of the housing stock, the loss of 20 per cent of the stock through war damage and the rising demographic pressures. The rent controls introduced in 1948 to cover pre-1948 dwellings in urban centres slowed rent rises substantially, but brought in their train the progressive dilapidation of older rented housing. In the period up to 1963, the State instituted a vastly expanded construction effort (see Table 5.1), the costs of which were met largely from the central government budget and from para-state credit institutions. To meet the crisis, the State adopted as its agents the *Habitation à loyer modéré* (HLM) social housing movement and the *Crédit foncier de France* (CCF), a State-owned building loan organization.

Turning first then to assistance for private sector construction, the subsidized sector covered individuals of average-to-modest income who constructed dwellings according to standard criteria. The CCF made mortgage loans of 70 per cent of cost, and particular housing types – the *logécos* – benefited from a State grant. As Pearsall (1983) reports, 1.6 million such dwellings were constructed and home ownership spread among a broad stratum of the population. The social housing sector, which provided lower-cost housing to rent or buy, expanded rapidly as a key element of the housing effort. Branches of the social housing movement were often associated with individual towns and cities, with mayors, councillors and prefects among their governors. They acted, therefore, as municipal agents, but being semi-autonomous they were free to act as developer, and to borrow and invest.

Subject to cost and design yardsticks, lower-rent housing was made available to those on municipal and departmental housing lists, the subsidy coming from two sources. The State loans were made at lower, fixed-interest rates for a 65-year period, to 90 per cent of cost. A second source was the '1 per cent employer' tax levied on wage bills, which enabled firms to nominate employees for social housing. Under this scheme, the HLM movement contributed greatly to overcoming the postwar housing shortage. By the early 1960s, it was responsible for 40 per cent of all new dwellings. The situation today is that the 1200 HLM organizations have built 2.5 million dwellings for rent and 1 million for sale (Pearsall, 1983). It should be borne in mind, however, that while these organizations are non-profit making, they should also not be loss-making; as a result tenants can be subject to substantial rent rises in times of high inflation. Clearly, the elderly without a pension, low-paid immigrants and marginal groups were not well covered by this system because they were insufficiently solvent.

The HLM organizations built apartment blocks to different standards, each with its associated rent level, (there being two superior categories above the 'ordinary' rent, and three types of cheaper accommodation for those rehoused from urban renovation and clearance programmes, as well as two types of housing for sale). And so this institutional channelling of families to apartment blocks according to means implied a pronounced social segregation by housing type. In addition, spatial segregation arose since much new construction was of the large-scale, tower-block estate type on the urban periphery. Here, developments of more than 100 dwellings were concentrated in a ZUP, benefiting from lower land prices. The SCIC provided much of the financing, and the SCET undertook site acquisition and preparation.

In the early 1960s housing shortages remained chronic in urban areas, physical and plumbing standards remained unsatisfactory and shanty towns mushroomed on the edge of major cities. Yet in 1963 the government announced a major housing policy change, which reflected the wider retreat from interventionism in favour of market forces. As one element in a major reform of the banking system, State budgetary support for private housing would be replaced by bank mortgage lending and a higher personal contribution. Thus, in the subsidized sector for private housing, a smaller CFF loan was to be accompanied by a bank mortgage arranged under a contractual home savings plan. This carries a moderate fiscal inducement and now represents the principal form of private housing finance (Heugas-Darraspen, 1985). Finally, these principles of reduced state support and greater market orientation applied equally to the HLM movement. The proportion met by grants was substantially reduced, and lower-interest construction loans were now made by the CDC, banker to the local authorities. The sector was exhorted to offer a wider range of housing, particularly to buy. The construction effort by HLM organizations reached its peak proportionately in the 1960s, but from 1968 onwards the progressive financial squeeze of rising interest rates and lower subsidies took its toll.

As we have seen, the late 1960s and early 1970s saw a fundamental change in public attitudes towards urban policy. The widespread disenchantment concerned both inner-city renewal schemes and tower-block developments alike. The scale, brutalism and density of the new architectural forms evoked a negative reaction, expressed commonly as an aversion to gigantic developments; many French came to prefer single-family housing. In the early 1970s, French residents began to leave the peripheral housing estates in large numbers, reacting in addition to the poor internal design, lack of noise insulation, and poor transport and service provision. This points very clearly to deficiencies in planning and housing policy, but the rising vacancy rates of apartment blocks began a spiral of dilapidation. As for the inner city, comprehensive redevelopment evoked vociferous and sometimes violent opposition (Castells, 1978), as poorer groups were displaced by commercial expansion schemes, whose deteriorating finances led to scaled-down social housing objectives. Displacement and dispossession were also typical in the conservation areas (*secteurs sauvegardés*), where the emphasis was placed on restoration of buildings of architectural merit with rehousing *in situ* receiving low priority. In Vieux Lyons, only one-fifth of existing residents remained, and in the Marais district of Paris, a price spiral and sharp rise in co-ownership resulted (Kain, 1981).

Housing finance was subjected to fundamental reform once again in 1977 (see p. 29), and most of the current system arises from the Housing Act of that year. Two major reports had laid the bases for the change: the Nora–Evenu Report stressed the importance of rehabilitation, while the Barre Report stressed the need to focus public resources on those in need, while letting rents move to market levels and thus reducing total state subsidies. Under the 1977 law, four principal forms of assistance replaced the previous system: these covered low-interest loans for the 'social' rented sector, two types of home purchase plan and the personal housing aid (APL), which was designed as a housing allowance for poorer tenants facing more market-related rent levels (Heugas–Darraspen, 1985).

In the event, the 1977 reform led to substantial burdens on the State in the guise of the APL, which in 1986 amounted to FF 20 bn, or over 50 per cent of housing aid. Rising real interest rates led to high rent increases and home-owner mortgage repayments, and so to an explosion in APL assistance. Vincent (1986) sees this itself as a factor in house-price inflation as demand for housing remained high for several years, rather than being choked off quickly by rises in interest rates.

Rehabilitation formed the second main thrust of the 1977 legislation, which provided three specific modes of assistance. Both public and expert opinion was in favour of a shift in policy, especially towards the maintenance *in situ* of poorer tenants. Historically, since 1945, two main systems of housing rehabilitation assistance had existed in France: the FNAH fund was designed to support voluntary initiatives among landlords. Far more successful was the PACT system, under which 350,000 dwellings were improved during the period 1945–74 (Pearsall, 1983). The associations were non-profit making, professional advisory bodies for rehabilitation, serving poor owner-occupiers in inner-city areas and landlords whose property there could be renovated as social housing for the existing disadvantaged population. Reforms in 1971 and 1975 introduced the *Association nationale pour l'amélioration de l'habitat* (ANAH, National Association for Housing Improvement) which, at department level, brings together landlords, tenants and state administration. The ANAH benefits from a tax on leasehold income and had a budget in 1984 of FF 1 bn. Most activity, especially that financed by the 1977 Act, is concentrated in designated rehabilitation areas (OPAH). In many cases the technical and advisory work is conducted by the PACT–ARIM associations. The rehabilitation assistance provided by the 1977 Act comprises improvement grants to landlords and owner-occupiers, and social assistance to tenants in order to moderate the effects of subsequent rent increases.

Heugas-Darraspen (1985) sees in this system a clear success: the OPAH system had been used increasingly selectively to sustain and expand social housing in older areas. In the context of conservation areas, drawing on the Fonds d'aménagement urbain, the OPAH is a flexible and socially-sensitive alternative to the secteur sauvegardé instrument, focusing on the rehabilitation of the ordinary housing stock as well as architectural restoration (Scargill, 1983). Over 100,000 dwellings per year have been improved (though this was only one-half the target figure of the 8th Plan). Expenditure by the ANAH had doubled to FF 956 million over the period 1978 to 1984 and the cost of the PALULOS and PAH grants rose to almost FF 3 billion in 1985.

The peripheral estates built in the 1950s and 1960s are, however, also often in need of rehabilitation, due to faults in the prefabricated construction, poor quality and to vandalism on the many estates caught in a cycle of poverty and alienation. The HLM movement in the 1980s has been caught in a process of spiralling deficits, as the high interest rates on borrowings burden its balance sheets, and as solvent tenants leave. The rehabilitation of such estates represents the greatest cost. There remain 1.3 million dwellings built before 1970 in need of rehabilitation, at an estimated cost of FF 55 bn. To cover this cost without drastic rent increases for tenants, the HLM organizations have rehabilitated blocks and filled them with poorer tenants qualifying for APL. The ensures a highly effective subsidy but exacerbates the 'ghetto' problem of many estates.

Finally, we turn to Housing Act changes under recent alternating governments. In general, the point of contention concerns the legal protection afforded to tenants; in addition, there are differences of emphasis in that the Socialist government favoured housing construction as an employment creation measure, while the Chirac goverment stressed sales of social housing to tenants. The legal protection in terms of security of tenure (outside the 1948 Act) and rent rises afforded to the 5 million tenants in the private sector was minimal before the Quilliot Law of June 1982. This legislation covered essentially security of tenure and the establishment of a joint body representing landlord/tenant associations to set permissible percentage annual rent rises. Far from being perceived as a conciliatory step, it antagonized property owners already subject to the new wealth tax and the withdrawal of tax allowances on rent incomes and capital gains. Inevitably, the supply of private rented housing dried up almost totally and new construction fell by one-quarter. Subsequent Socialist ministers Quilès and Auroux relaxed the rent rise controls, and Méhaignerie of the 1986 Chirac government reversed much of the remainder. Such a political football will naturally not be left alone by the Rocard government.

5.2.4 *Strategic planning for metropolitan regions*

The designation in 1964 of eight regional counter-magnet cities to Paris, and the appointment in 1966 of strategic planning organizations (OREAM) for most of these, reflected the desire of de Gaulle's government to channel growth to the regional capitals while constraining that in Paris (see p. 14). The objective of physical planning here was to promote the expansion of these cities, while helping to redress their traditional shortcomings in amenities and employment and residential conditions. Urban expansion brought with it a lowering of residential densities in the centre, and so this offered profitable private opportunities for large-scale commercial expansion schemes and associated public transport investments. Such ambitious projects posed enormous administrative and financial challenges. The intention was that the costs would be programmed in the national Plan, and the structure planning system instituted by the 1967 LOF would enable the metropolitan strategies to be implemented on the ground through the SDAU and the POS. Meanwhile, metropolitan planning authorities (District of the Paris region, OREAM), nominated by the State, would draw up strategic plans in accordance with the State's wishes.

This administrative organization reveals all the hallmarks of the centralist state; only in the 1970s and 1980s did regions and local authorities come to play an enlarged role. Typically, the strategic plans reflected central concerns and priorities, with very little local consultation in the early phases. This is apparent in the planning organization for the Paris region, where the planning authority, the District (which in 1966 became the Region), was controlled by government-nominated local councillors, who were wholly unrepresentative both politically and geographically (Doublet, 1976). Only in 1976, with the reform of the Paris region, did it gain greater legitimacy. In Lyons, an 'urban community', made up of the constituent communes, was created in 1966, but only began to exert real influence in the 1970s. The absence of an 'urban community' in the Marseilles region meant that local government was powerless to implement a unified strategy and in practice, communes competed ferociously against each other for projects.

Using the OREAM–Nord region, and specifically, Dunkirk, as his case study, Castells (1978) pursues a Marxist critique of such urban strategic planning. He argues that the State, in overriding local elected representatives, in dictating the essence of the strategy, and in refusing credits for local projects which do not match its own concerns, is promoting the interests of monopoly capital (in this case the steel, chemicals and cement groups). The true 'regional developers' are the giant manufacturing and construction groups, who replace the local bourgeoisie as the dominant class. Strategic planning becomes the institutionalized process whereby these conflicting class interests are mediated by planners, who see themselves as acting in the 'general interest'. Such a topic deserves lengthy treatment, but it is clear that the Dunkirk case represents such a stark clash of interests in exaggerated form. Elsewhere, the multiplicity of communes, with diverse interests, leads to complex bargaining strategies and renders inappropriate such a simplified class analysis.

One may say that the strategic plans for the city regions generally faced rather similar problems and produced rather similar responses. The overall context for these plans in the 1960s was one of rapid demographic and economic growth, which contained within it marked pressures for the decentralization of residence, of manufacturing and warehousing activities. These were accompanied by an emerging inner-city problem of loss of function and of commercial encroachment. The plans for the Paris region and Lyons shared much in common – high population and employment growth forecasts, a preference for channelling residential growth and employment to 'new towns', namely large suburban extensions to channel growth, ambitious commercial expansion and public transport plans, restructuring plans for the inner suburbs to produce a better residence–workplace balance and improved local service provision. A brief review of plan content shows their broad similarity:

(1) The Lyons strategic plan (1970) forecast a 50 per cent increase in population to the year 2000, and sought to accommodate this in a polymodal form by establishing two new towns east of a green belt. The suburbs were to be 'restructured' around secondary service and employment centres, and future growth would be focused along priority public transport axes, separated by green wedges. In harmony with the overriding objective of raising Lyons to the status of an international business and services centre, the decentralization of industry would be fostered while the commercial centre of La Part-Dieu (together with comprehensive redevelopment of the 'core' Presqu'île) would be pursued (Tuppen, 1986). Large-scale public investment projects of a new international airport at Satolas, the high-speed train service and a new local metro system would support this international role.

(2) The Paris regional plans display many of the same concerns. They sought a polycentric form for the city region, with a local balance of services and employment and an integrated high-speed public transport network which would unify the regional labour market. The key elements of the plan were to be the transport network itself, the 'new towns' and suburban 'restructuring poles' as important local employment and service centres. Taking an axial form, north-west to south-east, it was hoped that the new

city region would redress centre–periphery and east–west disequilibria (House, 1978; Moseley, 1980).

Finally, we mention the Marseilles plan. This was even more ambitious in its growth forecasts, but differed in the emphasis it placed on the imperative of developing a manufacturing sector to counteract endemic underemployment. New-town growth (l'Etang de Berre), the commercial centre and new motorway and underground rail systems remained, of course, compulsory elements (OREAM–PCA, 1974).

The intervening years of economic crisis and population stagnation have rendered invalid many of these assumptions: in all three cases outlined, scaled-down demographic forecasts have brought major modifications and cancellations of new-town and motorway projects. But the strategic plans all encountered other difficulties of implementation, which highlight problems inherent in the French planning and policy environment. Assessing the outcomes, Moseley (1980) writes of Paris (but these observations apply equally to Lyons and Marseilles) that the planners underestimated the pressures for the decentralization of jobs and residences; the rate of change to a service economy was also underestimated. The outcome was an increased imbalance between home and workplace, with no redressing of underlying geographical disequilibria in employment. There were difficulties in controlling the location of suburban housing; commercial expansion exacerbated the inner-city housing problem and rendered even more difficult the restructuring of older suburban centres. Hence one may dispute the claim that the objectives of the Paris regional plans were broadly achieved. Even the *Institut d'Aménagement et d'Urbanisme de la Région d'Ile de France* (IAURIF) (1979) speaks of the need for a nuanced assessment.

The French planning and policy environment presents many obstacles to the effective implementation of a regional schema. Most of these have already been discussed. First, the strategic plan often lacked a mandatory character and could only be implemented by moral persuasion. The hierarchy of plans from the structure plan through to the POS was typically incomplete, and so the strategy was often not translated into regulatory planning at the POS level. The central–local tensions stymied many schemes, and local government, as in Marseilles, was simply in no position to implement a metropolitan strategy (OREAM–PCA, 1974). Finally, there were also deficiencies in the policy instruments themselves. The poor control over land prices and the loopholes in the ZAC system led to comprehensive redevelopment in the inner city, which was quite at variance with what was originally planned. As we shall see subsequently, redevelopment led to expanded commercial schemes with precious little social housing. This inner-city office development, which was much denser than had been intended, conflicted with the employment location objectives of the plans themselves (Flockton, 1982).

The effects of these policy shortcomings have been to produce more a sprawl development than a channelled growth. Policies have failed fully to meet the challenge of restructuring the suburbs, and they have exacerbated inner-city tensions through accelerated social segregation and land and property speculation. In the recent years of slow growth, policy has changed to deal with some of the excesses. Notably, reindustrialization of the inner areas, rehabilitation and enhanced social housing programmes are now the watchwords (Paris Projet, 1980, 1982; Tuppen, 1986).

Of course, such a one-sided concentration on the deficiencies of planning and implementation distracts attention from the manifold achievements in French urban regions which the visitor finds so impressive. The airport, railway and motorway improvements, the new-town developments, the prestigious inner-city cultural and commercial projects leave a strong and favourable impression. As we have seen, however, this should not disguise the policy tensions and social conflicts resulting from urbanization and its control.

5.3 Inner-city renewal and rehabilitation

Slum condemnation and clearance had been pursued in the larger cities for decades, but with little vigour and even less coherence. In the mid-1950s, the Ministry of Reconstruction (later renamed Ministry of Construction) enunciated as its renewal objective the identification of inner-city areas suffering decay or under-utilization, with the purpose of providing modern public facilities and of promoting the enhanced central city functions which an expanding economy requires. Although 'balanced' development was the key, we may note that residential improvement is not mentioned here. In 1958, urban development by zone was introduced with the comprehensive redevelopment instrument of the ZRU.

In Paris, government approval was given in 1955 to what was to become the biggest and most controversial of the Paris region's renewal programmes – La Défense. The site lay immediately contiguous to the high-status residential and business districts in the west of Paris, and so represented the main central area extension ouside the historic core. A total of 750 ha were to be redeveloped and the shanty towns (*bidonvilles*) and craft workshops would be swept away in favour of new office construction. In 1958 a planning authority and development agency (EPAD) was created, its first tasks being to acquire land from a multitude of small landowners, and to provide for the resettlement of residents and artisans.

In Lyons, on the insistence of the Reconstruction Ministry's technical field service, two adjacent projects were given priority. Within easy reach of the city centre, on the Presqu'île, these concerned the La Part-Dieu barracks and the nearby Moncey area. Complete clearance was foreseen, and in 1958 the stated objectives for La Part-Dieu were for 'balanced' redevelopment comprising a state administration centre, 2800 dwellings, and schools and shops.

By the early 1960s a change of emphasis at Ministry level was apparent. Balanced renewal was giving way to the promotion of large business and commercial centres, with the associated radical improvements in public transport facilities. This policy shift can possibly be explained by the difficulties encountered in the urban renovation zones. Everywhere the ZRU formula was meeting fundamental difficulties. Deficits had arisen from expropriation delays, from a grave underestimation of infrastructure costs and from the land speculation which the very announcement of renewal had set in motion (Dauphin and Jacotey, 1974). Clearly, delays laid heavy debt burdens on the commune and meanwhile prices spiralled. The result of the mounting deficits was a scaling-down of plans and a budgetary retrenchment by the *Fonds national d'aménagement foncier urbain* (FNAFU, National Fund for Urban Land Management) fund from 1965. Doubtless a further factor was the public opposition to compulsory clearance and resettlement, when local politicians were fearful for their re-election prospects.

During the 1960s comprehensive redevelopment came to be associated more generally with commercial expansion schemes and profitable housing projects. A variety of factors may explain this phenomenon: the State's policy of counter-magnet cities, the low degree of policy control by local authorities, and the preference shown (by many municipalities, but not all) for partnership schemes involving private interests in the desire to limit public subsidy.

The policy of creating commercial centres in certain regional capitals was a clear symbol and instrument of the commitment to regional development, but it also offered an escape from the mounting deficits of the renovation projects. The La Part-Dieu development in Lyons was wholly revised in 1965. Any ambitions for the provision of social housing were dropped and 185,800 m² of office and retailing space were planned, in addition to major office buildings for public administration and the national radio corporation. In Marseilles, the planned commercial centre stretched from the central axis of the Canebière near the Old Port through the decaying central districts of Sainte-Barbe and Butte des Carmes to the Porte d'Aix. On 35 ha, the city's town planning authority, the AGM, was to provide 360,000 m² of administrative and retailing floorspace, and planned to serve this centre by a metro link and by rail and motorway connections at its northern boundary.

In Paris, the La Défense project was greatly expanded in 1970 when, to help meet the demand in the Paris region, the office space planned was doubled to 1.5 million m². In all of these cases, a further densification of the project, an ever-greater dependence on private capital and a more pronounced orientation to market demands were the response to rising public financial deficits. Such schemes also generated opportunities for the private sector.

An intrinsic element in this shift in strategy was the ZAC instrument introduced by the 1967 LOF, which stressed partnership with private capital. However, the emphasis on profitability and market orientation had been felt earlier. The powerful SCET and SCIC, which provide crucial technical and financial support to projects, had pressed for a greater market emphasis since the early 1960s. In cases such as Lyons though, munici-palities were anxious to limit their financial exposure and hence their degree of subsidy to projects. This automatically meant that the costs of public facilities and of land for social housing within these projects had to be met by land sales to the private sector. The SCET and SCIC, therefore, were acting as if they were private developers (Webman, 1982). And the low degree of policy control, which arises when the municipality acts only at arm's length, means that market forces come to determine the policy direction. Webman (1982, p. 124) quotes the director of the La Part-Dieu project: 'There was no rebuilding plan, no plan for the *ensemble*, no opportunity for programming the projects, for planning the investments'. Much clearly depended on the prevailing conditions in the property market and on office developers' willingness to invest.

In the highly inflationary years of the early 1970s, an office construction boom was reaching its climax, financed by lax credit policies and secured by highly inflated asset prices; the bubble burst with the oil crisis. During this period the price of land adjacent to public renewal operations had risen to such an extent that the character of the public projects had changed beyond recognition. The subsidy required for public housing would be too great, and so a change to commercial uses and to higher-quality housing was, in the absence of firm land-price control, unavoidable. Characteristically, renovation projects became more densely built, had more commercial space and less assisted housing. Social segregation involved the uprooting of poorer tenants to the periphery. Of some notoriety was the 'Place d'Italie' development on the Paris Left Bank, where the dense clustering of towers broke the inherited urban scale. The 'Fronts de Seine' development in the XVth *arrondissement* (ward) attracted the same criticism and had notably reduced social housing provision. In provincial cities, the pressures were similar: White (1984) describes the marked social and economic changes in the Saint Georges district of Toulouse. In Rennes, central commercial development and social segregation went hand in hand.

The collapse of the property market in 1974 gravely affected the large commercial centre projects. The Marseilles project was stopped with only one-third of the plan completed. The La Part-Dieu development was finally finished in much reduced form after 20 years, and the La Défense project had debts totalling FF 700 million in 1978. To counter a forecast final deficit of FF 1 billion, the government authorized the construction of a further 350,000 m² of office space.

In 1974, the policy response to mounting public demonstrations, even riots, was to tighten the ZAC regulations and to turn to rehabilitation, enabling the local population to remain *in situ*. The housing rehabilitation programmes proceeded apace in the years 1977–82. Pre-1949 dwellings were brought up to modern standards of amenity and 40 per cent of this older stock has now been improved. However, improvement has proved costly and substantial rent rises have been unavoidable, under even the 'social agreement' modernization loan system. On average, rent rises on completion have involved a doubling or trebling of rent levels, and in the case of a sale, a 50–100 per cent increase in price (Aballéa, 1986). In the eyes of critics, rehabilitation still brings social segregation because of the rise in housing costs, although after some delay.

Rehabilitation schemes face similar problems to those of redevelopment if there is a limited subsidy and a heavy dependence on market forces. Webman (1982) shows that, in the absence of a dynamism in the local property market, landlords are unwilling to rehabilitate. In contrast, in the presence of a strong underlying dynamic, possibly initiated by the local authority's improvement efforts, speculative pressures may then confound the social objectives of rehabilitation. Chambéry is a clear example, as Aballéa (1986) shows. Here the municipality undertook heavy rebuilding and compulsory purchase, while a local association of landlords and private investors (ACRI) merely carried out surface improvements, sufficient to release properties from rent control. Inevitably, a speculative process was set in motion, while the municipality was increasingly embroiled in very costly expropriation and rebuilding procedures.

5.4   Social and economic tensions in peripheral housing estates

The forbidding present-day social and economic problems in the high-rise suburban social housing estates were already evident in the form of 'new-town blues' in the late 1950s. Sarcelles, a huge housing development planted in a rural commune to the north of Paris, should have served as a clear warning. The OHLM of the city of Paris and the SCET and SCIC organizations all prevailed upon the municipal council to accept this outsize overspill development, using the ZUP policy instrument. Underdeveloped transport, commercial and cultural services all reflected the technical and financial inadequacies of the commune and its distance from the large, Paris-based organizations. With little local employment, this dormitory town began to exhibit the well-known neuroses of uprooting, depression and boredom, and any such sufferer came to be known as a 'Sarcellite' (Jannoud and Pinel, 1974). In the 1970s and 1980's, these problems were greatly exacerbated by rising unemployment, the steady replacement of French residents by immigrants and an accelerated decay of the building fabric; exasperation, aggression and economic precariousness became more characteristic traits.

The prize-winning 'Haut du Lièvre' estate on a windy plateau overlooking Nancy was begun in 1956 and sought to follow Le Corbusier principles. The two longest blocks in Europe (each 400 metres long and fifteen storeys high) were constructed and now house 10,000 people in 2800 HLM apartments. It appears that only in the more animated inner-city locations have Le Corbusier's '*ville radieuse*' principles known a certain success, as in Nantes and Marseilles. Elsewhere, in the urban periphery, where economic recession has compounded the design and service provision problems, a social crisis is evident. In the Haut du Lièvre estate, one-third of the flats are vacant, one-fifth of families have a single parent, there is a pronounced educational underachievement, and three-quarters of the population have an income of 70 per cent of the minimum wage (*Le Monde*, 30 November 1980).

All of these social characteristics are found at 'Les Minguettes' at Vénissieux, in the south-eastern suburbs of Lyons. Like the Sarcelles development which preceded it by ten years, a small community was swamped by a new ZUP overspill development, managed by 11 housing organizations, none of which was based in Vénissieux. Of the 62 towers of over 15 storeys, 44 were of one single design. By the early 1970s, the once-rapid influx of French residents turned into a very marked outflow (Tuppen and Mingret, 1986), compensated only in part by an inflow of immigrants. The clearing of the shanty towns and transit camps in the mid-1970s, and the creation in 1975 of the employers' contribution to the housing of migrant workers led to an influx of immigrants, and in particular those with large families (Gaspard and Servan-Schreiber, 1984). In 'Les Minguettes', 33 per cent are immigrants, and in 'Haut du Lièvre' 21 per cent are of Arab origin (excluding children born in France). Racial tensions, coming on top of the longstanding frustrations, led to serious riots in Vénissieux in 1981 and 1983.

A succession of interministerial groups have addressed the question. A group initiated in 1973 was given new impetus in 1978 when it was renamed '*Habitat et vie sociale*' (Habitat and Social Life), with the role of coordinating the activities of relevant ministries in the more dilapidated estates. At first, the focus was on the physical fabric, but it quickly became apparent that the social, economic and cultural aspects are interlocked. The problem required a high degree of co-ordination, as well as a long-term, substantial budgetary commitment. The Dubedout Commission, established after the 1981 Vénissieux riots, made plain that action would have to take place on a number of levels, and that the social and economic deprivation of inhabitants would have to be dealt with, in addition to questions of poor amenities and the modernization of the physical fabric. Thus initiatives for youth employment creation, training and the designation of educational priority areas have been introduced alongside administrative reforms which seek to link housing organizations and the social security system more closely with the municipalities. A commission for the social development of districts addressed the problems of the 23 worst estates. Most recently, in the context of decentralization, central government has established its own interministerial commission for cities (CIV) to define central policy on both inner-city and peripheral estate problems. This is backed by the Urban Social Fund, and the whole programme is called '*Banlieues '89*' (Suburbs '89).

The financial problems of the HLM organizations remain grave, however. Falling tenancy rates reduce rent income and raise communal heating bills, and buildings financed by a 50-year loan already demand substantial rehabilitation expenditure. The National Association of HLM Organizations estimated in 1981 that 300,000 dwellings were 'in danger' and another 300,000 in a critical situation. The practice of focusing rehabilitation on those blocks where tenants will receive personal housing allowances (APL) from the State does, of course, perpetuate the concentration of the poor and of immigrants. This may alleviate the pressing financial burdens of the OHLM, but in 1981 it was estimated that the rehabilitation of a tower block flat would cost FF 100,000 per dwelling. The assessed value was only 40 per cent of this figure. Clearly, a very high level of subsidy will be needed to resolve the question.

SIX

French Agriculture: The Paradoxes of Modernization

6.1 Introduction: An uncertain future

Decades of protectionism, from 1884 to the establishment of the Common Agricultural Policy (CAP) after 1958, meant that much-needed structural reforms in French agriculture, especially the evolution from a peasant agricultural to a larger farm size, were postponed to a more competitive era. And so, in the early postwar period, French agricultural structures and degree of mechanization had much in common with the pre-1914 era. Until 1960, France was a net food importer. For a country which has the best agricultural endowment of Western Europe, with a high acreage per head, generally good quality soils and a favourable climate, with large production reserves, this was indeed a poor result.

The transformation of agriculture in the postwar years, with a rapid upsurge in production and yields, especially from 1959 to 1974, has pushed France to its position as the largest producer in the European Community (EC) and the world's second largest food exporter. From 1960 to 1980, the volume of agricultural output rose by 64 per cent (though by only 27 per cent in the 1970s) and net value-added per worker tripled in real terms. In terms of the contribution of the farm and food industry to the trade balance, the much-criticized notion that it could become a 'green petroleum' to help compensate for energy import costs is now more widely accepted. This has, of course, been achieved at considerable cost in terms of export subsidies from Brussels and Paris. This performance reflects a substantial rise in yields per hectare and per head of livestock. From 1960 to 1980, wheat yields doubled, rising at 3.6 per cent per year, and barley yields rose 3 per cent per year. Over the 1970s, milk yields per cow tested rose by 3 per cent per year (Bergmann 1983). Underlying this transformation was the familiar pattern of tractorization, increasingly heavy use of fertilisers, biological improvements in seed and livestock and a generally much greater reliance on purchased inputs to raise yields. These biological, chemical and mechanical improvements imply a more intensive agriculture, in the form of a higher value-added/hectare and certainly a higher capital intensity. If

145

machines help to substitute for labour, the income per head of the remaining workforce can rise. In general, however, French agriculture remains of much lower intensity than the Dutch, Danish or German (milk yields, for example, are only 70 per cent of the Dutch) and so retains huge production reserves.

Though the farm and food sector has been one of France's star performers, the achievement has been marked by considerable strains and the outlook remains uncertain. Not only has structural change eliminated a host of marginal farmers, the future for the modernized and capitalist farms which remain is far from secure. The golden years of French farming from 1960–75 have been succeeded by a decade of difficulties, of fluctuating harvests, of stagnant incomes and variable trade results. Optimism has evaporated with the shift to slow economic growth, structural surpluses and the associated world trade tensions, and ever tighter budgetary restrictions. The growth rates of the 1960s, which eased structural adjustments, the abundant credit and favourable world markets have all gone, and France faces a severe task in using its comparative advantages to its benefit.

These difficulties render more acute the familiar constraint in which an advanced agriculture finds itself. Market equilibrium between supply and demand becomes ever more difficult, with a marked tendency to structural surpluses, which threaten a price collapse. The origins quite simply lie in the surfeited state of consumers in the West, who react little to falls in the price of foodstuffs. Meanwhile, technical progress expands the supply of food. This inherent tendency to overproduction, with the threat of a price collapse, is the justification for agricultural policy price-support schemes, such as the CAP. In the absence of expanding export opportunities, production capacity must be cut, releasing land and labour, or a more extensive mode of production achieved. If farmers are to avoid declining incomes, then the few who remain must each produce more. As a reward for their technical progress, farmers find that, in real terms, the price of their unit output is falling, to the benefit of the consumer. This is the paradox of modernization, or of technical progress (Klatzmann, 1978), which the modernizing farmer faces.

These difficulties of adjustment are plainly apparent in the structural changes which the once typically peasant, subsistence agriculture has undergone. The competitive pressures that are exerted, as the sector is incorporated into the market economy, produce an increasing differentiation in what was seen, perhaps sentimentally, as a relatively homogeneous social group. The 'three agricultures', first identified in France in the mid-1960s, consisted of the marginal farmer condemned to disappearance, of the capitalist farmer who can profit under existing cost and price structures, and of the modernizing farmer suffering under a burden of debt.

Broadly speaking, from 1950 to 1980, the number of French holdings fell by one-half and the average size almost doubled. Taking the population census definition of the farm labour force as persons active principally in agriculture (PAA), their numbers fell from 5.1 million in 1954 to 1.9 million in 1979 (i.e. 8 per cent of the active population). This represented a fall of 3.5 per cent per year in the early years, of 5 per cent per year from 1965 to 1975, and since then of 2.5–3 per cent per year.

These structural changes in no way encapsulate all the socioeconomic changes which have occurred in the agricultural sector. In terms of the economic organization of farmers, there has been a profound shift, in mentality as much as in economic behaviour, towards co-operative and producer group forms covering all aspects from credit, supplies and technical advice through to food processing and marketing. As we have noted, on the individual farm the production revolution in its biological, chemical and mechanical aspects has led to far greater capital intensity per person and per hectare. For the small producer, as in Brittany, this offers the prospect of survival by the intensification of production on a small acreage; mechanization increases the amount of effective labour available and so permits a specialization in labour-intensive branches, such as dairying. However, events of recent years have raised obvious doubts about this path to survival. Highly sensitive to borrowing costs and to the cost inflation of yield-enhancing purchased inputs, intensive farmers are squeezed in a scissor movement against the falling real prices per unit of output. Their future is further undermined by the imperative of a cut in production capacity, which will be targeted in part to achieve a less intensive, more extensive farming sector.

The principal solution to this conundrum has been seen for the past two decades to lie in the promotion of non-farm activity or diversification by regional development measures. Local non-farm employment speeds the adjustment in agriculture and helps sustain a denser rural population. As we shall see, French rural policy has been the most advanced in Western Europe, and counterurbanization trends – the 'urban exodus' – have brought a marked influx into rural areas. However, the most buoyant conditions are found on the outer metropolitan fringes; in isolated areas and thinly populated mountain areas, the long secular trend of depopulation continues unabated.

6.2 The farming revolution

6.2.1 Regional diversity and socioeconomic disparity

French agriculture is so diverse that it can be classified in a variety of ways: by production system, by economic criteria, by land tenure, by the age of

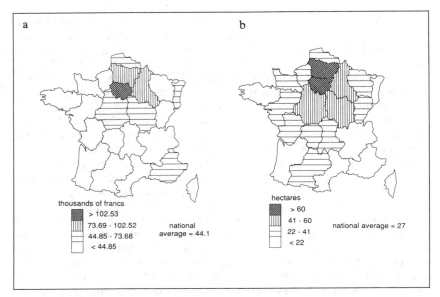

Figure 6.1   Agriculture. a, Gross farm income, 1978. b, Usable agricultural land per farm, 1985.

the farmer or by technical level. Though demographic and technical factors lend much to the degree of variation, natural conditions remain decisive. Regional specialization on the basis of natural attributes has indeed continued to grow (except in the case of factory farming) with technical progress and falling unit transport costs. The full range of natural conditions in France is evident in the designation of 425 small agricultural regions (Klatzmann, 1978). Other analysts classify France into five large regions or twenty-two administrative regions, which, though having no precise counterpart in terms of natural regions, nevertheless have statistical advantages.

Figure 6.1b shows the regional variation in farm size by farmed area. The large farm character of the Paris region and Picardy is apparent, while the small farm size typical of Brittany and Alsace (where 40 per cent of the farmed area belongs to farms of fewer than 20 ha), stands in contrast. Regions such as Rhône-Alpes and Aquitaine have somewhat larger farms but have still typically a smaller than average farm size. The Pays de la Loire and the Franche-Comté have a more medium-sized structure, while Languedoc, with its vines and extensive hill grazing, has both extremes of size.

Size of itself says little of the carrying capacity of the land according

Table 6.1   French farm size, 1955–85

Farm size	1955[1]		1970[1]		1985[2]	
	thousands	%	thousands	%	thousands	%
<1 ha	173.0	7.5	127.4	8.0	82.3	7.7
1–5 ha	648.8	28.1	328.7	20.7	180.7	17.1
5–10 ha	476.7	20.7	246.1	15.5	122.2	11.6
10–20 ha	536.0	23.2	359.7	22.6	193.2	18.3
20–35 ha	294.9	12.8	279.0	17.6	204.1	19.3
35–50 ha	82.5	3.6	115.4	7.3	113.4	10.7
50–100 ha	75.1	3.2	101.3	6.4	122.9	11.7
>100 ha	20.0	0.9	30.0	1.9	37.9	3.6
Total	2,307.0	100	1,587.6	100	1,056.9	100

[1] Usable agricultural land.
[2] Utilized agricultural land.

to climate, relief and fertility, and gives no indication of the degree of intensification practised (namely the application of labour, capital and other purchased inputs). These are encapsulated by the gross farm income per hectare or per labour unit, indicating the intensity of farm use. The notion of gross farm income reflects value-added in farming less financial charges and salaries but before profits tax and amortization of capital. Obviously, the vine, fruit and horticulture regions of the Midi and Alsace are apparent, but particularly noteworthy are the intensive farming systems of Brittany (livestock, dairying and early vegetables on small farms, together with factory farming) and of the Nord-Pas de Calais, where a high technical level in mixed farming is achieved on medium-sized farms. The great capitalist farms, specializing narrowly in wheat, maize, peas and sugar beet of the Paris region, the Centre and Picardy tend to show a median position given the relatively more extensive nature of cereal growing on large farms. Finally, the low intensity of farming in the mountainous zones (Vosges, Massif Central, Alps, Pyrénées) can only in part be detected here. On average, or smaller than average-size farms of permanent pasture, milk and cheese production, cattle and sheep-rearing are the characteristic activities.

The full breadth of income differences begins to be apparent as farm size is taken fully into account (Figure 6.1a). Average gross incomes (1978) in the rich departments of the Paris basin ranged from FF 100,000 to 170,000, while in the poorer departments incomes fell below FF 40,000 (INSEE, 1981). These divergences reflect in part the variable profitability of different branches of agriculture: per hectare, the gross income difference between sugar beet and grazing is of 3:1. Add to this the farm size difference, then the large arable farms have incomes of 780 (national average of 100) and the small, full-time, mixed farm, 43. Such a disparity between the Picardy cereal producer and the Aquitaine or Midi-Pyrénées small, mixed-farming holding would not be exaggerated. However, the richer zones are highly concentrated and the income variation (admittedly based on regional averages) is more subdued elsewhere.

Finally, we could classify farms by sociological or economic criteria. Here the high average age of farmers in the Massif Central, the South-west and South-east, together with the ratios of farms with or without a successor, conveys a sense of progress, stagnation or decline (Klatzmann, 1978). Bergmann (1982a) groups full-time farms according to the value of their output, which shows the degree of concentration of production. One-fifth of full-time farms produced 57 per cent of the total gross income of their group, while one-half produced only 13 per cent. Clearly, this overstates the degree of disparity, since in the latter group there are very many older farmers who have long ceased to invest and contract new debts, while within farm households there will also be substantial non-farm incomes. Le Roy (1986) prefers a typology based on 'economic' farming, 'social' farming and part-time farming (which is not synonymous with the popular notion of 'three agricultures'):

(1) 'Economic' farming comprises 500,000 farms which generate two-thirds of total production. Of these farmers more than one-half are of maturer years and have paid off their debts; the remainder fall into equal-sized classes of the 'rich', the 'newly installed' (and heavily indebted), and the factory farmers and producers under contract.

(2) The 'social' farming group, which accounts for 15 per cent of production, includes 400,000 farmers; one-half are pensioners and one-half are poor, aged over 50 years (in 1979) and with a holding of 10–15 ha in size.

(3) The part-time farmers number 300,000 and account for 20 per cent of production.

Kayser (1986) distinguishes between the large farmers, the medium modernizers and the marginal farmers. The large ones represent 5 per cent of the total, while there remain 207,000 full-time marginal farmers. The medium modernizers make up 51 per cent of all farms of over 5 ha (43 per cent of full-time farmers) and account for 54 per cent of income of the sector as a whole. A growing number of these feel deceived by modernization, although they do not contest the principle of productivity itself. They feel, however, in no sense remunerated for the costs they have borne.

6.2.2 The transformation of the farm sector and the problem of the modernizing farmer

In the struggle for higher incomes, the one-time self-sufficient peasant farmers have pursued a path of higher intensity, higher input, higher yield agriculture, which by its very nature renders them dependent on urban markets, on the Crédit Agricole bank, and on agribusiness firms as supplier and sometimes as customer. In seeking incomes comparable to those of the urban dweller, the farmer is also subjected to the competitive forces and risks of the market economy. As a small, autonomous producer, however, the farmer requires a strong producer organization to withstand the power of the highly concentrated agribusiness and retailing groups.

As we have noted, the transformation of French farming is based on technical, structural and organizational changes. The former leads to a growing capital intensity and to a sharp rise in the volume of purchased inputs. The number of tractors expanded from 30,000 machines pre-1939 to 1 million in 1964 and to 1.5 million in 1983 (Bergmann, 1983). The use of fertilizers quadrupled from the prewar years to 1962–5, and has since doubled. The volume of current purchased inputs (e.g. fuel, fertilizers, herbicides, seeds, animal feed) rose by 7.2 per cent per year from 1960 to 1973, and by roughly one-half of that from 1974 to 1980. Presently, purchased inputs represent about 37 per cent of the gross value of production. Yield-enhancing inputs and labour-substituting machinery raise land and labour productivity enormously, but they clearly render incomes highly sensitive to output volume and price, as well as to input costs. To achieve this expansion, farmers have become very heavily indebted. Bergmann (1982a) notes that the accumulated debts of French farmers amounted to twice their gross annual income. Though these borrowings are generally contracted at preferential interest rates from the Crédit Agricole, younger, modernizing farmers have faced crippling repayments in the recent years of abnormally high real interest rates.

To accommodate the rise in output and especially to bolster the power of the suppliers (i.e. the farmer) in relation to traders and processing and retailing groups, markets, wholesaling and producer-owned processing have been transformed out of recognition since the early 1960s. Over the last 25 years the obsolescent capacity and supply chains of the meat sector have been completely replaced, eradicating the multitude of middle-men and price rings. Similarly, in the fruit and vegetable sectors, *marchés d'intérêt national*, introduced in the early 1960s, have produced a price transparency and an access to markets for producers, which has had the desired effect of strengthening the suppliers' negotiating power. Co-operatives have a preferential position here. In dairying, 50 per cent of the volume processed and marketed is conducted through the channels of producer groups and co-operatives; in cereals, the proportion reaches 70 per cent and in table wines, 55 per cent.

The surest way of raising farm incomes per head is through labour migration from agriculture, and indeed, this 'structural' effect has been by far the dominant factor in the rise of farm incomes (Henry, 1981). The effect is in part purely one of larger shares for those remaining, but the greater acreage per farm which an improved farmer:land ratio implies, enables scale economies to be reaped in the optimal use of equipment, and a spreading of fixed overhead costs. Unit production costs are thereby reduced. We have considered the so-called 'rural exodus', which is often a misnomer since it reflects the age pyramid of owner-farmers, and the decision by the young not to enter farming as an occupation. Cases of owner-farmers abandoning farming for an alternative occupation are relatively few. As a direct result then of the contraction of the farm labour force, labour productivity grew annually at 5.3 per cent during the period 1958–80, and had a strongly favourable impact on farm incomes. The contraction has also brought land consolidation, with the dissolution of small farms and the transfer of land to expand the medium-sized farms. Since 1970, growth has been in the 50–200 ha groups (Table 6.1). Clearly, the growth has been in the family-farm sizes, and not in the 'capitalist' sizes, as some had feared: this is reflected in the steady fall in the proportion of farm labourers in the total farm workforce (Bergmann, 1983).

Looking to the future, the age structure of French farmers and the absence of inheritors in many small farms will lead inexorably to a release of land for farm consolidation. The 1980 census revealed that 40 per cent of male farmers were aged 55–75 years. Hence by the year 2000, there will have been a considerable structural change, leading to a farm capacity of 640,000 units or double the present size. There is some doubt as to whether all the land released will be consolidated to produce larger farms. Abandonment is becoming a problem, not just in less fertile areas, but also in the Paris basin. Much depends on the market outlook, farm income expectations and non-farm opportunities for the farmers and uses for the land itself.

Farm size is, however, an unsatisfactory proxy for income, and we have seen that income inequalities within the farm sector are wide, and certainly wider than within other occupational groups. The stagnation of farm incomes after 1974 resulted, at first, from poor harvests and, subsequently, from adverse market conditions and tighter Brussels price policies. This has hit most severely that substantial section of full-time farmers made up of younger farmers on transitional holdings, seeking to achieve a viable scale. We know, for example, that one-half of full-time holdings receive only 13 per cent of gross income (Bergmann, 1982a, 1983), but the breakdown of this group by socioeconomic status can only be estimated. Adverse conditions since the first oil crisis have intensified the struggle of the modernizing farmers to establish the economic viability of their holdings. As we have implied, intensification on a too-small holding leads to a suboptimal use of machinery, and exposes the producer more cruelly to the scissor movement of rising costs and falling unit prices. The margin of economic viability has therefore been rising and will continue to do so as the European Community grapples with the problem of overproduction.

The difficulties have been exacerbated by the practices of co-operatives, feed firms and public authorities alike since the mid-1970s. The co-operatives have come to favour the larger producer by demanding minimum quantity and quality conditions of their members, while the public authorities, with their policy of making loans and grants for farm modernization schemes, have concentrated assistance ever more strictly on farms exceeding the specified 'minimum farm size' (SMI). Finally, food-processing firms, which have contractual supply arrangements with farmers of a subregion, specify not only the deliveries but also the level of production costs to be attained, which naturally reflect those of the efficient farmer. Areas thus specialize in a certain type of production in order to supply the processor and the successful farmer becomes integrated into these new market relations.

Many discontented farmers turned to MODEF, the farmers' defence organization or, in Brittany, to the Regional Federation of Farmers' Unions (FRSEAD), which represented the modernizing sector. Allaire and Blanc (1982) point out that the 'third agriculture' does not comprise simply older farmers with no inheritor; in the years 1970–4 more than 60 per cent of new owner-farmers took over farms of less than 20 ha in size. In particular, they are concentrated in the hill and mountain areas where alternative local employment opportunities are rare.

The Socialist Party in opposition came to adopt a farm policy favouring redistribution towards the small, poor farmer. The latter was seen to be 'acapitalist' and not incorporated into the market economy. The prevailing model of development through intensification was dubbed 'productivist', which one might take to mean a high input–high output pattern of production pursued on modernized farms, dependent on state aid for their success (Allaire and Blanc, 1982). The first Socialist Minister of Agriculture, Edith Cresson, called in 1982 for a more self-sufficient, thrifty agriculture, which would generate employment in backward areas. One should, however, point out that the policy, had it not been curtailed, might have condemned newly installed farmers to a life with few prospects. The 'productivist' critique seems to miss the mark. For it is readily apparent, and will be seen to be so in the case of Brittany, that intensification is often pursued on small farms beyond a point that can be justified on efficiency grounds. The unpalatable conclusion is that only a larger farm, possibly farmed at a lower intensity per hectare, will generate satisfactory incomes.

6.3   French agricultural policy and the CAP

Having long protected their agriculture from foreign competition, French governments in the postwar period had to face up to the problems that arose as farmers embraced the possibilities of technical progress. The incorporation of the sector into the market economy exposed agriculture to new hazards – the rampant inflation of the postwar years and the fluctuations in farm product prices which were experienced with greater acuity as French farmers produced surpluses above French needs. Price policies and market organizations were established in the 1950s, and from 1960 innovatory structural policies were introduced to speed up the move towards greater efficiency.

Price policy and structural policy were later to become the two-pronged approach of the European Community's Common Agricultural Policy (CAP), a policy modelled closely on French practice and which reflected France's fundamental national interest in pursuing its agricultural comparative advantage in a Europe opened to West German industrial strength. Surprisingly, French agricultural representatives realized rather late their favourable position at that time under the CAP, and the period 1968–73 proved to be a golden one of high common prices and expanding export markets within Europe. The late 1970s were marked by poor harvests, stagnant incomes, battles over the EC organizations for specific products and, finally, by the threat of bankruptcy as the surpluses turned into mountains and lakes. The dissatisfaction of French farmers with the CAP became shrill, which is sign enough that the supposed benefits it confers on France have failed to materialize.

6.3.1   *French price support and structural policies*

The prototype for intervention agencies to buy in and store farm produce in the attempt to make prices firmer was that of the ONIC (National Office for Cereals) for cereals, set up by the Popular Front in 1936. Legislation in 1953 extended this form of market organization to all cereals, beef, milk, wine and sugar. To finance intervention and storage, a market organization fund, the FORMA, was established. These agencies were interprofessional in character, bringing together the farmers' representatives and the major buying groups. Surpluses of wine and milk were, however, emerging by the mid-1950s. Against the background of high inflation, there were widespread demonstrations clamouring for agricultural price indexation on the basis of farm input prices and the retail price index. The farm lobby's success here was brief, for the 1957 *Lalorbe Law*, which instituted price indexation, was abolished by the first agriculture minister of the Fifth Republic, Debré, in December 1958. The new government's emphasis was on technical assistance and structural change to achieve efficiency gains, and this approach governed the *Loi d'orientation agricole* of 1960, which heralded a new era of innovatory structural policy (Neville-Rolfe, 1984). Delays in the implementation of the 1960 legislation gave the young farmers' organization, the CNJA (see p. 5), their opportunity, and the occupation of the Morlaix subprefecture in 1961 brought the issue to a head. The 'Pisani' reforms, in the 1962 supplementary law, reflected the current of thinking of the CNJA. The organization sought to remedy land tenure difficulties and to embrace co-operative forms of production and marketing so as to give its members a countervailing producer power to that of the agribusiness groups and wholesalers. The CNJA saw these forms of economic organization as a 'third way' between capitalism and socialism. The new structural policy comprised:

(1) The creation of publicly financed, regionally-based bodies (SAFERs), which would intervene in the land market, using a pre-emption right, to acquire land for consolidation to create larger holdings. It was intended that SAFERs could intervene to dampen price speculation and so bring price levels closer to the productive value of the land. SAFERs would also intervene in land consolidation operations, where parcels of land were being regrouped.

(2) The creation of the development and welfare fund (FASASA) to provide retirement annuities to farmers of 65 years and more (later reduced to 60 years), with the grant linked where possible to the release of land to a SAFER. For family members and inheritors on marginal farms below the minimum size (SMI), retraining grants were made available.

(3) The communal farm group (GAEC) formula was created for the direct amalgamation of small farms into a larger producer group.

(4) Provisions for the creation of producer groups, especially the *société d'intérêt commun agricole* (SICA). To strengthen the market power of small producers, and to ward off the threat of their vertical integration into agribusiness firms, the SICA formula allowed the financial association of producer groups with co-operatives or private firms for the marketing of specific products. Under forward contracts, a supply of uniform quality would be agreed. This policy was supplemented by the 1964 *Loi d'économie contractuelle*, which sought to establish standard contracts between the interprofessional partners.

(5) Social insurance, particularly against illness, was instituted under a special regime for farmers.
(6) National and regional markets for meat, vegetables, etc. were to be established. These would rationalize the existing chaotic and obsolescent system, under which producers had little bargaining power. Their position was to be strengthened by the building of storage facilities which would enable them to hold produce off the market.

Finally, this array of legislation and policy instruments was complemented in 1973 by the introduction of an enterprise grant for young farmers, the *dotation d'installation aux jeunes agriculteurs* (DJA). This was designed to give financial assistance to young people entering farming in mountainous regions (later extended to a national coverage).

It was implicit in such a policy that marginal farms would disappear over time to further the enlargement of medium-sized farms. However, this reality was shrouded by the modernist euphoria which induced many small farmers to assume heavy debt burdens. Many small farmers whose farms were below the minimum size were excluded from cheap Crédit Agricole loans and from public grants; this made them bitterly aware of the constraints of small size. More immediately, widespread bankruptcies among Breton poultry and pork producer groups in the overproduction crisis of the mid-1960s brought home the fragility of many of these modernising endeavours. The extistence of the 'three agricultures' could not be ignored.

It would seem that these pioneering structural measures have been less effective than was hoped, partly for financial reasons, partly because they were 'commandeered' by the small-to-medium family-farm sector to ease their transition. Thus the retirement annuity (*indemnité viagère de départ-IVD*), which rose to 80,500 cases in 1969 before falling to 16,000 in 1977. This was used primarily to facilitate generation change on the family farm – the effects on land release were much smaller. Similarly, the GAEC provisions were proved disappointing, leading to the creation of a possible 109,000 groups by 1977. Of these, 84 per cent are family groupings, comprising primarily father and son, thereby easing the transmission of the inheritance, but having little to do with the intended merger of farms. The SAFER acquisitions have covered a steady 26 per cent of the land area offered annually for sale. Only 16 per cent of the land so acquired was bought under the pre-emption right. Although one-in-ten farmers may have benefited from land consolidation and new farm creations, generally the SAFERs' activities have not raised the farms in question to the level of viability (Chombart de Lauwe, 1979).

6.3.2 *France and the establishment of the CAP*

At French insistence, the Treaty of Rome's clauses concerning agricultural policy were specific and binding, such that a CAP would be formulated to further France's comparative advantage, and thereby act as a counterweight to West Germany's industrial strength. The decisions taken in 1962 embodied generally the high protection and market intervention principles of French prices policy; the degree of external protection and of price guarantees varied quite widely by product, however, French cereal producers would benefit from an unlimited price guarantee no matter how much they produced (unlike the previous French 'quantum' system) and the expectation was that the finally negotiated intervention price level would be significantly higher than the French level. The sugar beet producers would gain from higher prices and higher production quotas. In addition to common prices, the other fundamental principles on which France insisted – EC preference (so it could supply the Common Market) and financial solidarity (with a common fund, the EAGGF (European Agricultural Guidance and Guarantee Fund), to meet the support and administration costs) were achieved. After the six-month long 'empty chair' policy practised by France in 1965, concerning principally the 'Luxembourg compromise' question, the common financing was agreed, although as a *quid pro quo* common cereal prices were fixed nearer to the high West German levels. The financial arrangements came into force in 1971 and so price policy and many budgetary decisions came to be settled in Brussels.

It is interesting that the French dairy, cereal and beet farmers and their representatives failed at first to see the generosity of these arrangements. They viewed the negotiations cautiously, fearful that their decades-long protection would be at an end (Neville-Rolfe, 1984). The years 1968–73 witnessed unparalleled income growth and export sales, but in 1969, only one year after the completion of the Common Market, two events were to signal major future difficulties. The Mansholt Memorandum on the reform of EC agriculture pointed to the rise in self-sufficiency in foodstuffs and the signs of structural surpluses in milk, sugar and wheat. The spiralling budgetary costs could not be contained. This analysis was familiar; the huge production reserves in agriculture, the high guaranteed prices and the distorted hierarchy of prices (which favoured the cereal grower, the beet farmer and the milk producer), were all inducements to produce, which made the policy unsustainable. The prescription was drastic: a sharp cut in price levels (especially of products in surplus, so as to modify the relative prices between products in surplus and in deficit) and a sizeable cut in production capacity, eliminating marginal farms and withdrawing from production an area the size of Benelux. The French response, in the form of

the Vedel Commission report of 1969, was no more sanguine: it recommended the withdrawal from production of more than 8 million ha, a
reduction of the full-time farm labour force to 700,000 by 1985. Though
this was received with shock and bitterness, the evolution has in fact
followed this path, with 800,000 full-time farm workers in 1980 and a total
force in standard labour units of 1.5 million in 1985.

The currency turbulence of 1969, during which the French franc and the
Deutschmark were devalued and revalued respectively, ushered in the
system of 'green' currencies and monetary compensatory amounts (MCAs)
which has proved so damaging to the unity of the agricultural market. Since
1969 the existence of a single European farm price has been rare, and so
there has been no truly unified market. Currency changes have repeatedly
disrupted the agricultural market and governments have resisted the
consequences: a devaluation raises farm prices in domestic currency; a
revaluation reduces them. The first is inflationary, but a windfall gain for
farmers; the second, in reverse, cuts farm incomes. And so to avoid this,
'green' currencies were substituted for the commercial exchange rates, with
the result that a wedge was driven between the domestic farm price and the
price in international trade. At the borders, taxes and subsidies (MCAs) had
to bridge the gap. The crucial point is this: the lack of a common price level
means that the competitive countries can no longer penetrate other markets
successfully, and so France could not pursue its comparative advantage in
agriculture. France's sore grievance was that the 'positive' MCAs assist
strong currency countries such as West Germany, because they sustain a
very high domestic price level there, while imposing a tax on cheaper
(French) exports to West Germany. Meanwhile, high-priced West German
farm exports are subsidized to help them sell elsewhere in the Community.

It will be of no surprise that the system of MCAs has been profoundly
disruptive in the intervening years. While West German output has flourished and West Germany has developed a powerful agricultural export
industry (flouting the principle of comparative advantage), France has
simply held its European share, failing to capitalize on its agricultural
vocation. The West Germans and the Dutch have increased the intensity of
their livestock production manyfold, capturing parts of the French market,
while France's share in total EC red meat and dairy production has fallen
sharply (1962–77). Its share of vegetable production has likewise fallen.
The comparable figures for 1970–9 do, however, tell a more subtle story (Le
Roy, 1982). What Mahé and Roudet (1980) are voicing here is, in the first
instance, a criticism of the price hierarchy (or relative prices) in the EC. By
agreeing to a high cereals price, France has compromised its livestock
sector, which is dependent on cereals feed. The availability of very cheap
imported feeds, especially soya and corn gluten, which attract no import

duty, has favoured the intensive Dutch and West German livestock farms. The fact that they can flourish and export under the MCA system compounds the distortions.

At the national ministerial level, the 1970s saw a greater consensus developing over agricultural policy, in particular as a thoroughgoing corporatism came to be practised with the FNSEA acting as equal partner in decision-making. However, a succession of violent demonstrations kept the position of the livestock, pork, wine, sheep and fruit and vegetable producers in the public eye, all aggrieved at their less favourable CAP market organizations. Oversupply and its effects on prices, together with the currency distortions, threatened the livelihoods of these small producers. In brief, the disputes concerned:

(1) The small, poor livestock farmers, aggrieved at the high cereal feed prices which benefited the rich Paris basin producers, clamoured for a substantial rise in support prices for beef and milk, and for permanent intervention buying which would guarantee them a regular income. In 1973–4, Jacques Chirac earned himself the gratitude of the livestock farmers as he achieved these demands in Brussels and set up the interprofessional office for beef, ONIBEV. In addition he conceded direct subsidies to livestock farmers to cover the inflation in costs of purchased inputs from 1973.

(2) The pig farmers in Brittany, in the Corrèze and Touraine demonstrated in 1974 and again in 1979 and 1984. In part they were mollified by the livestock subsidies, but the problems of their branch relate to its strongly cyclical nature, the increase in factory-farming methods, and the MCA problem, which has left France open to subsidized imports from strong currency countries such as The Netherlands, West Germany and, at times, Belgium.

(3) The wine-growers of the South-west and Languedoc producing table wines have never hesitated to seek redress in times of glut or of cheap imports. Throughout this century in years of overproduction their livelihoods have been threatened, and more recently the threat of imports has been perceived to come from Italy, rather than Algeria. A large devaluation of the lira and the ending of MCAs on wine brought surplus Italian wine flooding into France. An illegal levy of 12 per cent was imposed in 1975 on Italian wine, sparking off the 'wine war'. The settlement of this in 1976 provided for more distillation of the surplus at public cost to the Community, and for the establishment, in France, of an interprofessional office for wine, ONIVIT. These measures have proved quite insufficient, as France has felt itself more recently forced to adopt a protectionist stance.

The distillation provisions were further reinforced in 1983 (Neville-Rolfe, 1984).

(4) The sheep-rearers of the Massif Central have long depended for their very existence on government subsidies channelled through their producer organizations and on strong import controls. To prevent cheaper British lamb from disrupting the home market, the French goverment, notably in the years 1978–80, defied the European Court by forbidding entry until a common sheepmeat regime had been instituted. As we shall see, this regime has done little to resolve the difficulties.

6.3.3   *Recent French policy under alternating governments*

Presidents Pompidou and Giscard both courted the farm vote and were never sparing in their praise of the family farm. It was not forgotten that agricultural policy was the jewel of the Fifth Republic. A veil was drawn over Debré's earlier assault on the farming establishment, as the FNSEA became closely incorporated into the decision-making machinery. Doubts came to be raised, however, over Giscard's approach, which embraced the farm and food sector as a totality; this raised the question of whether his economic liberalism would be applied to the farm sector, implying greater competition and a streamlining of supply links to the agribusiness consortia. The 1975 *Loi sur l'interprofession* sought to 'harmonize' relations between the agribusiness groups and the family farmer. In response to the second oil crisis of 1979, President Giscard coined the phrase 'green petroleum' to indicate French agriculture's vocation as a major contributor to the balance of payments. At the 1980 Annual Congress of the Agricultural Chambers of Commerce, Giscard spoke of the future for French agriculture as a 'world challenger, and strong exporter'.

The 1980 *Loi d'orientation agricole* reflected these economic and political imperatives. Presented as a charter for agriculture for the last two decades of the century, its impact bore no comparison with its 1960 and 1962 predecessors – in fact it was quickly replaced by Socialist legislation. Much was devoted to a tidying up of legislation, while the two new directives concerned the land market and the organization of the farm and food industry. The balance of payments contribution of the industry was to be strengthened by the expansion of a national marketing organization, and by easier export credit facilities. The land market proposals were too radical, confronting the attachment of the French to land rights. The original proposal sought to establish an agricultural land group (GFA) on family farms, in which inheritors would hold shares on which they would receive dividends. This was designed to replace the practice of payment for buying them out to co-inheritors by a newly installed farmer already burdened by these debts. Finally, the grants to encourage well-trained young people to enter farming were greatly increased (Le Roy, 1986).

The incoming Socialist government wished to implement its egalitarian, anti-'productivist' values in the agricultural sector, and to ensure that the sector made its contribution to a reduction in unemployment. The eradication of the notion of the 'third agriculture' was essential if the ideological current was to be reversed. Policies on incomes, social payments, marketing and advisory services were designed to help the survival of the smaller farmers (and by implication to reduce the competitive advantages and financial assistance given to larger ones). A symbol of this change was the abandonment of corporatism. The goverment distanced itself from the FNSEA, and welcomed the radical unions representing small farmers. Other than the overhaul of advisory services, there were three key objectives: the setting up of government agencies to act as marketing boards, the payment of solidarity assistance to poorer farmers, and the establishment of the Land Commission (*Le Monde*, 11 December 1982).

Agencies were to be established as marketing boards for each major product and came to replace the FORMA. They would channel all off-farm sales and would conduct the major marketing tasks, raise product quality and invest in processing, all in addition to their role as CAP intervention agencies. Here we see the idea of the network applied by product, having the effect of strengthening control over the domestic market. All farmers' trade unions, together with consumers and food industry employees, would be represented on these agencies, which was interpreted as a direct attack on the FNSEA's once dominant position in the producer organizations (Debatisse, 1986). Of key significance was the proposal that these agencies would redress income disequilibria in farming by reintroducing the old quantum system. Small producers would earn the high fixed prices, but large producers would face a sliding scale of prices according to quantity.

This quantum policy clearly conflicted with CAP provisions, as did other forms of assistance. In 1981 and 1982 the EC Commission ruled as incompatible with the Treaty a number of aids to livestock producers, as well as the 'solidarity assistance', which, though designed for the poorer, would have benefited 65 per cent of French farmers (Neville-Rolfe, 1984). Finally, the 'Office Foncier' proposal suffered the rapid fate of many of its predecessors, when challenging French attitudes to fixed property. It aspired to a nationalization of agricultural land, which would then be rented to farmers (Debatisse, 1986). Such proposals have a respectable progeniture but none has made progress. In practice, many of the proposals were defeated by the FNSEA, which succeeded in having Edith Cresson replaced as Minister by Rocard, hence signifying an end to this agenda.

6.3.4   *The reform of the CAP*

France has not benefited fully from the CAP, and indeed this has been a source of exasperation since 1973. The distortions of the price structure, favouring cereals over livestock, the free entry of cheap imported feedstuffs and the effects of the MCAs were the focus of criticism. It is, then, interesting to examine how French commentators and politicians hope to square the circle of pursuing an expansion of French agriculture on the basis of its comparative advantage within an overall policy framework increasingly marked by budgetary and output restraint. The abolition of positive MCAs and the imposition of a tax on imported oils, fats and feed command general agreement in France. The imposition of production quotas is seen as a direct threat, preventing French regions from closing the productivity gap. The differences seem to arise over price policy and its consequences. Bergmann (1982b) calls for a policy along the lines of the Mansholt Memorandum and Vedel Commission report: a substantial fall in the cereals price could still be borne by French cereals producers who would take up the export shares of less favoured EC producers. Cheaper cereals would benefit the livestock sector and assist dairy exports, but in many cases, particularly that of hill-farmers, more extensive systems of rearing would be needed. The structural changes which would ensue would only continue the trends of the 1970s. In contrast, Debatisse (1986), Minister of Agriculture in 1979–80 and always close to the FNSEA, favours a move to a two-stage pricing system. High guaranteed prices, sufficient to sustain the average farmer, would be paid for the quantities needed to supply the 'organized market', i.e. the Community, 'traditional' export markets and food aid, while on the 'free' world market, export prices would be those of that market.

The strategy of the French government in negotiations on reforms has been clear: to pursue price and production restraint at a European level, without damage to the basis of the CAP, while fostering French interests as an exporter. It is difficult to see in every case how the government, boxed-in, has pursued those objectives. Since the establishment of the European Monetary System (EMS), it has constantly sought to abolish positive MCAs and its long championing of an oils, fats and imported feed tax is understandable. These require, however, careful negotiation with the West German government, if the fundamental principles of the Community budget are not to be put at risk. The acceptance in 1982 by Edith Cresson of the principle of production thresholds for milk and cereals, followed by the decisions on milk quotas during the French presidency of the EC Council in 1984, however, attracted the full criticism of the farming community. With quotas, it is difficult to see how the advantaged French regions can expand at the expense of less fortunate EC regions. Meawhile, the Socialists' 'social' reorientation of policy achieved little and raised the spectre of a renationalization of agricultural policy under a plethora of social assistance programmes. The accession of Spain and Portugal to the Community remains a most daunting challenge to French wine, fruit and vegetables and olive oil producers. This explained Giscard's long-held opposition to their EC entry and the policy of Integrated Mediterranean programmes (IMP) was to some extent a sop to aggrieved French Mediterranean farmers. The French response has been to shift to higher quality output, which may have given them a temporary advantage for a few years.

6.4 Regional evolution

We have previously described the regional pattern in 1978 of gross farm income (p. 148). Looking at the regional evolution over the 1960s and 1970s, it is apparent that regional farm income disparities have widened slightly (using a standard measure of dispersion) and that, broadly speaking, the ranking of regions remains the same. Whether we compare gross income per farm from 1962 to 1978 or gross value-added per worker from 1968–9 to 1976–7, this conclusion holds, though in the latter case, the farm year 1976–7 would still reflect some of the effects of the drought, especially on the dairy sector.

There is then a certain rigidity in the picture of regional farm incomes, although individual regions have made some notable advances. The favoured cereal-growing regions of the Paris basin continue to show a value-added per head of twice the national average. The Champagne region though, has made great strides (cereal-growing using high fertiliser inputs, as well as in the wine industry). The horticultural and viticultural regions of Languedoc and Provence (PACA) continue to occupy a median position, joined now by Alsace, which has shown rapid improvements in its wine industry. Of the mixed farming/rearing regions, Brittany, with its higher-intensity model of farming, has moved close to the national average, while other polyculture/dairying regions of the West seem perhaps to have suffered from the drought conditions, or from milk overproduction (Poitou-Charentes). The traditionally poorer regions of the Massif Central, Franche-Comté (milk/beef) and the South-west and Rhône-Alpes (mixed farming/rearing) all remain low income regions (Henry, 1981).

This growth in value-added per head, and its regional variation, reflects a wide range of factors. The principal proximate causes are reductions in the labour force, and the scope for intensification of production (itself reflecting technical advances, input prices, demand, agricultural policy and regional comparative cost advantages). It is readily apparent that the geographical pattern of production and incomes will reflect transport costs, natural conditions and farm size. Their impact on production costs needs no elaboration. There are two further points to emphasize though. First, the better (worse) the natural conditions, the greater (fewer) the possibilities of switching to more profitable production systems. Second, size is in no sense a rigid constraint on income. Small farmers will tend to opt for labour-intensive production (with lower hourly incomes); large farmers will tend to adopt mechanized operations in more extensive cropping systems, which give higher labour incomes.

In making this static picture dynamic, the interrelationships become more complex. As dynamic factors, we can introduce technical change and associated changes in comparative costs leading to changing regional specializations. In general, technical change in conditions of self-sufficiency will lead to greater output and falling prices. Except in the cases of transport improvements, the introduction of more tolerant crops and irrigation/drainage (which promote new regional specializations), for example, technical change tends particularly to enhance the productive potential of more fertile regions (Badouin, 1979). Under the impact of technical change and falling real prices, the economic threshold of farm size rises, as does the threshold of economic production (meaning that more land becomes submarginal and should be found an alternative use). If an equilibrium between supply and demand is to be re-established, land and labour must be taken out of production to cut capacity (since the intensity of farming is price insensitive). It is here that the factor of agricultural policy impinges most strongly. A policy of high price guarantees, as practised under the CAP, will sustain the submarginal producer in relative poverty and give windfall gains to the large producer on favourable soils. Changes in that policy, which give direct aid to the submarginal farmer, must shift the burden of adjustment to the more efficient farmer (Weinschenk and Kemper, 1981). Hence under contemporary conditions, factors which facilitate the adjustment of size and production capacity are to be promoted: they lie in the external environment and in particular in non-farm employment opportunities. However, let us turn first to the regional impact of the CAP.

As previously remarked, the high producer prices and surpluses tolerated under the CAP have moderated the effects of competition in an oversupplied market. Inequalities are greater because an excess of marginal farms exists alongside large farms benefiting from windfall gains. As price guarantee payments are made according to volume of production, so the large farms of the northern regions benefit, while the extensive farming of more mountainous regions receives little market support. The level of farm incomes per head reflects quite closely the degree of EAGGF guarantee expenditure. In addition to the size of operations, however, the type of product is important: it is well known that CAP support varies very significantly according to product, with the 'northern' products of milk, sugar beet and wheat gaining the lion's share, and the more 'southern' products of fruit, vegetables, wine and sheepmeat gaining far less. The consequences for regional incomes are clear. Heavy milk support has contributed to the growth of Breton incomes; the shift towards cereals in the Paris basin, albeit a shift to a more extensive system, reflects the attraction of high cereal prices for those with a corresponding natural advantage and little surplus labour. In upland farms, the move to rearing on home-grown fodder reflects their weak competitive position as well as their principal natural attribute. The difficulties of the Languedoc wine-grower reflect the difficulties of this sector within the CAP, though more dynamic (and higher quality) viticultural and horticultural regions (Provence, Alsace, Champagne) have scarcely suffered from this disadvantage.

Within the farm sector proper, the level of regional demand, proximity to ports for imported feed (pork, poultry, eggs) and the competitive performance of regional supply, processing and marketing channels (fruit, vegetables, milk) are of considerable importance. More generally, though, it is the regional economic environment which has a major impact on farm incomes – transport and communications infrastructures, the level of technical services and, especially, the scale of non-farm employment opportunities, which will speed the release of labour from farming. It is of no surprise that regions of favourable economic environment have, on the whole, a high-income farm sector (Henry, 1981). Buoyant economic conditions foster structural change which enables a region to take advantage of CAP price levels and guarantees.

Having looked then at the regional evolution within the national framework and at the underlying forces for differentiation, we turn to two contrasting regional studies, of Brittany, and of zones of poorer natural conditions.

6.4.1 *The Breton model and its difficulties*

Technical progress under conditions of stagnant demand leads to the thwarting of farmers' income expectations, while condemning them to the modernization route; this is amply seen in the Breton case. In spite of the dynamism of Breton agriculture since 1950, the much-vaunted Breton model of agricultural development has produced such strains and disappointments that peasant demonstrations have occurred frequently. The pig rearers siege of the subprefecture of Brest in 1984 echoes the siege of Morlaix during the 'artichoke war' of 1961. Added to these have been the pig rearers' battles of 1974, and the milk producers' strikes of 1964 and

1972. Violent political demonstrations can produce temporary benefits, but they do little to change the underlying severity of the constraints. In the race to modernize, the 'progressive' small farmer faces the severest financial difficulties, while the threshold of economic viability rises inexorably to condemn increasing numbers to the category of the marginal farm. The pressures for structural adjustment have been inexorable. During the years 1954 to 1984, the active farming population has fallen by two-thirds, but Brittany still has the densest farm population, at two to three times the national average, and an average farm size three-quarters that of the national average.

From the early 1950s, Breton farmers showed a great willingness to innovate and modernize, to embrace the CNJA creed of group agriculture and to accept the co-operative model of organization from the supply stage through to food processing and marketing. Without any doubt, co-operative producer organizations have reached their highest level of development in Brittany. The strong, Catholic JAC campaigned tirelessly for this 'third path', which lent itself to a heavily overpopulated agricultural region, where small producers had little market strength. And finally, men of the region such as Gourvennec and Leclerc championed the cause of the producer organization, as an alternative to domination by large agribusiness interests.

As early as 1952, the first group ventures were set up in the guise of technical advice groups (CETA). From their direct experience of the 'artichoke war', and led by Gourvennec, the growers of early vegetables in north Finistère set up the first of the multi-purpose co-operatives, the SICA of Saint Pol de Léon, in 1961. Through the siege of the Morlaix sub-prefecture in 1961, the north Finistère producers pressured the goverment into applying the 1960 *loi d'orientation agricole* and so secured the future of their co-operative which, from 1964, came to be the exclusive representative of the local vegetable producers. Two forms of producer grouping introduced by the 1960 law – the machinery-sharing group (CUMA) and the farm amalgamation group – were taken up most enthusiastically in Brittany in the 1960s. Membership of co-operative groups became the densest, covering all vegetable producers, three-quarters of poultry farmers and one-half of pig farmers (Canavet, 1976). The auction, where bidding takes place for the whole of the supply (and which can be held back in totality in the case of a low price level), has become standard. The SICA of Saint Pol, one of the three largest French co-operatives, all of which are Breton, has accomplished much. In addition to its expected role, it has established an economic council covering all producer groups in north Finistère. To foster regional development, it set up a research and pressure group, the SEMEN-F, in 1963, which has pushed through the development of the deep-water port at Roscoff and campaigned for modernized telephone and expressway networks.

For the overpopulated, small farming areas typical of much of Brittany, the option of a greater labour and capital intensity offers the only medium-term means of achieving higher incomes, given the poor farmer:land ratio. Breton farming has evolved from largely autonomous, subsistence polyculture and rearing to production for the market, specializing more narrowly in one or two branches of intensive farming, for example Léon spring vegetable producers. On the livestock side, the move towards intensive poultry rearing after 1955 was followed in the 1960s by pig rearing and in the 1970s by veal and bullock rearing. To help meet the animal feed needs and to sustain a great expansion of milk production, two fodder revolutions succeeded each other: first, rye grass grown on temporary pasture and, subsequently, maize growing for silage.

The intensity of Breton agriculture is apparent from its share of national output and its regional specialization. The value of output per hectare is well over twice that of the French average, and during the 1970s grew faster than any other European region. The structure of Breton output by value is overwhelmingly based on animal products, with only 6 per cent coming from early vegetables. Well over one-half comes from milk and pork equally, and 15 per cent from poultry. Breton farmers produced 20 per cent of national milk output, 45 per cent of pork, and 35 per cent of eggs (INSEE, 1981). Brittany had by far the greatest regional rise in milk output – 82 per cent during the period 1971–83. In pig rearing, especially, but also in poultry and egg production, Brittany has secured a pronounced regional lead: however, this has involved a marked concentration among producers, involving the elimination of the smaller holding. This intensification reflects, to an extent, the regional comparative advantages of intensive fodder growing and labour availability; however, these no longer exert such a powerful effect, given the availability of bought-in feed, and the rapid industrialization of these branches on factory-farming lines.

We come then to the strains in this Breton model of development whereby the small farmer produces along intensive lines. Only to a lesser extent do these difficulties originate in Brussels; more importantly, they concern the strains of structural adjustment and the erosion of the region's comparative advantage. The social differentiation among farmers has increased and there can be little doubt that the philosophy of co-operative forms of organization in agriculture has been unable to save the uneconomic holding. By discriminating against the small producers, co-operatives attract the criticism that they operate like any private firm. Disenchantment began in 1965 with the bankruptcy of small pig and poultry producer groups when overproduction appeared. This was the spur to the creation in

1966 of a regional federation of farmers' unions, the FRSEAO, which also voiced Breton grievances against the distorted CAP price structure and the absence of price regionalization to compensate for Brittany's peripheral position. The FRSEAO played a vigorous role in May 1968 and became aligned with one of France's two main trade unions, the *Confédération Française Démocratique du Travail*. Seeking price regionalization and prices guaranteed to offer a living wage, the FRSEAO adherents saw themselves as 'peasant workers', and proletarianized (Canavet, 1976). The membership of this radical grouping was recruited from among the debt-ridden, modernizing farmers, rather than from the poor, marginal farmers. Much is made of the subjection of such farmers to the food and feed industries. More broadly, though, the situation reflected the deepening problem of high interest rates and falling real prices in the more adverse economic conditions of the 1970s.

A keener commercial awareness among co-operatives led to fusions, interco-operative production agreements and, above all, to minimum quality and quantity conditions imposed on suppliers. The small farmers found themselves increasingly excluded or disfavoured and those dependent for their incomes on small milk deliveries faced a stark future. Increasing differentiation between producers is the inevitable result of this competitive system, especially given the economies of scale available in factory farming. A sizeable minority, the marginal farmers, now achieve minimal or negative net incomes per head, while it is common for the modernizing farmers to have debt/asset ratios of 50–75 per cent (Canavet, 1976).

Finally, there is the matter of the profound dissatisfaction with the structure and workings of the CAP. In addition to the price distortions and absence of price regionalization, other issues led to violent unrest in 1984. The decisions on milk quotas were still to come (and their effect has been profound, if uneven). The grievances of the Breton farmers had three proximate causes: the decision by the EC to forbid any further subsidy for the transport of Breton produce by rail; a collapse of poultry prices; and the unresolved dispute over the MCA distortions to the trade in pigmeat. Concerning the latter, there is no guaranteed intervention price for pork, and MCAs have enabled producers in stronger currency countries (West Germany, The Netherlands) to achieve higher selling prices on exports to France by way of an MCA subsidy, while they benefit from cheap bought-in animal feed. The Breton producer seems to be caught between sinking prices and rising production costs. The main pork producer co-operative in the Côtes-du-Nord at Lamballe (COOPERL), has experienced a shake-out of producers and a collapse of investment (*Le Monde*, 2 February 1984). As a final comment, it has to be said that these difficulties in the intensive rearing sector reflect a fragility in the chosen path of intensification. As highly mechanized factory farming techniques become the norm in these branches, so the comparative advantages of Brittany – intensive fodder-growing and abundant labour supply – become dangerously eroded. The severe competition facing Breton poultry producers from their Brazilian counterparts is merely one illustration: it will also be apparent that small farmers elsewhere who follow this intensification route will tend to face similar difficulties.

6.4.2 Regions of poorer natural conditions

Regions of poorer natural conditions, though diverse, present a particular problem for French agricultural and regional policies; for long the subject of depopulation because of their poor endowment and marginal economic viability, they are seriously constrained in their attempts to increase farm efficiency and incomes. Natural conditions impose pastoral and improved fodder systems, yet their principal products of beef and sheepmeat, milk and cheese, have all been in temporary or permanent surplus, which has led to a price collapse of several years' duration. If the resolution of European overproduction is to be found in extensification and capacity cuts, how can the further depopulation of these regions be avoided?

The disadvantaged zones, as officially designated, comprise four categories: high mountain, middle mountain, piedmont and other disfavoured areas. Though the ten natural regions concerned vary in their natural and socioeconomic charcteristics, in terms of area and in numbers of farms, over three-quarters fall into the four zones of the central plateaus north and south, the Centre, Morvan and the South-west (see Figure 7.1). In total, the disfavoured zones have 35 per cent of the French farmed area, with farms of slightly less than average size (though with very few small farms), an older workforce and one-third of the total headage of cattle. Rather schematically, one may distinguish the 'other disfavoured' zone by its higher fodder crop proportion, and by its emphasis on fattening in addition to milk. The high and middle mountain zones show an overwhelming preponderance of permanent pasture, and tend to focus on milk, nursing calves, cheese and mutton (comprising 30 per cent of the total French sheep flock). Seventeen departments here depend on milk for between 30 and 50 per cent of value of production, and in Doubs (Franche-Comté) and the Loire (Massif Central) for well over one-half of value of production. Herds remain small by French standards, but their concentration in larger herds reflects economic pressures. As we shall see, these sectors have experienced chronic difficulties for some years, with sharply falling prices in real terms.

Even within these upland zones there are, however, marked regional differences in income and productivity. In the ten departments of the Massif Central, for example, farms of national average size achieved a far lower performance in terms of yields (a milk yield of only three-quarters the national average and a gross income per hectare of only two-thirds). In more difficult natural conditions, the Pyrenean and Alpine dairy farmers achieve milk yields equal to or higher than the national average (Livet, 1980). Clearly, then, sociological factors and questions of technique lie behind these performances. Livet (1980) dismisses the level of mechanization as a factor in the lower performance of the Massif Central; rather, the problem of low rate of technical innovation can be detected in the low degree of improved grassland and in the age composition of the workforce. Age itself is not, however, of unvarying significance: in the Ariège (Pyrenees), one of the oldest workforces achieves satisfactory yields.

If we turn to the severe competitive difficulties facing farmers in these regions, we can recall the position on the milk, beef and sheepmeat markets. The system of milk quotas is slightly less constraining in disfavoured zones, but has, nevertheless, had severe consequences. The option of modernization of dairying through expansion, to overcome the relative backwardness of the sector, has been blocked by quotas. Second, the slaughter premium on dairy cows has caused a glut in the beef market and brought the inevitable price collapse (Debatisse, 1986). Of course, taking a long-term view, this ruining of livestock rearers may contribute to a future shortage. Particularly hard hit by this price collapse have been the 90,000 rearers of nursing calves of the livestock nursing region, which covers the northern half of the Massif Central and its northern extension. During the past decade, producer prices have fallen by 30 per cent in real terms, with a consequent stagnation in output.

The 'lamb war' between Britain and France has also had a notable effect on the economic viability of these areas. With 70 per cent of total French flocks, farms in these disadvantaged zones possess large flocks and show a strong tendency for concentration of rearing in larger units. However, the hard-won benefits of the EC sheepmeat regime have proved largely illusory as prices have continued to weaken, falling below cost, with the consequences of a slowly falling output over the 1980s. Though French producers receive a year-end 'headage' payment per ewe, which makes up the difference between the average market price and a guide price, prices have been falling under a flood of cheaper imports from the UK. As no MCAs are imposed on the sheepmeat trade, the weakening pound has enabled British producers to penetrate the French market. At the head of the list of French complaints is the continuing scale of concessionary imports of New Zealand lamb into Britain, and the claim that the British variable premium is a far more efficient system of deficiency payment than its French counterpart. Meanwhile, the cost to Brussels of market support for sheepmeat rose by 80 per cent between 1983 and 1986.

The exaggeration of the crisis for the rearing and dairying sectors in the poorer regions can now been seen in an abandonment of these branches and a weakening of land prices (*Le Monde*, 28 July 1987). The 1979–80 census showed, for example, that more than 60 per cent of dairy farmers and cattle rearers were aged over 50 years, and one in two had no successor. A marked reduction of their numbers is therefore inevitable over the coming decade. Public policy has attempted for many years to tackle these difficulties, approaching the problem in the wider context of regional development and, sectorally, within the framework of farm assistance. The zones, as de-limited, correspond to the areas in which more favourable agricultural assistance is available. This can, for example, take the following forms:

(1) the grant per head of livestock;
(2) the installation grant for young farmers is markedly higher in the mountain zones;
(3) subsidies for livestock sheds are higher in disfavoured zones;
(4) assistance is given for the collection of milk and for the improvement of milk quality;
(5) the lower-interest loans for installation and modernization are more favourable (Le Roy, 1986).

The revitalization of mountain farming systems will depend in part on better pasture management, especially of communal lands. There are also detailed regional programmes for land consolidation and improved local processing and marketing.

SEVEN

Rural France: Then and Now

7.1 Images of rural life

For over half a century from the end of the nineteenth century until the mid-twentieth, it was the peasantry which dominated rural France after the disappearance of artisans, shopkeepers and workers from the countryside. Rural France represented unchanging agrarian values of solidity, attachment to the land and private property, and an economy and way of life untouched by capitalist imperatives of efficiency and productivity. For the urban bourgeoisie, the countryside was usually equated with expeditions to another land or youthful memories of idyllic summer holidays. In Renoir's *Partie de Campagne* (1936), a *petit bourgeois* family discovers the delights of a virtually unspoilt nature on its annual outing by the banks of the Marne. Over a decade later in the early postwar years, Leenhardt's *Les Dernières Vacances* (1947) introduces the destructive effects of a Parisian property developer into a corner of Provence where two children lose their cherished holiday home due to the financial ineptitude of their father. Capitalism has now begun to make its imprint felt.

Despite these almost caricatural images of the rural world, attempts to promote a capitalist agriculture in the interwar years were made in some areas. When this process gained pace in the 1960s, the image of the countryside began to alter from the disparaging descriptions of boredom and idiocy, to be replaced gradually by the utopian vision of a peaceful realm and new forms of sociability that the urban world has lost, just at the time when rural areas were beginning to acquire the modernity and comforts of urban existence. The neo-rurals, in the aftermath of '68, discovered in the countryside all that they rejected in the absurdity of urban life in capitalist societies. Most of the early settlers sought marginal areas in the process of being abandoned, where they could find fulfilment in a return to the land and its ancestral rhythms and customs, for example in the Cévennes (Léger and Hervieu, 1978).

It is often assumed that rural change emanated from urban values which were adopted by closed communities divorced from a global society. In effect, the ownership of land as the fundamental source of rural values and

172

reproduction of the peasantry never existed in local societies in which conflict with the larger society was absent (Bodiguel, 1986, pp. 101–2). Rural societies did not simply change as a result of the penetration and progressive integration of urban and industrial values; the first initiatives were spearheaded by groups from within the local society. The State, through its panoply of rural and regional development measures, sometimes in opposition to, at other times in collaboration with local interests, pushed through a transformation that would integrate the rural domain into a national and international economy.

7.2 Demographic revival

After 30 years of rural decline, the 1975 census indicated the beginning of a reversal of population decline (see Figure 1.3b). Closer inspection of this trend shows that, while the net migration residual has been substantially reduced, it was primarily due to in-migration into rural communes near urban agglomerations, the ZPIUs. The population of these communes rose by more than 1.28 per cent per annum, with an appreciably higher increase of 41 per cent in the ZPIUs of the Paris region for the period 1968–75 (Hervieu, 1978, p. 226). Furthermore, the loss of the young and of the rural workforce continued unabated during these years.

Even by 1982, when the census indicated for the first time in over a century, demographic expansion in rural communes as a whole, it was still largely taking place in rural communes of the ZPIUs, which now totalled 8.8 million inhabitants. This included 16 per cent of the population compared to the 10.5 per cent in rural communes outside the ZPIUs. Thus 74 per cent of rural communes within the ZPIUs gained population between the 1975 and 1982 censuses, compared with only 39 per cent of those outside the ZPIUs (Kayser, 1984, pp. 300–1). In fact, the population outside the ZPIUs continues to decrease, in particular in the most rural areas of the Auvergne, the Limousin and the Centre region, as well as in the whole of Corsica where the loss amounts to 2–7 per cent per annum.

It has become common to speak of this France as '*La France du vide*' (empty France), almost in the vein of 'the French desert', in an attempt to alert and mobilize public opinion. Nevertheless, although demographic vitality comprises an aspect of local dynamism, it cannot be equated with desertification in an economic sense or the potential for the survival of local societies. There is no direct relationship between population growth and economic and social integration in sparsely populated areas (Mathieu and Duboscq, 1985). The only general characteristics of this type of area is its ageing population and a deterioration in the provision of public and private service (p. 11). Indeed, in several of Mathieu and Duboscq's case studies, such as the Causse Méjean in the southern Lozère, or the Piège, formerly a poor agricultural area in the Aude, a dynamic and modernized agriculture has evicted marginal groups; in the Piège this has left a social void due to extremely rapid depopulation. Nor can we apply a simple cut-off point beyond which there is no hope of reversing the situation. Some areas, at one time nothing more than rural wastelands, have witnessed a demographic renewal, for example, Barre des Cévennes, with an increase of 62 inhabitants between 1975 and 1982. Here, the refusal of a number of young people to leave and the return of others, partly in response to the economic crisis, have contributed, as in other rural areas, to demographic, economic and social revitalization.

7.3   Rural diversity

More than ever, rural areas now contain a multitude of activities and a diversity of social groups, each with its own specific geography. The radical change in agricultural production has resulted in a new social stratification, with a majority of the rural population belonging to the middle category. While farmers still own 70 per cent of usable land, they have now become a minority, albeit substantial, in rural areas. A series of new activities (industrial and artisanal production), the growth of tourism and leisure pursuits and the settlement of urban dwellers have produced new social groups that outnumber farmers in many areas. In rural communes outside the ZPIUs, farmers and agricultural workers constitute only 41 per cent of the active population. The image of a totally distinctive rural France in social terms is thus no longer tenable.

From the mid-1970s, workers (34.8 per cent of the active population in 1975) overtook the agricultural population (25.9 per cent farmers and 5.0 per cent farm workers in 1975), although the former were frequently of rural origin themselves (Bodiguel, 1986, p. 156). One in three rural inhabitants were thus industrial workers, a presence that is most noticeable in eastern and northern France, Rhône-Alpes, the southern Breton coast and the urban periphery around cities such as Toulouse, Bordeaux, Perpignan and Caen (Chapuis, 1978, pp. 140–1). In some cases, industrial centres are not linked to urban zones, as in the Choletais in the Vendée. This is a zone of dense and highly specialized industrial production, characteristic also of parts of the Ile de France and the Nord. Elsewhere, and in particular in the densely populated West, stretching from Basse Normandie, Brittany, Maine and the Charente Maritime, an area of industrial decentralization, industrial employment is important, though not specialized (Chapuis, 1978, p. 142). Again, it would give a false picture of rural industrial production to view it as nothing but an extension of traditional industries.

Indeed, much of the production, often using female labour, is concerned with intermediate and consumer goods and construction, for example, Moulinex in Normandy, SEB in the Côte d'Or and Leroy-Somer in Poitou-Charentes.

The growth in the number of white-collar employees, more closely associated with small towns (*bourgs*), has also been a feature of rural change. On the one hand, employees and civil servants have increasingly disappeared from villages, while increasing in small towns with the expansion of services (Kayser, 1986, p. 55). It is also in the larger rural communes that artisans and other self-employed persons are most common. In some of the most rural regions, small-scale artisan production has been enriched by the presence of neo-ruralites who have helped to create a network for marketing products outside of the region and to tourists. Examples of this are the *Maison du Lozère* or CORSIDA in Corsica. The building of homes for the new rural population (permanent and secondary residences) and the children of farmers has also given a boost to artisans such as masons, plumbers and carpenters. While the proportion of artisans in the population varies according to the type of settlement, the main differentiation lies between regions of early industrialization and those of more recent industrialization and diversified agriculture. In the former the provision of consumer items passes more readily through large-scale distribution channels, for example in the North and the East, while in the latter the level of artisan activity occupies a more important place, as in the Centre, the West and the South-west (Bachelard, 1986).

The revival of artisan activity was made possible by the arrival of the largest group contributing to rural demographic expansion, namely residents who work in urban areas and those who own secondary residences. Full-time residents have made their presence felt most strongly in the rural communes of the ZPIUs, or in what Keyser and Schecktman-Labry (1982, p. 28) call the 'third zone' of the urban fringe, where urbanization confronts an agricultural system and a fully functioning rural society. We return to this zone in our discussion of local politics and land use conflict (p. 176). However, many urban commuters are in reality the children of villagers; this accounts, to a great extent, for the large working-class population in rural areas.

The construction of secondary residences has also generated employment, though of a more seasonal nature. From 1962 to 1982, the number of secondary residences increased by 130 per cent, amounting to 2.3 million residences in 1982 concentrated within a 150 km radius around Paris and Lyons, on the Breton and Mediterranean coasts and in the Alps, where these are now as numerous as primary residences. Again there is a difference between the newly built secondary residences, characteristic of the coast, mountains and zones within 50 km of large cities and inhabited by the better-off, and those in more distant areas, where the house is likely to have been inherited (Mathieu, 1978). In some rural areas, secondary residences have not been accepted by the local population and have provoked a xenophobic reaction, as in Corsica.

Rural change has been most intense in regions of generally rapid economic growth, near large towns and cities and in larger villages, roughly those with at least 800 inhabitants. In the wake of diversification and new demands, previously dominant groups have not always been able to control land use. In addition, a series of directives and legislation have guided the use of the rural environment, for example protected environmental zones and regional parks. Other planning measures, such as the *contrat de pays* (local contract) and the POS, while not compulsory for communes with less than 10,000 population, have been adopted by many, and consequently sparked off numerous conflicts over land use.

7.4   Local conflicts and politics

Two trends can be observed in local political life in recent years. Nationally, the number of mayors from the agricultural sector declined from 45.4 per cent in 1971 to 39.6 per cent in 1977, and slightly increased to 40 per cent just before the 1983 municipal elections. Lamarche (1986, p. 83) argues that this signifies the loss of interest by farmers in the management of their communes and their participation in other institutions, such as the chambers of agriculture, co-operatives and agricultural unions. While new preoccupations have emerged and the agricultural population has decreased, this does not inevitably lead to loss of political control, even when farmers only constitute a minority. If we take the case of the departments of the Gard and the Hérault, farmers held all the seats in the 640 fully rural communes in the 1953 municipal elections; 30 years later they still controlled a majority, albeit slim, of councillors' seats (52.2 per cent), despite their much reduced presence, which amounted to only one-quarter of the population in rural communes outside the ZPIUs (Bernard and Carrière, 1986, p. 242).

At the same time, local elections were increasingly politicized and contested by new social groups. Probably the height of electoral opposition to agricultural interests occurred in the 1977 elections with the advent of a number of middle-class associations. New housing, secondary residences and tourist activities all presented threats to agricultural land, and sometimes engendered conflicts on the issue of whether to sell land. In the so-called 'third zone' of the urban fringe, conflict is most likely to break out where urbanization is either blocked or contained. In other cases, it has led to alliances being formed between farmers and the new social groups, all of them anxious to preserve the rural quality of the locality, and thus to prevent new developments (Kayser, 1982, pp. 82–3).

However, some of the most vehement and organized resistance in rural areas has been directed towards state projects in which fundamental ecological or regional issues are at stake. For example, the battle of the 103 farmers against the appropriation of Larzac by the army or the opposition by the inhabitants of Plogoff in Brittany to the construction of a nuclear power station, are just two instances (see p. 20). It is interesting to note that Larzac was represented on television programmes in the early 1970s as an empty plateau, a desert (Dressler-Holohan, 1978, p. 192). On the other hand, environmental protection using regional and national parks is not always warmly received: in Barre des Cévennes, where the residents have often expressed opposition to the national park, they accused the State of taking away their rights to decide land use in a commune where half the land is under the park's jurisdiction (Mathieu and Duboscq, 1985, p. 44).

7.5 Rural planning

Starting from sectoral projects in agricultural and large-scale irrigation schemes in the 1950s, rural planning broadened to include environmental and social objectives within integrated local policies (Clout, 1987). Geographically as well, by the mid-1970s a whole array of policy measures had brought every type of zone under the umbrella of rural planning and had progressively incorporated the whole of the rural area into a national space (Figure 7.1). Three different rural areas can be identified (Mathieu, 1982) in terms of their integration into the market economy. These extend from the highly integrated, for example the Beauce and modernized agricultural areas in Brittany; those with potential which hold out the possibility for further development; and third, zones minimally integrated, though not totally abandoned, and in which the physical and social fabric has deteriorated, for example parts of the Massif Central, Pyrénées and Southern Alps. In more recent years, and especially since decentralization, the emphasis on local initiatives and planning has led to a planning system that is able to respond to specific needs and situations.

The first large-scale rural management bodies, established in the late 1950s and early 1960s, stemmed from initial attempts at more active state intervention, aimed at developing and integrating selected rural areas that showed a potential for more intensive market production. These rural planning corporations were of mixed-economy status, often engaged in costly irrigation and water supply control (Gascogne, Languedoc, Provence), or water management combined with land reclamation (Atlantic

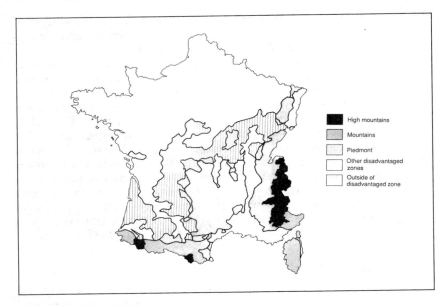

Figure 7.1   Disadvantaged rural areas (agricultural regions).

marshes and Corsican plain). Later on, vast coastal development schemes for tourism were initiated. However, the type of redevelopment seen on the Languedoc coast, where a number of large resorts were created, never came to fruition in Corsica, due to active local protest in the 1970s (Kofman, 1981).

The second phase of rural programmes involved the appointment in 1967 of commissioners for rural renovation zones, whose purpose was to stimulate action by DATAR and the field services of government ministries. The first areas designated under this programme were those suffering from agricultural overpopulation in which industrial decentralization had already resulted in industries moving in to take advantage of the cheap and plentiful labour supply (see p. 102). To these zones were later added mountainous areas – marginal areas that were of little interest to private investment, where more diversified activities based on forestry, tourism and rest homes could be combined with some agricultural activity. These semi-marginal zones were often endowed with an overall regional plan, for example the Cévennes, where the rural development plan was based on the physical planning legislation of 1967 and 1970. These plans combined the objectives of employment diversification, service provision and environmental protection but, as we have seen, the strong hand of the State in regional and national parks was very much in evidence. State planning agencies were able to exert considerable power in determining who could take up farms within their geographical area, and in this way they incorporated sections of the population who were dependent on their subsidies, such as the neo-rurals (Léger and Hervieu, 1978). In all, six national parks in high mountain areas, covering 2.3 per cent of national territory, and twenty regional parks, generally in areas of low population density (5.2 per cent of national territory), have been created.

The policy for mountain zones had its origins in the 1961 legislation, and later in the mountain renovation zones. These zones were once again modified following the designation in 1977 of disadvantaged zones, which implemented an EC Directive on less favoured areas, permitting special subsidies to be granted there. The maintenance of basic services in thinly populated areas also came under state control in 1976. Finally in 1979, an interministerial fund, the FIDAR, was established to address the problems of fragile rural zones that have frequently been equated with abandoned agricultural areas suffering rapid population decline. However, Aitchinson and Bontron (1984) conclude, as do Mathieu and Duboscq (1985) that there exists a great deal of variation in the processes causing fragility and generating crises. Localities, too, adjust and respond in many different ways, which reflect the transformation of agriculture, the composition and identity of local communities and the articulation between local and global systems (Renard, 1984). In some areas, agriculture has been almost completely replaced by another activity, such as tourism, as in the Alps. Although this had led to a demographic revitalization, it has posed ecological problems due to the neglect of the environment. In other areas, on the contrary, as highly specialized agriculture or forestry has become the dominant economic force (southern Morvan in Burgundy, the Landes). Yet, in others, such as Bellegarde in the Creuse (Limousin), a polycultural system retains some aspects of the peasant economy. It has not been able to stop a continual decline and ageing of the population, and is thus highly vulnerable. In some localities, as in the Causse Méjean (Larzac), a development strategy has emerged from within the middle peasantry; in others, as on the Sornac plateau (Corrèze), government assistance has always been sought.

The most recent legislation, the 1983 law for the development and protection of mountainous zones, was seen as a sort of tool box that could be adapted to specific situations, for each of the seven mountainous areas is endowed with its own structure plan. Its innovative aspect lies in the practice of decentralist planning, in which the intercommune charters (1983) replaced the previous rural plans (PAR) and protected environmental zones. However, the National Council for Mountain Areas, which was created by this legislation, never met during Chirac's term of office (*Le Monde*, 22 March 1988), and so the full potential of this legislation has not been translated into action.

Currently, the major concern is the fate of rural communes in the Europe of the 1990s dominated by the major cities. Rural areas are increasingly left to sort out their own futures using the intercommune charters and local development initiatives constituted around artisans and small- and medium-sized firms. They are still dependent on national agencies and outside planners to draw up plans and have thus benefited least from decentralization, unlike the larger urban communes with more resources (see p. 128).

BIBLIOGRAPHY

Aballéa, J. (1986) 'L'habitat ancien, un nouvel enjeu'. *Problèmes Economiques*, **1978**, 25–9.

ADEF (1983) *Les enjeux de la fiscalité foncière*. Paris: Economica.

Aitchinson, J.W. and Bontron, J.C. (1984) 'Les zones rurales fragiles en France: une approche méthodologique'. *Bulletin de la Société Neuchâteloise de Géographie*, **28**, 23–55.

Allaire, G. and Blanc, M. (1982) *Politiques agricoles et paysanneries*. Paris: Le Sycomore.

Amiot, M. (1986) *Contre l'Etat. Les sociologues*. Paris: Edition de l'Ecole des Hautes Etudes en Sciences Sociales.

Ardagh, J. (1988) *France Today* (rev. ed.). London: Penguin.

Arnaud, C. (1988) 'Le logement, vitrine des ségrégations sociales'. *Le Monde Diplomatique*, **415**, 20–1.

Aydalot, P. (1978) 'L'aménagement du territoire. Une tentative de bilan'. *L'Espace Géographique*, **4**, 245–53.

Aydalot, P. (1983) 'Redistribution spatiale des activités'. *Les Cahiers Français*, **212**.

Bachelard, P. (1986) 'L'artisanat: l'indispensable polyvalence'. *Pour*, **109**, 79–83.

Badouin, R. (1979) *Economie et aménagement de l'espace rural*. Paris: PUF.

Barrère, P. and Cassou-Mounat, M. (1980) *Les villes françaises*. Paris: Masson.

Barzach, M. (1988) 'La famille, assurance-vie de l'Europe'. *Le Monde*, 4 May.

Batiot, A. (1982) 'The political construction of sexuality: the contraception and abortion issues in France, 1965–1975'. In Cerny, P. (ed.) *Social Movements and Protest in France*. London: Frances Pinter.

Bauchet, P. (1986) *Le plan dans l'économie française*. Paris: Economica.

Béaud, M. (1985) *La politique économique de la gauche*, Vol. 2. Paris: Syros.

Berger, A. (1975) *La nouvelle économie de l'espace rural*. Paris: Cujas.

Berger, S. (1987) 'Liberalism reborn: the new liberal synthesis in France'. In Howorth, J. and Ross, G. (eds.) *Contemporary France. A Review of Interdisciplinary Studies*. London: Frances Pinter.

Bergmann, D. (1982) *Les transformations structurelles de l'agriculture française depuis 1950*. Paris: INRA.

Bergmann, D. (1983) 'French agriculture: trends, outlook and policies'. *Food Policy*, November, 270–86.

Bernand, M.C. (1986) 'Nouveaux languedociens – nouveaux notables? Les élus locaux du Gard et de l'Hérault 1953–1986'. In Bernard, M.C. and Carrière, P.,

Géographie électorale du Languedoc-Roussillon, 1981–1986. Montpellier: Espace Rurale, no. 7, pp. 229–69.

Béteille, R. (1986) *La population et le social en France*. Paris: Ellipses.

Bodiguel, M. (1986) *Le rural en question*. Paris: Harmattan.

Bouchet, J. and Savy, M. (1982) 'Décentralisation des activités et aménagement du territoire'. *Problèmes Economiques*, **1787**, 2–8.

Bourdieu, P. (1985) *Distinction. A Social Judgement of Taste*. London: RKP.

Boyer, R. (1987) 'The current economic crisis. Its dynamics and its implications for France'. In Ross, G. and Hoffman, S. (eds.) *The Mitterrand Experiment: Continuity and Change in Modern France*. Cambridge, Mass.: Polity Press, pp. 33–53.

Braudel, F. and Labrousse, E. (eds.) (1982) *Histoire économique et sociale de la France. 1950 à nos jours*, Vol. 3. Paris: PUF.

Brémond, J. and Brémond, C. (1984) *L'économie française face à la crise*. Paris: Hatier.

Brunet, R. (ed.) (1987) *La vérité sur l'emploi*. Paris: Larousse.

Bunyard, P. (1988) 'The myth of France's cheap nuclear energy'. *The Ecologist*, **18**, 4–8.

Calmès, R. *et al.* (1978) *L'espace rural français*. Paris: Masson.

Canavet, C. (1976) 'L'évolution récente de l'agriculture bretonne: de l'agriculture paysanne à une agriculture intégrée au mode de production capitaliste'. In *L'agriculture bretonne*.

Capdevielle, J., Dupoirier, E., Grunberg, G., Schweisguth, E. and Ysmal, C. (1981) *France de gauche vote à droite*. Paris: Fondation Nationale des Sciences Politiques.

Capul, J.Y. and Meurs, D. (1988) *Les grandes questions de l'économie française*. Paris: Nathan.

Caron, F. (1981) *Histoire économique de la France XIX–XX siècle*. Paris: A. Colin.

Carré, J.J., Dubois, P. and Malinvaud, E. (1976) *French Economic Growth*. Oxford University Press.

Castells, M. (1978) *City, Class and Power*. London: Macmillan.

CERA and INSEE (1987) *Atlas de la Basse Normandie*. Caen: CERA.

Chafer, T. (1982) 'The anti-nuclear movement and the rise of political ecology'. In Cerny, P. (ed.) *Social Movements and Protests in France*. London: Frances Pinter.

Chapuis, R. (1978) *Les ruraux français*. Paris: Masson.

Charbonnel, J.M. and Lion, J. (1988) 'Protection sociale et pauvreté'. *Problèmes Economiques*, **2079**, 11–17.

Chombart de Lauwe, J. (1979) *L'aventure agricole de la France*. Paris: PUF.

Clerc, D. and Chaouat, B. (1987) *Les inégalités en question*. Paris: Syros.

Clout, H. (1987) 'France'. In Clout, H. (ed.) *Regional Development in Western Europe*, (3rd edn.) London: David Fulton.

Cohen, E. (1986) 'Nationalisations: une bonne leçon de capitalisme'. *Problèmes Economiques*, **1972**.

Collins, D. (1988) 'A more equal society? Social policy under the Socialists'. In Mazey, S. and Newman, M. (eds.) *Mitterrand's France*. London: Croom Helm.

Coulmin, P. (1986) *Décentralisation. La dynamique du développement local*. Paris: Syros.

Crozic, M.F., Desrez, S. and Hérin, R. (1987) 'Les profils sociaux des collèges et des lycées en Basse Normandie'. In *GéoSociale*, **4**. Caen: Centre de Publications de l'Université de Caen.

Dacier, P. *et al.* (1985) *Les dossiers noirs de l'industrie française*. Paris: Fayard.

DATAR (1987) *La politique régionale européenne en France*. Paris: DATAR.

Dauphin, D. and Jacotey, C. (1974) *Propriétaires et constructeurs devant l'urbanisme et l'action foncière*. Paris: Delmas.

Debatisse, M. (1986) *Agriculture: les temps difficiles*. Paris: Economica.

Derycke, P.H. (1979) *Economie et planification urbaines*. Paris: PUF.

Desplanques, G. (1985) 'Modes de garde et scolarisation des jeunes enfants'. *Economie et Statistique*, **176**, 27–40.

Doublet, M. (1976) *Paris en procès*. Paris: Hachette.

Dressler-Holohan, W. (1978) 'Gardarem lou Larzac'. *Autrement*, **14**, 192–204.

Dressler-Holohan, W. (1985) 'Le statut particulier de la Corse à l'épreuve de la réalité insulaire'. *Les Temps Modernes*, 1479–1517.

Eck, J.F. (1988) *Histoire de l'économie française depuis 1945*. Paris: A. Colin.

Estrin, S. and Holmes, P. (1983) *French Planning in Theory and Practice*. London: Allen and Unwin.

Ferrier, J.P., Guglielmo, R., Krier, G., Porte, G., Rinaudo, Y. and Lacoste, Y. (1986) 'Provence-Alpes-Côte d'Azur'. In Lacoste, Y. (ed.) *Géopolitiques des régions françaises*, Vol. 3. Paris: Fayard.

Findlay, A. and White, P. (eds.) (1986) *West European Population Change*. London: Croom Helm.

Flockton, C. (1982) 'Strategic planning in the Paris region and French urban policy'. *Geoforum*, **13**, 193–208.

Flockton, C. (1983) 'French local government reform and urban planning'. *Local Government Studies*, Sept./Oct., 65–77.

Flouzat, D. (1984) *Economie contemporaine*, Vol. 3. Paris: PUF.

Fourastié, J. (1979) *Les trentes glorieuses*. Paris: Fayard.

Frémont, A. (1978) L'aménagement du territoire. La pratique et les idées'. *L'Espace Géographique*, **4**, 245–53.

Frémont, A. (1988) *France, La géographie d'une société*. Paris: Fayard.

Gaspard, F. and Servan-Schreiber, C. (1984) *La fin des immigrés*. Paris: Seuil.

Gauron, A. (1983) *Histoire économique et sociale de la Cinquième République*, Vol. 1. Paris: La Découverte.

Gehring, J.-M. and Saint-Dizier, C. (1986) 'Lorraine'. In Lacoste, Y. (ed.) *Géopolitiques des régions françaises*. Paris: Fayard.

Gervais, M., Jollivet, M. and Tavernier, Y. (1976) *La fin de France paysanne de 1914 à nos jours*. Paris: Seuil.

Girard, A. (1981) 'L'école: mythes et réalités'. In Reynaud, J.D. and Grafmeyer, Y. (eds.) *Français, qui êtes-vous?* Paris: La Documentation Française, pp. 407–19.

Gloaguen, J. (1986) 'La fin des grandes usines'. *Le nouvel économiste*, 5 Séptembre.

Gollac, M. and Laulhé, P. (1987) 'La transmission du statut social'. *Economie et Statistique*, No. 199–200, 85–93.

Goubet, M. and Roucolle, J.L. (1981) *Population et société française 1945–1981*. Paris: Sirey.

Granelle, J.J. (1975) *La valeur du sol urbain et la propriété foncière*. Paris: Mouton.

Granelle, J.J. (1976) 'L'évolution du prix des terrains à bâtir dans quelques agglomérations'. *Promotion Immobilière*, **33**, 21–4.

Gravier, J.-F. (1947) *Paris et le désert français*, Paris, Le Portulan.

Green, D. with Cerny, P. (1980) 'Economic policy and the governing coalition'. In Cerny, P. and Schain, M. (eds.) *French Politics and Public Policy*. London: Methuen, pp. 159–76.

Guillauchon, B. (1986) *La France contemporaine: une approche d'économie descriptive*. Paris: Economica.

Hall, P.A. (1985) 'Socialism in one country: Mitterrand and the struggle to define a new economic policy for France'. In Cerny, P.G. and Schain, M. (eds.) *Socialism, the State and Public Policy in France*. London: Frances Pinter.

Hanley, D., Kerr, A.P. and Waites, N. (1984) *Contemporary France. Politics and Society since 1945* (2nd edn). London: RKP.

Hannoun, M. and Templé, P. (1975) 'Les facteurs de création et de localisation des nouvelles unités de production'. *Economie et Statistique*, **68**, 59–70

Hantrais, L. (1982) *Contemporary French Society*. London: Macmillan.

Hargreaves, J. (ed.) (1987.) *Immigration in Post-War France. A Documentary Anthology*. London: Methuen Educational.

Hayward, J. (1986) *The State and the Market Economy*. Brighton: Harvester Press.

Hénin, P.Y. (1986) L'emploi: les enseignements théoriques et pratiques des années récentes'. *Problèmes Economiques*, **1989**, 24–9.

Henry, P. (1981) *Etude des effets régionaux de la PAC*. Brussels: EC Commission.

Hérin, R. (1987) 'Le retard scolaire en Basse Normandie. Essai d'interprétation'. In *Géosociale*, **4**, Caen: Centre de Publications de l'Université de Caen.

Hervieu, B. (1978) 'Le village mort-vivant'. *Autrement*, **14**, 225–31.

Hervieu-Léger, D. (1987) 'Socio-religious change in France: trends in French Catholicism'. In Howorth, J. and Ross, G. (eds.) *Contemporary France. A Review of Interdisciplinary Studies*. London: Frances Pinter, pp. 111–29.

Heugas-Darraspen, H. (1985) 'Le logement français et son financement'. In *Notes et Etudes Documentaires*. Paris: La Documentation Française.

House, J. (1978) *France: An Applied Geography*. London: Methuen.

IAURIF (1979) 'Réflection sur lé schéma directeur de la région d'Ile de France'. *Cahiers de L'IAURIF*, **56–7** (Paris).

INSEE (1981) *Statistiques et indicateurs des régions françaises* (Annexes du projet de loi de finance pour 1981). *Les Collections de l'INSEE*, R45–460.

INSEE (1982) *Recensement général de la population*. Paris: INSEE.

INSEE (1985) *Enquête sur l'emploi*. Paris: INSEE.

INSEE (1986) *Femmes en chiffres*. Paris: INSEE.

INSEE (1987) *Données sociales*. Paris: INSEE.

Jannoud, C. and Pinel, M.H. (1974) *La première ville nouvelle*. Paris: Mercure de France.

Julien, C. (ed.) (1988) *Le libéralisme contre les libertés*. Paris: Le Monde Diplomatique.

Kain, R. (1981) 'Conservation planning in France: policy and practice in the Marais, Paris'. In Kain, R. (ed.) *Planning for Conservation*. London: Mansell.

Kayser, B. (1984) 'Subversion des villages français'. *Etudes Rurales*, **93–4**.

Kayser, B. (1986) 'Le village recomposé'. In Programme Observation du Changement Social, *L'esprit des lieux*. Paris: Editions du Centre National dela Recherche Scientifique.

Kayser, B. and Schecktman-Labry, G. (1982) 'La troisième couronne périurbaine: une tentative d'identification'. *Revue Géographique des Pyrénées et du Sud-Ouest*, **53**. 27–34.

Keating, M. and Hainsworth, P. (1986) *Decentralisation and Change in Contemporary France*. Aldershot: Gower.

Keeler, J. (1985) 'Corporatist decentralization and commercial modernization in France: the Royer law's impact on shopkeepers, supermarkets and the State'. In Cerny, P. and Schain, M. (eds.) *Socialism, the State and Public Policy*. London: Frances Pinter.

Kesselman, M. (1980) 'The economic analysis and programme of the French Communist Party: consistency underlying change'. In Cerny, P. and Schain, M. (eds.) *French Politics and Policy*. London: Methuen.

Klatzmann, J. (1978) *L'agriculture française*. Paris: Seuil.

Kofman, E. (1981) 'Functional regionalism and alternative regional development programmes in Corsica'. *Regional Studies*, **15**, 173–81.

Kofman, E. (1982) 'Differential modernisation, social conflicts and ethno-regionalism in Corsica'. *Ethnic and Racial Studies*, **3**. 300–12.

Kofman, E. (1985) 'Regional autonomy and the one and indivisible French Republic'. *Environment and Planning C*, **3**, 11–25.

Laborie, J.P. *et al.* (1986) 'Industrialisation et aménagement du territoire'. *Problèmes Economiques*, **1973**.

Lafay, G. (1987) 'La spécialisation française: des handicaps structurels'. *Les Cahiers Français*, **229**.

Lajugie, J. (1979) *Espace régional et aménagement du territoire*. Paris: Dalloz.

Lamarche, H. (1986) 'Localisation, délocalisation, relocalisation du milieu rural'. In Programme Observation du Changement Social, *L'esprit des lieux*. Paris: Editions du Centre National de la Recherche Scientifique.

Lambert, Y. and Willaime, P. (1986) 'La vie religieuse: nouveaux modes d'insertion locale'. In Programme d'Observation du Changement Social, *L'esprit des lieux*. Paris: Editions de Centre National de la Recherche Scientifique.

Larkin, M. (1988) *France Since the Popular Front. Government and People 1938–1986*. Oxford University Press.

Léger, D. and Hervieu, B. (1978) 'Les immigés de l'utopie'. *Autrement*, **14**, 48–70.

Le Monde (1986) *La France des régions*. Paris: Le Monde.

Le Monde (1988a) *Bilan du septennat. Alternance dans l'alternance*. Paris: Dossiers et Documents.

Le Monde (1988b) *L'élection présidentielle*. Paris: Dssiers et Documents.

Le Roy, P. (1981) 'Données pour une politique agricole française'. *L'Agriculture d'Enterprise*, Jan.–Feb.

Le Roy, P. (1982) *Le problème agricole français*. Paris: Economica.

Le Roy, P. (1986) *L'avenir de l'agriculture française*. Paris: PUF.

Lipietz, A. (1980) 'Polarisation-interrégionale et tertiarisation de la société'. *L'Espace Géographique*, **9**, 33–42.

Livet, R. (1980) *Les nouveaux visages de l'agriculture française*. Paris: Les Editions Ouvrières.

Mahé, L.P. and Roudet, M. (1980) 'La politique agricole française et l'Europe verte: impasse ou révision?' *Economie Rurale*, **135**, 1/1980, 12–24.

Malinvaud, E. (1983) *Réexamen de la théorie du chômage*. Paris: Calmann-Levy.

Malinvaud, E. (1986) 'Les causes de la montée du chômage en France depuis vingt ans'. *Problèmes Economiques*, **1989**,

Mallet, S. (1969) *La nouvelle classe ouvrière*. Paris: Seuil.

Martin, J.P. (1983) *Effects of the Minimum Wage on the Youth Labour Market in North America and France*. OECD Occasional Papers. Paris: OECD.

Mary, A. (1987) 'De l'identité scolaire locale. Eléments pour une typologie de collèges du Calvados'. In *GéoSociale*, **4**. Caen: Centre de Publications de l'Université de Caen.

Mathieu, N. (1978) 'Le phénomène "résidences secondaires" '. *Autrement*, **14**, 40.

Mathieu, N. (1982) 'Questions sur les types d'espaces ruraux en France'. *L'Espace Géographique*, **11**, 95–110.

Mathieu N. and Duboscq, P. (1985) *Voyages en France par les pays de faible densité*. Paris: Editions du CNRS.

Matteaccioli, A. (1981) *Diversité régionale et cohérence nationale*. Paris: Economica.

Mazey, S. and Newman, M. (eds.) (1987) *Mitterrand's France*. London: Croom Helm.

Michalet, C.A. (ed.) (1984) *L'intégration de l'économie française dans l'économie mondiale*. Paris: Economica.

Michelat, G. and Simon, M. (1985) 'Déterminations socio-économiques, organisations symboliques et comportement électoral'. *Revue Française de Sociologie*, 32–69.'

Mormiche, P. (1986) 'Consommation médicale: les disparités sociales n'ont pas disparu'. *Economie et Statistique*, **189**, 19–38.

Morvan, Y. (1985) *Fondements d'économie industrielle*. Paris: Economica.

Moseley, M. (1980) 'Strategic planning and the Paris agglomeration in the 1960s and 1970s: the quest for structure and balance'. *Geoforum*, **11**, 179–223.

Muet, P.A. and Fonteneau, A. (1984) 'La politique conjoncturelle de la gauche: la relance contrariée'. In *Cahiers Français*, **218**.

Neville-Rolfe, E. (1984) *The Politics of Agriculture in the EEC*. London: Policy Studies Institute.

Nivollet, A. (ed.) (1982) *La décentralisation*. Paris: Les Cahiers Français, 204.

Noin, D. (1974) *L'espace français*. Paris: A. Colin.

OECD (1987) *France*. Paris: OECD Economic Surveys.

OREAM-PCA (1974) *L'aire métropolitaine marseillaise*. Marseilles: OREAM-PCA.

Paris Projet (1980) *Schéma direct d'aménagement et d'urbanisme de la ville de Paris*, no. 19–20. Paris: Ville de Paris.

Paris Projet (1982) *Politique nouvelle de la rénovation urbaine*, no. 21–2. Paris: Ville de Paris.

Parodi, M. (1981) *L'économie et la société française depuis 1945*. Paris: A. Colin.

Pascallon, P. (1981) 'Redéploiement industriel et développement régional' *L'Espace Géographique*, **10**, 74–6.

Pavy, G. (1980) 'Le retournement de l'année 1965'. In Mendras, H. (ed.) *La sagesse et le désordre*. *France 1980*. Paris: Gallimard.

Pearsall, J. (1983) 'France'. In Wynn, M. (ed.) *Housing in Europe*. London: Croom Helm.

Pinçon-Charlot, M. and Rendu, P. (1988) 'Les hauts fonctionnaires face aux enjeux scolaires de leurs enfants'. *Revue Française de Pédagogie*, **83**, 51–6.

Potel, F. (ed.) (1985) *L'état de la France et ses habitants*. Paris: La Découverte.

Pottier, C. (1984) 'Facteurs de rééquilibrage spatial de l'emploi industriel: les régions françaises face à la crise'. In Aydalot, P. (ed.) *Crise et espace*. Paris: Economica.

Preteceille, E. (1988) 'Decentralisation in France: new citizenship or restructuring hegemony?'. *European Journal of Political Research*, **16**, 409–24.

Prost, A. (1987) 'L'évolution de la politique familiale en France de 1938 à 1981'. *Mouvement Social*, **129**, 7–28.

Quinet, E. and Touzéry, L. (1986) *Le plan français: mythe ou nécessité?* Paris: Economica.

Reece, J. (1979) 'Internal colonialism: the case of Brittany'. *Ethnic and Racial Studies*, **2**, 275–92.

Renard, J. (1984) 'Changement social et sociétés rurales'. In Collectif Français de Géographie Sociale et Urbaine, *Sens et non-sens de l'espace*. Paris: 215–26.

Renard, V. (1980) *Plans d'urbanisme et justice foncière*. Paris: PUF.

Rey. H. and Roy, J. (1986) 'Quelques réflexions sur l'évolution électorale d'un département de la banlieue parisienne: la Seine–Saint–Denis'. *Hérodote*, **43**, 6–38.

Rioux, J.P. (1983) *La France de la Quatrième République. L'expansion et l'impuissance 1952–1958*. Paris: Seuil.

Rioux, J.P. (1987) *France Fourth Republic 1944–1958*. Cambridge University Press.

Saint Julien, T. (1982) *Croissance industrielle et système urbain*. Paris: Economica.

Scargill, I. (1983) *Urban France*. London: Croom Helm.

SCEES (1980) *Recensement général de l'agriculture française: 1979–80 les premiers résultats*. Paris: SCEES.

Schain, M. (1987) 'The National Front in France and the construction of political legitimacy'. *West European Politics*, **10**, 229–52.

SESSI (1987) 'L'implantation étrangère dans l'industrie au 1.1.1985'. *Chiffres et Documents*, **62**, Paris: SESSI.

Stoffäes, C. (1985) 'The nationalizations: an initial assessment 1981–1984'. In Machin, H. and Wright, V. (eds.) *The Economy and Economic Policy under Mitterrand 1981–84*. London: Frances Pinter.

Tabard, N. (1987) 'Espace et classes sociales' In INSEE, *Données Sociales*. Paris: INSEE.

Tafani, P. (1986) 'Corse'. In Lacoste, Y. (ed.) *Géopolitiques des régions françaises*, Vol. 3. Paris: Fayard.

Terrail, J.P. (1984) 'Identité ouvrière. Mouvement ouvrier d'hier et aujourd'hui'. *Société Française*, **13**, 13–22.

Thélot, C. (1982) *Tel père, tel fils?*. Paris: Bordas.

Tilly, C. (1979) 'Did the cake of custom break?. In Merriman, J. (ed.) *Consciousness and Class Experience in 19th Century Europe*. New York: Homes and Meier.

Touraine, A. (1983) 'State and social forces in Socialist France'. *Telos*, 55, 179–85.

Tuppen, J. (1983) *Economic Geography of France*. London: Croom Helm.

Tuppen, J. (1986) 'Core periphery in metropolitan development and planning: socio-economic change in Lyon since 1960'. *Geoforum*, 17, 1–37.

Tuppen, J. and Mingret, P. (1986) 'Suburban malaise in French cities'. *Town Planning Review*, 57, 187–201.

Vedel Commission (1969) *Perspectives à long terme de l'agriculture française, 1969–1985*. Paris: La Documentation Française.

Verdié, M. (1987) *L'état de la France et ses habitants*. Paris: La Découverte.

Vincent, M. (1986) *La formation du prix du logement*. Paris: Economica.

Viveret, P. (1985) 'The resolution of inequalities in a period of austerity'. In Morris, P. (ed.) *Equality and Inequalities in France*. Nottingham: Association for the Study of Modern and Contemporary France.

Weber, E. (1976) *Peasants into Frenchmen. The Modernization of Rural France, 1870–1914*. Stanford, Calif.: Stanford University Press.

Webman, J.A. (1982) *Reviving the Industrial City*. London: Croom Helm.

Weinschenk, G. and Kemper, J. (1981) 'Agricultural policies and their regional impact in Western Europe'. *European Review of Agricultural Economics*, 8, 251–81.

White, P. (1984) *The West European City*. London: Longman.

Zukin, S. (1985) 'The regional challenge to French industrial policy'. *International Journal of Urban and Regional Research*, 9, 352–67.

PLACE INDEX

189

SUBJECT INDEX